D0976400

ideologies

ideologies

An Analytic and Contextual Approach   Larry Johnston

broadview press

Canadian Cataloguing in Publication Data

Johnston, Lawrence Walker, 1955-
   Ideologies: an analytic and contextual approach

ISBN 1-55111-067-9

1. Political science — Philosophy. 2. Political science — History. 3. Ideology.
I. Title.

JA83.J65   1995   320.5   C95-932749-5

Broadview Press
Post Office Box 1243, Peterborough, Ontario, Canada K9J 7H5

in the United States of America:
3576 California Road, Orchard Park, NY 14127

in the United Kingdom:
B.R.A.D. Book Representation & Distribution Ltd.,
244A, London Road, Hadleigh, Essex. SS7 2DE

Broadview Press gratefully acknowledges the support of the Canada Council, the Ontario Arts Council, the Ontario Publishing Centre, and the Ministry of Canadian Heritage.

PRINTED IN CANADA

Contents

Preface

IF ONE OF THE BASIC SUPPOSITIONS OF this book is true, much in it will soon become out of date, and many of the comments in it will seem either ill-considered, or rather strange. This will be because the political context changes, and what seems appropriate to me to say now, will seem inappropriate to all of us five, ten, or fifteen years from now. For example, a major ideological battle that has dominated much of the twentieth century – the struggle between capitalism and communism – seems decisively over now. Many of the treatments of ideology in the post-war period – particularly in the United States – were dominated by this Cold War reality, but looked at today, less than a decade from the fall of the Berlin Wall, they seem to dwell too much on a conflict no longer at the forefront of our political experience. Similarly, it is sometimes difficult to convey to students the enormity in this century of fascism, an ideology that most of my teachers, if not contemporaries, have also tended to treat as exhausted or failed. And yet in 1995, the most popular Italian politician heads the former neo-fascist party, and ex-communists form part of most governments in Eastern Europe. In the market research for this book, many commentators spoke of the importance of Islamic fundamentalism, some suggesting that this is 'the greatest threat to democracy today.' Have defenders of 'the West' (advanced liberal democracy) and its values simply transferred their opposition and their fears from the communist threat to a fundamentalist threat? Does ideology, too, abhor a vacuum?

This book came about because of a suggestion that a chapter I had written for an introductory text – *Democracy and the State* (1994) – could well be expanded to form the basis for a more focused book on ideology. Much of that chapter has survived here, but much is new also, and all has been revisited and re-examined in the context of a much broader treatment of the subject matter. My method has been to approach ideologies as existing at the intersection of political history and political philosophy; ideas are shaped by the contexts in which they are articulated, debated, and transmitted. Each of the chapters in this book attempts to treat ideas within particular historical or social contexts, and it is the continuities and discontinuities in contexts which provide the dynamic that explains the consistency of ideologies as well as their evolution and transformation. Some readers of the chapter on which this is based found the discussion of liberals, conservatives, liberal conservatives, and conservative liberals confusing. This may be so, but then the reality, considered across generations and cutting across national boundaries, is also confusing.

In the West we have experienced at least three centuries of liberalism and conservatism, and almost two of socialism — to expect that they would remain fixed and susceptible of one easy explanation is to have a very innocent view of the way ideas fare in the real world. Nonetheless, I have attempted to avoid the tendency to multiply distinctions and labels unnecessarily, and having made certain distinctions in early chapters, have also sometimes collapsed them later for the sake of clarity.

Much of the interest of reviewers of this book when it was still a proposal was with either the new and emerging ideologies, or with those which stand outside the mainstream of Western political culture with its focus on conservatism, liberalism, and socialism. Accordingly, I have devoted two chapters to the examination of these rivals, one to those which challenge from within, especially feminism and environmentalism, and one to those which challenge from outside the liberal-democratic consensus, most of which can be grouped under the heading of authoritarianism. In this last respect, while I treat nationalism and religious fundamentalism in the same chapter as authoritarianism, I do not intend to suggest that it is only in authoritarian regimes that nationalism and religion are significant. Rather, nationalism and religion function differently in democratic liberal regimes than they do in authoritarian regimes, and the reader will find many references to nationalism and religion in the chapters which focus on liberal democracy.

I do apologize to those who wished to see here discussions of racism, sexism, heterosexism, tribalism, and even post-modernism. My bias has been (at least) twofold: one, to present as ideology systems of thought which have some *public* currency, where the public refers to normally educated non-specialists in the field; and two, to present those ideological currents most relevant to students in Canada and the United States. Moreover, racism, sexism, and heterosexism, seem to me to be terms usually indicating attitudes which are reflected in individual behaviour, not propositions about ends and means that are the basis for discourse, argument, and rational justification.

The fragments of ideological statement provided are to be approached as just that, fragments, morsels which ideally will serve to whet the appetite of students for more extensive passages which will be found only by returning to the sources from which these have been drawn.

My appreciation for support, comments, suggestions, and feedback, is due to Ed Andrew, Ron Blair, Joy Esberey, Paul Kingston, Susan Solomon, and especially to my wife, Ailsa Hanson. Thanks also to two anonymous reviewers, to Betsy Struthers for her thorough copy-editing, and to Don LePan and Michael Harrison at Broadview.

Chapter One

Definitions and Dimensions

IDEAS MATTER IN POLITICS. We may wish to debate how much they matter, or in what way they play their role, but to deny them any significance would be to declare the futility of all political discourse. It would be pointless to study politics, to read or write political prose, or even to engage in political activity, if the notions which animate such practices were utterly spurious. It is possible to see how important ideas are by comparing the very different political possibilities that exist in various countries, whether the issue is capital punishment, or abortion, or freedom of the press, or regulation of the marketplace. What people believe about politics, about the state and society, about government and power and authority, and rights and equality and opportunity – all these beliefs make a difference to what happens in the real world. The very different experience (at least up to the present) of Canada and the United States with regulating handgun ownership, or the success of European socialist parties put beside the relative failure of their North American counterparts, or the fragility of Italian coalitions compared with Switzerland's stable governments – each of these examples is testimony to the influence of patterns of belief that are, in each country, somewhat unique.

Every society possesses a **political culture** (and often, political sub-cultures), this broad term encompassing many elements which concern the intellectual dispositions (beliefs, attitudes, values) people have about political life or objects. A political culture is an aggregate like "the public" or "society": it indicates a collection of the ideas of the individuals who comprise a community. For this reason it is something independent of the ideas of any *particular* individual(s). Each of us reflects, more or less, the political culture of the society we inhabit or have been raised in, and this "more or less," as well as the ways in which we acquire political culture, can be particularly challenging to measure and demonstrate. Social scientists are intrigued by political culture because they believe that what people think about the political world shapes their behaviour, their consent, or

Fig 1.1 Definitions of Ideology

"In its ... much more important sense, it [ideology] is used to refer to a set of closely related beliefs or ideas, or even attitudes, characteristic of a group or community."
(Plamenatz, 1970:15)

"Ideologies share two principal characteristics: an image of society and a political programme. The image renders society intelligible from a particular viewpoint. Aspects of the social world are accentuated and contrasted to illustrate both how the whole *actually* operates and *ideally* should be organized. The specific social image forms the core of each ideology. From it radiates a programme of action: prescriptions of what ought to be done to ensure that social ideal and actual reality coincide. Prescriptions vary in accordance with the specific image of the good, or properly arranged, society."
(Eccleshall et al, 1984:7)

"An ideology may be – but need not necessarily be – coherent, systematic, and rational. If it is fairly persistent and pervasive, in the sense that a particular point of view or orientation occurs whenever an individual, group, or organization engages in action or discussion on any given subject, the bias takes on the shape of 'ideology.'"
(Groth, 1971:1)

"An *ideology* consists of a systematic and all-embracing political doctrine that claims to give a complete and universal theory of people and society, and to derive therefrom a program of action.... Of particular importance in the modern era is the role of ideologies as political belief systems that can be used to mobilize people for action."
(Funderburk and Thobaben, 1989:1)

"*An ideology is a value or belief system accepted as fact or truth by some group.* It is composed of sets of attitudes toward the various institutions and processes of society. It provides the believer with a picture of the world both as it is and as it should be, and, in so doing, it organizes the tremendous complexity of the world into something fairly simple and understandable. This is the point of the word *system*; ideologies are organized or patterned beliefs."
(Sargent, 1987:2)

"First, a political ideology is a reasonably coherent pattern of ideas about politics and government.... Second, a political ideology succeeds in simplifying these ideas considerably. To do this, it relies heavily on verbal and non-verbal symbols. Finally, a political ideology provides a program, and incites action.... A one-sentence definition might therefore be: 'Political ideology is a form of thought that presents a pattern of complex political ideas simply and in a manner that inspires action to achieve certain goals.'"
(Skidmore, 1989:7)

their level of tolerance. It is often suggested that political culture defines the boundaries of political activity within a polity, and in this way limits the realm of political possibility. Within any given society certain policies are seen to be legitimate, others not; debate, competition for authority, and the actual implementation of policy will generally occur within the boundaries of acceptability defined by the political culture. To be a communist or socialist has just not been "possible" in the United States in the way that it has in many other Western democracies. Many Americans view with suspicion the kind of government-funded health care that Canadians take for granted, or even venerate.

There are many different aspects of political culture that political scientists study, from its transmission through processes of socialization, to the role of mass media and polls in shaping public opinion. Within this book we are concerned with the substantive families of ideas that inhabit political cultures, that is to say, with the various "isms" of politics which are captured by the term **ideology**.

A: IDEOLOGY DEFINED

Among political science terms, **ideology** is infamous for being employed in many different ways. Sometimes ideology is used descriptively to indicate particular types of beliefs or belief-systems, and sometimes normatively: in a negative way ideology is contrasted with more elevated (philosophy) or objective (science) thought, or in a positive way compared to unprincipled or merely pragmatic politics. As I have done elsewhere, I will define ideology here as follows:

An ideology is a more or less consistent set of beliefs about the nature of the society in which individuals live, and about the proper role of the state in establishing or maintaining that society.

Fig 1.2 A Contemporary Philosopher On Ideology

"I take any ideology to have three key features. The first is that it attempts to delineate certain general characteristics of nature or society or both, characteristics which do not belong only to particular features of the changing world which can be investigated only be empirical inquiry.... Two closely related queries can always be raised about this feature of an ideology: What is the status of statements about these general characteristics and how do we show such statements to be true or false? And what is the relationship between the truth or falsity of such statements and the truth or falsity of scientific or historical claims about the character of empirically investigable processes and events?

The second central feature of any ideology is an account of the relationship between what is the case and how we ought to act, between the nature of the world and that of morals, politics, and other guides to conduct.... it does not merely tell us how the world is *and* how we ought to act, but is concerned with the bearing of the one upon the other....

... [T]he third defining property of an ideology is that it is not merely believed by the members of a given social group, but believed in such a way that it at least partially defines for them their social existence. By this I mean that its concepts are embodied in, and its beliefs presupposed by, some of these actions and transactions, the performance of which is characteristic of the social life of that group."
(MacInytre, 1978:5-6)

This definition has much in common with others (see Figure 1.1), and it indicates several features about ideology that other commentators have also noted.

SYSTEMATIC

The first of these is that ideology is **systematic** (or displays coherence), but often incompletely so. In other words, beliefs about one topic are related to beliefs about another, different subject. For example, beliefs about the nature (real or ideal) of society, may be connected somehow to beliefs about the role(s) to be played by the state in society, and this in turn informs beliefs about a particular matter of policy such as gun control. Thus, even though I may believe that access to guns contributes to crime and is generally detrimental to social peace, if I believe strongly enough that the state should have a very limited role in society, I may oppose all or most forms of regulation concerning firearms. My opposition would be very different from that of someone who simply "likes guns" and enjoys possessing them. This latter opposition, unlike the former, would not be ideologically motivated. Ideologically informed opposition to gun control might be linked, say, to a pro-choice position on abortion or to scepticism about government activity in the economy. Someone who is merely a gun collector and opposes regulation of their ownership may well desire or accept government regulation or activity in other areas. The difference in the two cases is the more or less systematic connection of the ideas on particular issues to larger, more general positions. It is sometimes useful to think of ideologies as sets of answers to a variety of questions, ranging from the very general and abstract to the concrete and particular. The systematic organization and connection of such questions and answers is a typical feature of an ideology, as we will see shortly when we turn to specific cases.

NORMATIVE AND PROGRAMMATIC

Secondly, ideologies are **normative**. They are to a large degree, if not primarily, beliefs about how the world *ought* to be. This normative dimension is something ideologies share with political philosophy, and something which makes ideology suspect for all those who believe that thought should be "objective" and that normative questions do not permit "objective" answers. A related dimension of ideology, but not necessarily of philosophy, is that it orients action or requires change in the world. Activity is a matter of following up on the normative beliefs contained in ideology. To believe that the world should be a certain way is one thing; to attempt to make it so is something further. Ideologies typically offer or inform a program of action that seeks to transform the world from the way it is, into what (for the ideology) is its ideal constitution. (Conversely, the ideology may seek to protect a valued way of life from change.) This is the practical or **programmatic** orientation of ideology. The very ability of ideologies to guide or even incite political activity, is one principal feature that makes them interesting to social scientists.

PERSPECTIVE

In addition to promoting a specific view of how the world should be, an ideology very often presupposes definite notions about what the world *is*, or employs unique concepts to explain or make sense of the world of experience. For example, both radical feminism and Marxism draw upon the normative principle of equality, and each seeks to eradicate the inequality it identifies in the world. It is also the case that the equality envisaged by feminism is different from (although not necessarily incompatible with) the equality envisaged by Marxism. Just as striking, though, is the different way in which feminists and Marxists identify the world in which they find inequality. The primary concept Marxists have used to describe and explain the social relations of society is that of **class**. In identifying class relations, Marxists claim to reveal the structure of modern social and political reality. For radical feminists, the structure of social reality is provided not (or not primarily) by class, but by **patriarchy**, the historical subjugation of women by men through socially-constituted gender relations. This does not mean that feminists deny the existence of the economic or material relations that Marxists indicate by the term *class*; it is simply that they argue that these are not the *essential* relationships. The point of this example, then, is that ideologies can operate as different ways of seeing and understanding the social world(s) we inhabit.

One of the most influential treatments of ideology, that provided by Marx (see Figure 1.3), made much of how ideology provides a way of seeing the world. Being a materialist (and a determinist materialist at that), Marx believed that our ideas are rooted in our material or economic activity. Marx also believed that society is composed of classes, based on the organization of production, and that in a capitalist, private property society, the two principal classes are owners (the *bourgeoisie*) and workers (the *proletariat*). The ruling ideology of any society will be the ideology which protects and reflects the interests of the dominant economic class, *even though* it may not be presented or understood by its adherents in such terms. Two aspects of Marx's treatment of ideology have been employed by others who might agree with him on little else: one is the connection (often hidden) of ideas with interests, the other the notion that ideologies are partial views of social and political reality, and in this partiality or bias are incomplete or even untrue (see Figure 1.4). And of course, it is not necessary for ideas to be true to be powerful, or to regulate activity. As a socialist who believed in the eventual triumph of the proletariat through a revolution that would create a classless society, Marx believed that all ideologies were false, except that of the proletariat (that is to say, only Marxism was true). The sociologist Karl Mannheim took Marx's view of ideology as "interested," but argued that the same partiality or lack of objectivity applies to Marxism. In Mannheim's view, *all* belief systems are "ideological," and thus partial and interested; only intellectuals can achieve objectivity by means of their ability to combine several perspectives. Mannheim's treatment of ideology was a pioneering work in what has become known as the "sociology of knowledge." In this field examination is made of the *function* performed by ideas, whether ideology, or science, or religion, rather than an analysis of their content. For the

Fig 1.3 Marx's View of Ideology

"The ideas of the ruling class are in every epoch the ruling ideas: i.e., the class which is the ruling *material* force of society is at the same time its ruling *intellectual* force. The class which has the means of material production at its disposal, consequently also controls the means of mental production, so that the ideas of those who lack the means of mental production are on the whole subject to it....

If now in considering the course of history we detach the ideas of the ruling class from the ruling class itself and attribute to them an independent existence, if we confine ourselves to saying that these or those ideas were dominant at a given time, without bothering ourselves about the conditions of production and the producers of these ideas, if we thus ignore the individuals and world conditions which are the source of the ideas, then we can say, for instance, that during the time the aristocracy was dominant, the concepts honour, loyalty, etc., were dominant, during the dominance of the bourgeoisie the concepts freedom, equality, etc. The ruling class itself on the whole imagines this to be so. This conception of history, which is common to all historians, particularly since the eighteenth century, will necessarily come up against the phenomenon that ever more abstract ideas hold sway, i.e., ideas which increasingly take on the form of universality. For each new class which puts itself in the place of one ruling before it is compelled, merely in order to carry through its aim, to present its interest as the common interest of all the members of society, that is, expressed in ideal form: it has to give its ideas the form of universality, and present them as the only rational, universally valid ones."
(*The German Ideology*, MECW, 1976: V, 59-60)

most part, our concern in what follows will be with the content of political ideologies, rather than with their social function.

THE COHERENCE OF IDEOLOGY

Three elements of ideology are closely related, and, at the risk of oversimplification, form the core of any ideology: an idealization, a diagnosis, and a prescription. There is, in idealization, the development or presentation of an ideal or mode, against which the existing world is then compared, resulting in a diagnosis. Depending on the distance between ideal and reality, the ideology is employed to construct a program designed to bridge that gap: this is prescription. This explains in part at least why ideologies are systematic; actions are

Fig 1.4 Ideologies as Partial World-views

"Indeed Marx and Engels are the originators of what became a widely accepted theory of ideology – that ideologies are interrelated systems of false ideas, false consciousness."
(Gould and Truitt, 1973:1)

"An ideology may be partial; it may consist of ideas and attitudes that relate only to a part of reality. Indeed, ideologies are nearly always partial. Or, perhaps I should say, the word 'ideology' is nearly always used to refer to a particular sphere of thought and not to thought generally."
(Plamenatz, 1970:18)

"Commentators have speculated at length about the epistemological status of ideologies. Can their relative truth-content be determined by rational inquiry? Is it possible to rank ideologies on an ascending scale of falsity with, say, fascism, as most of us would prefer, at the top? Or are ideologies equally invalid because they each distort social reality from some specific viewpoint? Is ideological knowledge a flawed and disreputable form of knowledge: a pathological or false consciousness that is antithetical to the true consciousness represented by science and philosophy? Or are science and philosophy themselves saturated with ideological assumptions which shape the investigations, and slant the conclusions, of their practitioners? And, if so, is completely accurate, objective or impartial social knowledge attainable?"
(Eccleshall et al, 1984:27)

necessarily and not accidentally linked both to the existing conditions encountered in reality, and to more general, abstract conceptions of what is ideal. Similarly, it is not accidental that much of the focus of ideologies and of much of the debate between them, is upon the way they see or explain the existing world. To press the medical analogy, the prescription is only as good as the diagnosis, and it is over the latter that many of the fiercest ideological battles have been fought.

One interesting consequence of the debate over diagnosis is a frequent loss of clarity concerning the ideal towards which the ideology strives. If an ideology is an itinerary for getting from "here" to "there," then logically the first thing needed is an idea of where "there" is. Ideologies, though, are often better at describing "here," and in identifying their means of "travel," than they are at

Fig 1.5 Right and Left

The terms "right" and "left" can be confusing to students, and this in part is because people do not always use them consistently or in the same way. The origin of these terms, like that of the term "ideology," is found in the French Revolution. Members of the parliament (the National Assembly) of the first French Republic were seated according to their ideological positions; those most radical to the left of the presiding officer, and those most conservative to right, with others arrayed in between as appropriate. By *radical* here, we mean those most disposed towards immediate and drastic change in society, and by *conservative* those most committed to maintaining the *status quo*. One employment of the terms "right" and "left," then, is to indicate dispositions towards fundamental or drastic change – but this use can create confusion (Fascist parties, for example, often desire drastic change, but are placed on the far right of the political spectrum). In revolutionary France, the radicals were early socialists and radical liberals; the conservatives were the nobility, monarchists, and political groups committed to the pre-revolutionary social arrangements. There is a long tradition, then, of identifying the left with socialism, and the right with conservatism, – liberalism constituting a "centre." In the twentieth century communism was added to the "extreme left" and fascism to the "extreme right." Obviously this is consistent with our usage of radical and conservative only where the context fits. In this text, "the right" refers to conservative parties or ideologies, and "the left," refers to socialist parties or ideologies.

locating their destination. This is understandable in that the ideal is the most abstract element of the ideology while the present state of affairs is most immediate, most palpable. Ideologies can be quite general (if not vague) about their ultimate goal(s), but the more their strength rests upon discontent with the existing state of affairs, the less this handicaps them. Many of the distinctions between various ideologies of "the left" have to do with competing diagnoses of the ills of contemporary capitalist society, and with competing prescriptions as to the best way of reforming or transforming capitalist society into something more appropriate. When it comes to describing post-capitalist society, leftist theories become much more general – and much more alike.

The implication here is that ideologies are fundamentally critical in their orientation: while this is often true, it is not universally so. Many ideologies are essentially critical of the existing social and political arrangements, the *status quo*, and have presented programs for radical change. But ideologies may also justify a *status quo* and present a program that resists fundamental deliberate change. When an ideological consensus emerges in a society, ideology may be much less about creating social change or transformation than about presenting competing solutions to problems, or managing change brought about by other circumstances. Mannheim called belief systems that seek to change the *status quo*, "utopian," and those which defend it, "ideological."

To the degree that ideologies do take a critical stance, situations may lead to unlikely allies. Ideologies quite opposite in their view of the ultimate good may be united in their denunciation of the *status quo* (for example, socialists and liberals opposing a military dictatorship). By the same token, specific policies or issues may attract support from competing ideological parties because each interprets the likely effect of such policies differently. Occasionally, both prefer some form of the policy in question to what currently exists (in this way some elements of both "the right" and of "the left" have supported the principle of a guaranteed annual income to replace the current patchwork of programs comprising the "welfare state.")

B: THE CONTENT OF IDEOLOGY

We have identified three aspects of an ideology: its **vision**, its **perspective** on the world, and its **program**. The first two of these are elements which ideology shares with political philosophy. Any political philosophy — or ideology — has a vision, and a way of comprehending reality, but a political philosophy is typically less clear than is an ideology about a particular program of action. In this sense ideologies are political philosophies geared for action. It is important to realize that much of the content of ideology is drawn from philosophical sources, and obviously, most often from those thinkers preoccupied with political philosophy. The content that ideology acquires from philosophy and elsewhere, may be approached as an hierarchy of beliefs or propositions, beginning with the most general and abstract and working down to the more specific and practical. These are often presented as categorical or "either/or" questions, an example of a very abstract question being "do you believe in custom or reason?" and an example of a very specific one being "do you believe in the right of women to access to abortion?" (Some questions may be more accurately framed as involving degrees of consent rather than compelling a choice between two alternatives. For example: "how important do you think custom and reason are, respectively?") The notion that these convictions constitute a hierarchy is based on the observation that beliefs about specific issues are often associated with particular answers to more general questions. Individuals who think reason is more reliable or useful than custom will be more likely to support proposals for the reform of traditional institutions, and it is probably a safe bet that those who oppose women's access to abortion place a greater value on some other good than they do on individual liberty.

It is also a reliable rule of thumb that the more general or abstract an issue, the more it can tell us about individuals' ideologies, and conversely, the more specific or practical a topic, the less it reveals about the ideology of its supporters or detractors. Someone whose belief system gives a high priority to tradition or custom is, all else being equal, a conservative; someone who greatly values liberty and equality of opportunity is very likely a liberal. On the other hand, support for lower taxes or opposition to prayer in schools could come equally from conservatives or liberals depending on the more general aims they have or the more abstract principles by which they are motivated. American liberals, for example, might oppose prayer in schools on the grounds that it violates the freedom of conscience of individuals who are not believers or are simply uncomfortable with public prayer. Conservatives might oppose the same measure on the basis that it violates the traditional separation of church and state set out in the American constitution. By contrast, in Canada (with the exception of the province of Newfoundland, which is debating the status of its constitutionally guaranteed parochial schools), the issue might excite neither liberals nor conservatives.

To outline and explain adequately all the possible issues on which ideologies diverge would be impossible here, and would anticipate much of the discussion in the remainder of this book. It is feasible, though, to present three categories of issues on which ideologies diverge, and *some* of the particular questions within each category that are perennial matters of ideological debate. The significance of these categories and the controversies involved with each will only be clear once we proceed to examine ideologies in subsequent chapters.

A. BELIEFS ABOUT SOCIETY AND THE PLACE OF INDIVIDUALS
The end(s)/purpose(s) of human life, of life in society.
The role of God/the Church in society.
Collectivism versus individualism.
Hierarchy versus equality.
Human nature as fallible versus human nature as infinitely perfectible.
The primary unit of identity: tribe, race, family, etc.

B. BELIEFS ABOUT THE STATE AND ABOUT THE NATURE AND STRUCTURE OF POWER
The end(s)/purpose(s) of government.

What makes authority legitimate:
> the place of tradition, religion, reason, law.

The form of power:
> absolute monarchy, responsible government, republicanism.

Ideas of justice:
> the rule of law, rights, equality.

Ideas of democracy:
> participation, representation, accountability.

The extent of the state:
> totalitarian versus activist versus limited versus minimal.

C. BELIEFS ABOUT SPECIFIC AREAS OF GOVERNMENTAL POLICY

economic policy:
> private versus collective or public property, regulation of the market, redistribution.

social policy:
> education, welfare, health care.

public morality/social order:
> crime and punishment, firearms control, sexuality, gender, race.

foreign policy:
> interventionism versus isolationism, nationalism versus internationalism.

In suggesting at the outset that ideologies are systematic, and in identifying and exploring in subsequent chapters the ideologies which go by names such as **liberalism, conservatism, socialism, populism,** and **feminism**, we are observing that the beliefs people hold about the catalogue of topics just listed are not randomly chosen, but display certain tendencies or patterns. For example, Figure 1.6 attempts to show that individuals who believe human nature is fallible are more likely to be disposed towards tradition than those who believe human nature is progressively perfectible, and who, accordingly, will believe in the power of human reason. Continuing, the traditionalists will be more likely to support monarchy and be suspicious of too much public participation in politics; the rationalists will favour republicanism and endorse democratic activity. As Figure 1.7 indicates, collectivists will stress equality and be more favourably disposed to public property than individualists, who will tend to stress rights and the inviolable character of private ownership. It is the existence of these kinds of tendencies or patterns that allows us to identify ideologies at all.

FIG 1.6

HUMAN NATURE

is fallible	is perfectible
supports tradition	supports reason
supports monarchy	supports republicanism

FIG 1.7

COLLECTIVISM	INDIVIDUALISM
stresses equality	stresses rights
supports public property	supports private property

C: THE CONTEXTS OF IDEOLOGY

Typically, ideologies are popular in a way that philosophers and their systems may not be. Many people who consider themselves liberals have never heard of Hobbes or Locke, let alone read their works. Yet to be a liberal is to adhere to an ideology first articulated most forcefully in the philosophies of these two thinkers. Being oriented to political *practice*, then, and being accessible to the general educated public, are two facets of ideology that distinguish it from political philosophy. The third, and in the view of this author, one of the most central points to grasp about ideology, is that it is largely shaped by its situation within shifting contexts. There is much about ideology that we cannot make sense of unless we pay particular attention to the way ideology reacts to specific circumstances. It is this fact which allows us to explain why conservatives in countries like Britain and the United States want government to give greater freedom to market forces, while conservatives in Eastern Europe resist reforms that would do just that. Or why conservatives in the twentieth century are often difficult to distinguish from those whom the early nineteenth century recognized as liberals. There are three levels of context to which we must refer our ideologies.

THE GENERAL SOCIAL AND HISTORICAL CONTEXT

Ideologies are the products of broad changes in the nature and composition of society, in ways that cut across national boundaries and carry through generations or centuries. J. M. Roberts [1980] has argued that the dominant theme of human history in the last two thousand years has been the rise and fall of world domination by Western Europe. Although much of the history since World War II signals the eclipse of Western Europe, it is still true that political models and principles produced by European culture provide the standard for most nations outside of the Islamic world. This is not to suggest the superiority of European culture, but simply to note its historical dominance and the political legacy that period of dominance has given the world; political history *has been* Eurocentric in some important ways which we cannot ignore unless we turn our back on history.

European political history may be divided into three broadly defined periods – **classical antiquity**, **medieval society**, and **liberal modernity** (see Table 1.1) – but it is the passage from the second to the last of these that most interests us here. In the next chapter we will discuss the liberal revolution as a watershed separating the medieval period from modernity. The mix of ideologies we will identify as the "first generation" is in its essentials a product of that revolution and its effects.

THE SPATIAL CONTEXT

This refers to the places – the nations or communities – within which specific ideologies and political cultures develop. The ideological universe we will map in subsequent chapters is a much larger place than any (or at least most) actual political culture(s). Within any given society, an ideology or two will dominate, a couple others may compete, while the rest are absent or so marginal as to elude the acquaintance of most citizens. Our comments above about gun control in the United States and Canada, or about the success of socialism in Europe and its absence in the United States, reflect the fact that the ideological landscape in each of these settings is distinct. Why some ideologies flourish and

Table 1.1 Western European Political History

	Classical Antiquity 400 BC - 400 AD	Medieval Age 400 - 1400	Modernity 1400 - ?
Form of Government	Polis to Empire	Feudal fiefdom to nation-state (absolute monarchy)	Constitutional monarchy to representative government to liberal democracy
Central moral-political concepts	virtue citizenship	natural law divine right	Popular sovereignty individual rights
Economic modes	slavery military agricultural	agrarian military commercial	commercial industrial market activity
Religion	pagan	Catholic Christianity	from Christian pluralism to secularism
Intellectual approach	philosophical	scholastic	scientific

others remain obscure within any country is no doubt a function of the history of that country, of its citizens and their cultural experience. The success in the United States of liberal conservatism with its distrust of the state is no doubt in part rooted in the birth of that country through revolution against a perceived tyrannical power. The viability of tory and socialist parties in Europe in the past has probably owed something to the clarity with which class is perceived in formerly feudal societies. Each case deserves to be considered on its own merits.

Nonetheless, attempts have been made to explain similarities in ideological experience, in particular the experience of "new" societies, one-time colonies of Europe such as Canada, the United States, Australia, New Zealand, and South Africa. The ground-breaking work here was Louis Hartz's *The Founding of New Societies* (1955), which offered a theoretical explanation for the ideological landscapes of "New World" societies based upon their relationship to the founding "Old World" societies. Hartz's theory was applied to Canada by Kenneth McRae, and re-applied by Gad Horowitz in his article "Conservatism, Liberalism, and Socialism in Canada" (1966), a central work comparing the nature of ideology in Canada and the United States. This work has been so influential that political scientists in Canada still often refer to the Hartz-Horowitz thesis. To paraphrase it adequately in the short space left in this chapter is not possible, and students are advised to consult the original.

THE TEMPORAL CONTEXT

Ideologies are ever-fluid, changing in response to political events and social circumstances. To be a liberal for example, changes its meaning in the United States after the Depression and the Roosevelt New Deal. How will ideologies that sustained themselves in the context of the Cold War re-define themselves in its absence? It is as much because of shifting temporal contexts as anything else, that the meanings of liberalism, conservatism, and even socialism have been impermanent. That is why we examine each of these ideologies at least twice, in the guise of first and second "generations." Similarly, the emergence of new ideologies like feminism and environmentalism (ecologism) reflects changing circumstances, but we describe them as a "third generation" to indicate that there is perhaps more continuity here with previous ideologies than may be indicated by new names.

In turning to specific ideologies, we will highlight for each the **vision**, the **perspective**, and the typical elements of a **program**. But we will begin in each case by examining the context in which the ideology arose, and by which it was defined. Much of what we have said in this first chapter is of necessity very general, and the succeeding chapters should make it clearer. Nonetheless, it might be well for students, to return and read this chapter once more, after becoming acquainted with the individual ideologies.

SUGGESTED READING:

Bell, Daniel. (1960). *The End of Ideology*. New York: Free Press of Glencoe.

Eccleshall, Robert, Vincent Geoghegan, Richard Jay, and Rick Wilford. (1984). *Political Ideologies: an Introduction*. London: Hutchinson.

Funderburk, Charles, and Robert G. Thobaben. (1989). *Political Ideologies: Left, Center, Right*. New York: Harper & Row.

Gould, James A., and Willis H. Truitt. (1973). *Political Ideologies*. New York: Macmillan.

Groth, Alexander J. (1971). *Major Ideologies: An Interpretative Survey of Democracy, Socialism, and Nationalism*. New York: John Wiley.

Horowitz, Gad. (1966). "Conservatism, Liberalism, and Socialism in Canada: An Interpretation." *Canadian Journal of Economics and Political Science*. 32, no. 2.

MacIntyre, Alasdair. (1978). *Against The Self-Images of the Age*. Notre Dame: University of Notre Dame Press.

Mannheim, Karl. (1936). *Ideology and Utopia: An Introduction to the Sociology of Knowledge*. London: Routledge & Kegan Paul.

Plamenatz, John. (1970). *Ideology*. London: Macmillan.

Sargent, Lymann Tower. (1987). *Contemporary Political Ideologies*. Seventh Edition. Chicago: Dorsey Press.

Skidmore, Max J. (1989). *Ideologies: Politics in Action*. New York: Harcourt Brace Jovanovich.

Chapter Two

Ideologies: First Generation

INTRODUCTION:
THE CONTEXT OF MODERN IDEOLOGY

CONTEMPORARY NORTH AMERICANS are heirs of a great revolution that occurred in Europe between three and five hundred years ago. (With some qualification, the same could be said of the citizens of Great Britain, France, Germany, the Netherlands, Belgium, Switzerland, Austria, Italy, Norway, Sweden, Iceland, Denmark, New Zealand, and Australia.) This revolution was the transformation from medieval community to liberal society, a multi-faceted transformation – economic, cultural, religious, scientific, even psychological. One of the significant political results of that revolution was the birth of ideology, and why that should have been so deserves our consideration. Secondly, this revolution produced certain ways of thinking or arguing which have remained true of (almost) all the ideologies produced since this time of upheaval.

The association of the birth of ideology with the emergence of the modern era is not a simple coincidence, nor is it a necessarily obvious correspondence. The world had seen competing systems of thought before, particularly in the classical period, when thinkers were Stoics or Sceptics or Epicureans; were these competing systems not ideologies? One essential difference is the development, in the modern period, of a "mass society," or of a "popular culture." In the modern age, systems of thought are not simply debated by a few philosophical professionals, but become, to a degree they never could in the classical period, the property of non-intellectuals. Ideologies inform, animate, and sometimes mobilize the broad public across class lines (something that becomes all the more true once literacy spreads and a general education becomes possible); indeed, Marx's concern with "bourgeois" ideology was that it was held by far more than just the bourgeoisie. In this way, the modern emergence of ideology reflects the penetration of ordinary life by political ideas which were once the privileged realm of a small, educated elite. It is indeed appropriate that the first modern ideology — liberalism — opposed the existence and dominance of such an elite.

Ideology was born, then, in the transformation of Western European society from the feudal nature in which it had existed for centuries into what we recognize as liberal modernity. It is *liberal* modernity because liberalism was the set of beliefs advocating, informing, and justifying this significant set of social and political changes. The ideologies which have competed with liberalism have had an axe to grind with the social and political reality of modern society, even if, as we shall see, they have become often very comfortable within that society. Before we examine liberalism and its opponents, we need to highlight several features of the transformation I have called the "liberal revolution," because these events and their consequences have become part of the background for all ideologies.

FEUDAL SOCIETY

Feudal society was a product of the encounter of tribal chiefdoms with the remnants of the Roman state. Authority was fragmented (something which marked the medieval period until late in its development) and usually exercised by local nobles, whose position often reflected military rank or prowess. Although there were attempts to reunite Western Europe by reconstituting the Roman Empire, a medieval emperor was at most a "chief of chiefs" rather than someone who personally governed the "empire." This last point is important, for medieval authority was largely personal.

The personal nature of authority in the medieval period is indicated by the dominance of traditional justifications. (Hereditary monarchy, a product of this period, is a classic example of the selection of leaders on the basis of custom or adherence to "accepted ways.") At the same time, there was considerable effort on the part of leaders to secure claims to charismatic authority: the "divine right of kings" is a theory that claims leaders are anointed and justified by God in their exercise of power. The religious unification of Europe under Catholic Christianity meant that rulers claimed justification under the same God, and that medieval politics often focused upon the relationship between the state and the Church. For the most part, weak, fragmented political power was complemented by a universal Church exercising considerable authority in a variety of contexts. Rulers sought favour from the Church in order to enhance their legitimacy, while the Church often required the power of the local state in order to enforce authoritative decisions or policies. The desire of either church or state to have the upper hand or final word set the stage for many of the conflicts of medieval times.

Feudal society was a collection of communities, very alike in some respects, different in others. Most individuals were peasants, engaged in subsistence agriculture and the performance of obligations to lord and to Church. In return, peasants received protection from the lord against assault or invasion and hope for salvation through the mediation of the Church. These reciprocal obligations were an essential feature of feudal society and its own justification; while the preponderance of the weight of these obligations fell upon the peasantry, their rationale was held to be the common good of the community for which the feudal lord was ultimately responsible. The mutual obligations between nobility and peasant mirrored the relationships between different levels of nobility. Medieval society presented an **organic hierarchy**, hierarchical because it was a structure of unequal resources and power, but organic in that the various components were linked by mutual obligations and duties. Power and authority also reflected this organic hierarchy. An emperor's power and authority depended on his ability to coerce or influence the princes and kings, which depended on their ability to coerce or influence the lesser nobility, and thus ultimately on *their* control of the peasantry — the final source of labour and production. Much of the medieval period was occupied by struggles among the nobility to establish their position within this hierarchy of claims and obligations, struggles usually settled by battle. Similarly, the laws promulgated by a king would only extend so far as his ability to enforce them, or as far as the willingness of his vassals to enforce them on his behalf. These vassals, in turn, would make and enforce their own laws to the extent of their ability. While in theory, law might announce common standards for a kingdom, in practice, law would be as fragmented as political power, and on a local level would reflect the traditional practices and customs of the community.

Feudal society was also very rigid, that is, not characterized by social mobility. Social position, high or low, was inherited, and with it a set of obligations and rights specific to that rank. Feudal society represented and reinforced a web of connections between entrenched social positions. This was a durable form of life, lasting for centuries, yet accommodating development and change within. The rigidity and durability of feudal society also meant that when powerful forces of social change arose in the fifteenth and sixteenth centuries, they could not be reconciled with the structure of this society, but required a social and political revolution ushering in a radically different form of life.

The medieval period ended when various forces became strong enough to dissolve the bonds which had held together the feudal structure. Sometimes change was gradual, and sometimes there were explosive developments; feudal society dissolved in nations at various times with different speed. For example, the transformation was relatively gradual and complete in Britain by the end of the seventeenth century, exploded violently in France in 1789, was not complete in Germany until well into the nineteenth century, and came to Russia early in our own century. For our purposes here, it is possible to discuss briefly three moments in the dissolution of feudal society and in the emergence of liberal modernity: the Reformation, the Enlightenment, and the rise of the market economy. All three continue to mark contemporary Western culture and society.

THE REFORMATION

The Reformation refers to the breakdown of the religious (and cultural) dominance of the Catholic Church. It is dated from Martin Luther's rebellion in 1517, but this was only the first in a series of reactions against the practices and theology of the Roman Church, reactions which established various Protestant sects and caused widespread social unrest, including several wars between and within states. The rise of Protestantism between the sixteenth and eighteenth centuries shattered the unity of the religious life of Western Europe and so undermined the authority of one of its central institutions, the Catholic Church. Conversion to one of the Protestant religions was a useful way for rulers to establish their own independence from the Church at Rome, and an opportunity to shape laws and practices free of ecclesiastical influence. Rulers of either confession found religion a useful pretence, or the basis of a duty, to make war against rulers of the opposite conviction. Most immediately though, for the ordinary individual, and for the eventual development of ideology, the establishment of reformed Christianity (which failed to become established in some nations — i.e., France, Spain, Italy) brought an increased measure of individual freedom through liberation from the authoritative obligations and duties imposed by the Catholic Church, and an increased emphasis on individual conscience and self-direction. This challenge to the religious and theological *status quo* had tremendous political significance (and a radical, revolutionary potential), although Luther himself called for continued obedience to civil authorities.

THE ENLIGHTENMENT

If the Reformation was a revolution against the traditional (Catholic) Church, the **Enlightenment** was a revolution against traditional philosophy and science, a movement that sought to understand the world and humanity on a new, more rational basis. Medieval philosophy and its accounts of natural scientific phenomena were marked by what is called Scolasticism. Education in the medieval period was provided, almost without exception, by men of the Church teaching in schools where the priesthood and nobility were educated. Accordingly, medieval thought was concerned to give an account of the world that was consistent with Catholic theology. For example, following the Biblical account of creation, Scholastic science taught that the earth is the centre of the universe, a teaching challenged by the Polish astronomer Nikolas Copernicus, whose observations led him to conclude that the planetary bodies revolve around the sun. Telescopic observations by the Italian astronomer Galileo confirmed Copernicus's theory, but under extreme pressure from the Church, Galileo was forced to recant (deny) his own findings.

It should not surprise us, then, that the Enlightenment — a new, non-theological way of thinking — followed on the heels of the Reformation. But the Enlightenment flourished not only because the Church's influence waned, but also because the new explanations of the world could be applied practically and be demonstrated as superior to traditional accounts. Indeed, the Enlightenment was by no means confined to Protestant thinkers. New ways of understanding led to new ways of doing, and where human practice confirmed these revelations, theology had to give way. The term "Enlightenment" covers several, often opposing approaches to understanding the world — idealism, empiricism, rationalism, utilitarianism, materialism, etc. Our interest is with two themes common to these various movements. One is the growth of a "scientific" approach to understanding the world. Science bases explanation upon experience, in particular on the critically controlled experience which results from the development of an experimental methodology; indeed, critical reflection on experience was perhaps the kernel at the heart of the Enlightenment.

Secondly, stemming from this kernel, was the **scepticism** of the Enlightenment. By this, we mean the disposition to take nothing for granted, to question, probe, and challenge existing ways of thought in order to uncover and eliminate error, weakness or inconsistency. All traditional theories or explanations, whether scientific, religious, political or moral, were open to challenge — and in fact were challenged. The Enlightenment has been called the "Age of Reason," and this emphasis on the capacities of human rationality informs both the adoption of scientific methodology and the sceptical approach to all received doctrines. The fundamental premise of all Enlightenment thought is that human experience, whether in the natural world or in social life, is accessible to human reason, and explicable in rational terms.

The Enlightenment was extremely corrosive of feudal society because it challenged all existing ways of living and the justifications offered for them. In the face of reason, one cannot justify political institutions by simply saying "that's the way it's always been"; the arrangements of society, like all others, are open to inspection on the grounds of their rationality. Understanding life rationally also carries with it the imperative to organize and conduct life rationally; in the context of traditional institutions this often had revolutionary implications. Many of our key political ideas — liberty, equality, popular sovereignty, the rule of law, rights, etc. —are products of the critical reflection on political experience conducted by Enlightenment thinkers. More immediately, the Enlightenment proposed that each individual has in their* reason a capacity for reflecting upon the world in which they live, for judging that world, and ultimately for changing it.

In short, together the Reformation and the Enlightenment overthrew the intellectual unity and hegemony of the middle ages, opening the way to diversity and contest of belief systems. In this way the path was cleared and in some measures the means and justifications provided, for the development of ideology.

THE MARKET ECONOMY

If the Reformation and the Enlightenment were revolutions in the way in which humans thought and believed, revolutions which had great impact on the spheres of human action, by contrast, the growth of the market economy was a revolution in the organization of practical life that also had impact on human culture. By "market" we mean the exchange of goods, services, and labour in transactions between individuals. A market economy exists when economic activity is undertaken primarily for the purpose of exchange in the market. Thus we can observe that feudal society had market activity — individual transactions of labour, goods and services — but was not a market economy, because most economic activity was for the purposes of immediate consumption or authoritative transfer (e.g. taxes to the landlord, or tithes to the church). Feudal peasants engaged in market activity only on a limited basis, and only after other ends such as feeding and clothing themselves and the payment of feudal obligations had been met. Markets need buyers as well as sellers, and feudal

---

* In this text, plurals are often used in "agreement" with words such as "each" and "every"; while such usage violates dictates of eighteenth–century grammarians, it is in accord with usage from Chaucer to Milton, and is a convenient way of avoiding the sexism of allowing "he" or "him" to represent both male and female, and of avoiding the undeniable awkwardness of "he or she," "his or her," etc.

peasants generally had little or nothing to spend or trade in the marketplace. The consuming class was the nobility and those wage labourers in the employ of the nobility, together constituting a very small proportion of the population. Market activity in feudal society was largely limited to basic necessities that required craftsmanship (tools, utensils), or luxury articles imported from other places. Thus markets existed throughout the feudal period, but were not the central focus of economic activity or production. About the sixteenth century, this began to change. A market economy could not develop without the erosion of feudal relations, and as the market economy grew, it in turn eroded what remained of feudal society.

A market economy has two fundamental requirements which feudal society could not meet: that economic production be undertaken for the purpose of exchange in the market, and that individuals obtain the goods they consume through purchases in the market. It was necessary, then, to transform the rural, self-sufficient production of feudal society into a predominantly urban market-oriented production. Ideally, even agricultural production would be reorganized on capitalist rather than traditional lines. An emerging market thus challenged the very basis of feudal society — the relationship between lord and peasant. As the extent of market activity grew, it required the transformation or elimination of feudal institutions, practices, and structures. For example, production for the marketplace requires the ability to hire labourers to produce goods or commodities. To develop a market in labour requires displacing peasants from subsistence agriculture and paying them a wage for engaging their labour in some other form of production. To displace peasants from the land requires freeing them from feudal obligations to the lord and Church. As with the Reformation and the Enlightenment, the growth of a market economy meant dissolving the bonds which held together feudal society, and thus tied individuals to their place within this organic, traditional society.

As may have become obvious, the Reformation, the Enlightenment, and the emergence of the market economy were not wholly separate events, but mutually reinforcing. It is difficult to imagine the growth of the market occurring as rapidly as it did without the social and cultural changes brought about by the other two revolutions. For example, in contrast to the emphasis placed by the Catholic Church upon the virtues of poverty and the potential sinfulness of riches, several variants of reformed Christianity regarded the accumulation of worldly goods as a sign of upright character. The market required a moral revolution through which it could be seen as proper for ordinary individuals (non-nobles) to be concerned with the acquisition of wealth; the Reformation helped accomplish this revolution. Likewise, the diminution of the power of the Church, generally a conservative institution, generally weakened resistance to social change. The Enlightenment was also of great practical importance to the economic transformation of Europe. The market economy could not have become so dominant without the development of processes of manufacture and the reorganization of social labour around production for the market. The practical side-effect of the new scientific rationalism of the Enlightenment was an explosion of technology, tangible in the inventions which sparked the Industrial Revolution. Science not only provided new ways of transforming raw materials and new kinds of goods, but a way of problem-solving which allowed for continual innovation, invention, and improvement on existing designs. Not coincidentally, those whose interests were served by the changes being brought about in society found in Enlightenment philosophy the concepts and arguments with which to justify the new and undermine the traditional. The rising middle class (neither peasantry nor aristocracy) created by the emerging market was often quick to embrace the Reformation and the Enlightenment, finding in these ammunition for their assault on traditional privilege and rigid political structures. With the language and concepts of the Reformation and Enlightenment, and recognizing the new opportunities created by economic change, they constructed an ideology — liberalism.

A. LIBERALISM

Liberalism is the first modern ideology, and as yet the dominant ideology of the contemporary age. [fn. It is important not to confuse ideologies with political parties; see Chapter Eight] As noted, the context in which liberalism was born was that of reaction to the feudal structures of medieval society. From the mid-seventeenth to the early nineteenth centuries, liberalism received systematic articulation and refinement by a series of philosophers and political activists.

THE STATE OF NATURE

The liberal reaction against the organic, hierarchical structure of feudal society is seen clearly in a conceptual device that appears frequently as a starting point in early liberal thought: the "state of nature." This was a (usually) hypothetical construct of how humans would live, singly or together, in a condition without political authority or other ordering institutions (see L1-L3). This type of speculation illustrates clearly three characteristics of liberalism: (a) the liberal focus on and primary valuation of **the individual**, (b) the **artificial** nature of **society** in the liberal view, and (c) the **rational, instrumental** character of political institutions, which liberals have sought to justify on the basis of their service to the self-interest of individuals. If medieval society embodied the

The State of Nature:
Thomas Hobbes:

[*For Hobbes, given human nature (L1), the state of nature is a condition of war (L2), which humans would gladly escape by acknowledging a common political authority (L4).*]

L1 "So that in the first place, I put for a general inclination of all mankind, a perpetual and restless desire of power after power, that ceases only in death. And the cause of this, is not always that a man hopes for a more intensive delight, than he has already attained to; or that he cannot be content with a moderate power: but because he cannot assure the power and means to live well, which he has present, without the acquisition of more."
(*Leviathan*, Chapter XI)

L2 "Hereby it is manifest, that during the time men live without a common Power to keep them all in awe, they are in that condition which is called war; and such a war, as is of every man, against every man.... In such a condition, there is no place for industry; because the fruit thereof is uncertain: and consequently no culture of the earth; no navigation, nor use of the commodities that may be imported by Sea; no commodious building; no instruments of moving, and removing such things as require much force; no knowledge of the face of the earth; no account of time; no arts,; no letters; no society; and which is worst of all, continual fear, and danger of violent death; and the life of man, solitary, poor, nasty, brutish, and short."
(*Leviathan*, Chapter XIII)

John Locke:

[*With a more conventional view than Hobbes, Locke sees the state of nature as something which can become a state of war, but is not necessarily such.*]

L3 "[W]e must consider what state all men are naturally in, and that is, a *state of perfect freedom* to order their actions and dispose of their possessions, and persons as they think fit, within the bounds of the law of nature, without asking leave, or depending upon the will of any other man.
A *state* also *of equality*, wherein all the power and jurisdiction is reciprocal, no one having more than another ..." (*Second Treatise*, §4)

dominance of social structure over individuals, then liberalism is the political philosophy of individualism; political community, or what liberal thinkers called "civil society" is somewhat artificial, something we establish from our initial position as individuals in order to improve our personal well-being (see L4-L7). Correspondingly, in the liberal view, social structures are reasonable instruments (that is, they are means we devise with our reason) that ought to maximize our well-being. Liberal thinkers have differed in identifying the character of this well-being (security, pleasure, self-determination), but they have agreed that it is the well-being of individuals which political society is ideally designed to secure. The verb "secure" is important here, for early liberals believed the state should provide a framework of laws and order within which individuals could safely pursue their self-interest (see L8-L12). They did not believe that the state should actually provide the tangible means of well-being to individuals. Early liberal thought, then, is not only about self-interest, but about self-reliance and self-regulation.

LIBERTY AND A LIMITED STATE

The typical medieval citizen was enmeshed in a web of responsibilities, duties, requirements, and sometimes privileges, with respect to church, state, family, class, etc. By contrast, liberalism put considerable emphasis on freedom or liberty (see L13-L16). For liberals, we are by nature free, but surrender some of our liberty to live in society with others, a surrender made in exchange for some other good, like security. (By nature, for liberals, we are also equal, but this receives less emphasis; see L17-L19). Government, or the limitation on our liberty which government involves, is seen by liberals as a necessary evil, and they are concerned to limit the extent of any limitation on personal liberty (see L20-L21). Increasingly, this liberty came to be expressed or defined through appeal to individual **rights,** which are claims sometimes made against other citizens, but also and most importantly, against the state (see Chapter Five below). Rights, in effect, put limits on the state, and a central political tenet of liberalism is the notion of a limited state, something clearly conceived in opposition to the absolute monarchies of the late feudal period. Instead of government being the property of *an* individual, it is — in theory — to serve the interests of *all* individuals, and to ensure this, liberals argued for limits on the state. Such limits could be achieved by removing certain subjects from the compass of state authority (as in the device of rights), or by giving greater control over government to the individuals whom government is supposed to serve (as through democracy). Either path embodies the notion of **constitutionalism,** and constitutionalism in turn implies **popular sovereignty.**

The Creation of Civil Society
Thomas Hobbes:

L4 "Lastly, the agreement ... of men, is by covenant only, which is artificial: and therefore it is no wonder if there be somewhat else required (besides covenant) to make their agreement constant and lasting; which is a common power, to keep them in awe, and to direct their actions to the common benefit.

The only way to erect such a common power, as may be able to defend them from the invasion of foreigners, and the injuries of one another, and thereby to secure them in such sort, as that by their own industry, and by the fruits of the Earth, they may nourish themselves and live contentedly; is, to confer all their power and strength upon one Man, or upon one Assembly of men, that may reduce all their Wills, by plurality of voices, unto one Will: which is as much as to say, to appoint one man, or Assembly of men, to bear their person; and every one to own, and acknowledge himself to be author of whatsoever he that so beareth their person, shall act, or cause to be acted, in those things which concern the common peace and safety; and therein to submit their wills, every one to his will, and their judgements, to his judgement. This is more than consent, or concord; it is a real unity of them all, in one and the same person, made by covenant of every man with every man, in such manner, as if every man should say to every man, *I authorize and give up my right of governing myself, to this man, or to this assembly of men, on this condition, that thou give up thy right to him, and authorise all his actions in like manner.* This done, the multitude so united in one person, is called a commonwealth, in Latin *civitas*. This is the generation of that great Leviathan, or rather (to speak more reverently) of that *mortal God*, to which we owe under the *immortal God*, our peace and defence." (*Leviathan*, Chapter XVII)

John Locke:

L5 "I moreover affirm, that all men are naturally in that state [of nature], and remain so, till by their own consents they make themselves members of some political society ..." (*Second Treatise*, §15)

L6 "Men being, as has been said, by Nature, all free, equal and independent, no one can be put out of this estate, and subjected to the political power of another, without his own *Consent*. The only way whereby any one divests himself of his natural liberty, and *puts on the bonds of civil society* is by agreeing with other Men to join and unite into a community, for their comfortable, safe, and peaceable living one amongst another, in a secure enjoyment of their properties, and a greater security against any that are not of it.... When any number of men have so *consented to make one community* or government, they are thereby presently incorporated, and make *one body politic*, wherein the *majority* have a right to act and conclude the rest." (*Second Treatise*, § 95)

L7 "And thus that, which begins and actually *constitutes any political society*, is nothing but the consent of any number of freemen capable of a majority to unite and incorporate into such a society. And this is that, and that only, which did, or could give *beginning* to any *lawful government* in the world." (*Second Treatise*, § 99)

Constitutionalism is the notion that there are established, understood rules concerning the exercise of power and authority, and that those who exercise power and authority respect these rules. In practice this means a set of limits or restraints on the scope of governmental authority or power, and the rules that provide this restraint embody a constitution, the most fundamental law of a polity. Clearly, constitutionalism is liberalism's response to the arbitrary, personal nature of absolute power as it developed at the end of the feudal period.

Popular sovereignty is the notion that the authority (or power) of the state is traced ultimately to the people who are governed within that state. Public authority is entrusted to elites by the people and is to be exercised for their (the people's) interest. In those thinkers who employed the devices of a state of nature, popular sovereignty was indicated by the supposed "creation" of government through a collective agreement called a "social contract" or "covenant," and with this agreement individuals were supposed to pass from a natural state without government to a civil state with rational, accountable government. In time, the device of the state of nature fell out of fashion in liberal thought (neither history nor social science support it), but the notion of popular sovereignty did not, and developed into the more familiar concept of democracy.

Early liberals, though, were somewhat uneasy about democracy, and looked for other constitutional means of keeping rulers in check. In Britain, liberals (called Whigs) pushed for **responsible government**, a struggle culminating in the so-called Glorious (or Whig) revolution of 1688, which led to a system of responsible government that has been the model for most of the world's parliamentary constitutions (which are the majority of the world's democracies). Re-

The Ends (Purposes) of Government
Thomas Hobbes:

L8 "The Office of the Sovereign, (be it a monarch, or an assembly) consists in the end, for which he was trusted with the Sovereign power, namely the procuration of *safety of the people*; to which he is obliged by the Law of Nature, and to render an account thereof to God, the Author of that Law, and to none but him. But by safety here, is not meant a bare preservation, but also all other contentments of life, which every man by lawful industry, without danger, or hurt to the commonwealth, shall acquire to himself.

And this is intended should be done, not by care applied to individuals, further than their protection from injuries, when they shall complain; but by a general providence, contained in public instruction, both of doctrine, and example; and in the making, and executing of good laws, to which individual persons may apply their own cases."

"... A good law is that, which is *needful*, for the *good of the people*, and withall *perspicuous*."
(*Leviathan*, Chapter XXX)

John Locke:

L9 "The great and *chief end* therefore, of men's uniting into commonwealths, and putting themselves under government, *is the preservation of their property*."
(*Second Treatise*, §124)

L10 "**Political power** then I take to be *a right* of making laws with penalties of death, and consequently all less penalties, for the regulating and preserving of property, and of employing the force of the community, in the execution of such laws, and in the defence of the common-wealth from foreign injury, and all this only for the public good." (*Second Treatise*, §3)

James Mill:

L11 "We may allow, for example, in general terms that the lot of every human being is determined by his pains and pleasures, and that his happiness corresponds with the degree in which his pleasures are great and his pains are small. Human pains and pleasures are derived from two sources: they are produced either by our fellow men or by causes independent of other men. We may assume it as another principle that the concern of government is with the

former of these two sources: that its business is to increase to the utmost the pleasures, and diminish to the utmost the pain, which men derive from one another."
(*Essay on Government*, I)

L12 "[T]he interest of the community, considered in the aggregate or in the democratical point of view, is that each individual should receive protection, and that the powers which are constituted for that purpose should be employed exclusively for that purpose."
(*Essay on Government*, V)

---

sponsible government means that the political executive is not able to act without the support of a majority in the legislature (the chamber of representatives). This made England a constitutional monarchy, and established the supremacy of Parliament.

A different approach, but with the same goal, was the advocacy of **mixed government**, or of a **separation of powers**, as embodied in the American constitution (see L22-23). Through history, mixed government had meant tempering government by one (monarchy) with government by the few (aristocracy) and by the many (democracy). This was the model for the American constitution of a President, Supreme Court, and Congress, with two distinctions. As a republic, the government by one was embodied in the office of a President rather than a monarch, and we should note in passing that for many liberals only a republic will do; monarchy, constitutional or otherwise, is an unacceptable feudal remnant. Secondly, instead of putting a check on monarchy, the designers of the American constitution (primarily James Madison), were liberals seeking to keep democracy in check.

Whether they advocated responsible government or separate branches of government kept honest through checks and balances, liberals tended to agree on the necessity of **representative government** (see L24-L25). An important part of the state, for some liberals the supreme part, the legislature, should be composed of representatives of the people. Here too, we should note that many early liberals had a very narrow view of who should be entitled to sit in the legislature or vote for such representatives. It was not a large step though for liberals to move, as they eventually did, from advocating representative government to advocating representative democracy as the surest means of preserving citizens' liberty.

Liberty
Thomas Hobbes:

L13 "By Liberty, is understood, according to the proper signification of the word, the absence of external impediments: which impediments, may often take away part of a man's power to do what he would; but cannot hinder him from using the power left him, according as his judgement, and reason shall dictate to him.

... The Liberty of a Subject, lies therefore only in those things, which in regulating their actions, the Sovereign has permitted: such as is the Liberty to buy, and sell, and otherwise contract with one another: to choose their own abode, their own diet, their own trade of life, and institute their children as they themselves think fit; and the like.

... As for other liberties, they depend on the silence of the law. In cases where the Sovereign has prescribed no rule, there the subject has the liberty to do, or forbear, according to his own discretion."
(*Leviathan*, Chapter IV)

John Locke:

L14 "But though this [the state of nature] be a *state of liberty*, yet it is *not a state of licence*, though man in that state have an uncontrollable liberty, to dispose of his person or possessions, yet he has not liberty to destroy himself, or so much as any Creature in his possession, but where some nobler use, than its bare preservation calls for it. The State of Nature has a Law of Nature to govern it, which obliges every one: And Reason, which is that Law, teaches all Mankind, who will but consult it, that being all equal and independent, no one ought to harm another in his Life, Health, Liberty, or Possessions."
(*Second Treatise*, §6)

L15 "*Freedom of men under government*, is, to have a standing rule to live by, common to every one of that society, and made by the legislative power erected in it; a liberty to follow my own will in all things, where the rule prescribes not; and not to be subject to the inconstant, uncertain, unknown, arbitrary will of another man."
(*Second Treatise*, §22)

Charles Secondat, Baron de Montesquieu:

L16 "It is true that in democracies the people seem to act as they please; but political liberty does not consist in an unlimited freedom. In governments, that is, in societies directed by laws, liberty can consist only in the power of doing what we ought to will, and in not being constrained to do what we ought not to will.

We must have continually present to our minds the difference between independence and liberty. Liberty is a right of doing whatever the laws permit, and if a citizen could do what they forbid he would be no longer possessed of liberty, because all his fellow-citizens would have the same power."
(*Spirit of the Laws*, Book XI, Part 3)

ECONOMIC LIBERTY

As important to the early liberals as *political* liberty was *economic* liberty. This is a notion perhaps better expressed by the term *market autonomy,* meaning that the state leaves unregulated the private economic transactions of individuals (see also Chapter Five). Again, this may be seen more clearly in contrast to the feudal economy, which was heavily regulated by both church and state, and which entailed a variety of authoritative transfers of resources from citizens to state and church. The classic liberal statement on economic matters has been considered the "laissez faire" doctrine of minimal government activity in the marketplace. (What "laissez faire" advocates often fail to acknowledge is that market society does not "just happen," but requires a variety of supportive policies and activities to be undertaken by the state —e.g. rules governing exchange, enforcement of contracts, stable currency, etc. In its early days, liberalism was as much about creating the conditions for a market society to flourish as it was about letting the market do its own thing.)

TOLERANCE

In addition to political and economic liberty, liberalism came to argue also for social or moral liberty. The most famous statement of this strain of liberalism remains John Stuart Mill's essay *On Liberty*, which is about freedom of opinion, belief, and lifestyle. These concerns are consistent with an ideology of individualism; if individual well-being requires political and economic liberty, why should it not also entail social or moral liberty? In asking such questions, how-

Equality
Thomas Hobbes:

L17 "Nature hath made men so equal, in the faculties of body, and mind; as that though there be found one man sometimes manifestly stronger in body, or of quicker mind then another; yet when all is reckoned together, the difference between man, and man, is not so considerable, as that one man can thereupon claim to himself any benefit, to which another may not pretend, as well as he."
(*Leviathan*, Chapter XIII)

Thomas Jefferson:

L18 "Whenever there is in any country, uncultivated lands and unemployed poor, it is clear that the laws of property have been so far extended as to violate natural right. The earth is given as a common stock for man to labour and live on. If, for the encouragement of industry we allow it to be appropriated, we must take care that other employment be furnished to those excluded from the appropriation. If we do not the fundamental right to labour the earth returns to the unemployed."
[*letter to James Madison*, October 28, 1785]

L19 "We hold these truths to be self-evident: that all men are created equal; that they are endowed by their Creator with inherent and inalienable rights; that among these are life, liberty, and the pursuit of happiness; that to secure these rights, governments are instituted among men, deriving their just powers from the consent of the governed; that whenever any form of government becomes destructive of these ends, it is the right of the people to alter or to abolish it, and to institute new government, laying its foundation on such principles, and organizing its power in such form, as to them shall seem most likely to effect their safety and happiness."
(from *The Declaration of Independence*)

ever, J. S. Mill went further than many previous liberals had been prepared to go (see L26). Liberal thinkers had hitherto often been quite conventional in their beliefs about public morality; while they had been unwilling to accept these beliefs merely because they were hallowed by convention or custom, nor had they simply rejected them. Instead, liberals had generally sought rational justifications for existing moral conventions or legal restrictions based on morality. It is only since Mill's time that liberals have been typically tolerant of moral and religious difference or plurality; one of the colloquial uses of "liberal" reflects just this notion of tolerance or open-mindedness.

This attitude of tolerance has often been extended by liberals into their approach to international affairs. Because the primary unit of identity for liberals is the individual, and because civil society is conceived of as something created, an artifact of human reason, the nation-state receives less attention or stress within liberalism than within some other ideologies. In fact, the liberal is drawn in two opposing directions away from the nation. On the one hand, the liberal tends to support local autonomy, self-determination, and in federal countries (and liberals tend to approve of federalism as a means of accommodating diversity) a certain amount of decentralization, if not outright advocacy of states' or provincial rights. In the other direction, and there is certainly no contradiction here, the liberal is inclined, all else being equal, to internationalism, which may be expressed practically in various ways. One, political, is participation in and support of international organizations promoting universal peace and prosperity. Another, equally political, is the stance of withdrawal from world conflicts and of non-engagement in matters not directly affecting the nation's citizens (see L27). Economically, the liberal's internationalism is expressed in a desire for free trade and a distaste for tariffs and other restrictions on the free flow of goods and services.

RATIONALISM

A final point to note is the importance of *reason* in liberalism, which espouses not simply individualism, but a *rational* individualism. Here the contrast is with the traditional character of feudal society, and we need simply recall liberalism's roots in that rationalist revolution known as the Enlightenment. The concern for representative, limited government is a belief that individuals can be protected from arbitrary, irrational authority through rational, predictable government. The market can be seen as a rational alternative to medieval rules and regulations. Liberal ethical theory looks to rational principle rather than traditional justification. In all these ways liberalism supposes that government, politics, and social life generally can be ordered by human reason in ways that will make individuals better off than they might otherwise be (see L28-L29).

The Dangers of Government
Montesquieu:

L20 "Political liberty is to be found only in moderate governments; and even in these it is not always found. It is there only when there is no abuse of power. But constant experience shows us that every man invested with power is apt to abuse it, and to carry his authority as far as it will go....

To prevent this abuse, it is necessary from the very nature of things that power should be a check to power."
(*Spirit of the Laws*, Book XI, Part 4)

James Mill:

L21 "Whenever the powers of government are placed in any hands other than those of the community—whether those of one man, of a few, or of several—those principles of human nature which imply that government is at all necessary imply that those persons will make use of them to defeat the very end for which government exists."
(*Essay on Government*, III)

Separation of Powers
Montesquieu:

L22 "When the legislative and executive powers are united in the same person, or in the same body of magistrats, there can be no liberty ... Again, there is no liberty, if the judiciary power be not separated from the legislative and executive."
(*Spirit of the Laws*, Book XI, Part 6)

Limited Government
James Mill:

L23 "For though the people, who cannot exercise the powers of government themselves, must entrust them to some one individual or set of individuals, and such individuals will infallibly have the strongest motives to make a bad use of them, it is possible that checks may be found sufficient to prevent them.... It is sufficiently conformable to the established and fashionable opinions to say that upon the right constitution of checks all goodness of government depends."
(*Essay on Government*, VI)

Representative Government
John Locke:

L24 "But *government* into whatsoever hands it is put ... however it may have power to make laws for the regulating of *property* between the subjects one amongst another, yet can never have a power to take to themselves the whole or any part of the subjects' *property*, without their own consent.... 'Tis true, governments cannot be supported without great charge, and 'tis fit every one who enjoys his share of the protection, should pay out of his estate his proportion for the maintenance of it. But still it must be with his own consent, *i.e.* the consent of the majority, giving it either by themselves, or their representatives chosen by them."
(*Second Treatise*, §139-40)

Thomas Jefferson [*writing to Madison about aspects of the proposed constitution of which he approved*]:

L25 "I like the power given the Legislature to levy taxes; and for that reason solely approve of the greater house being chosen by the people directly. For though I think a house chosen by them will be very illy qualified to legislate for the Union, for foreign nations etc., yet this evil does not weigh against the good of preserving inviolate the fundamental principle that the people are not to be taxed but by representatives chosen immediately by themselves."
[*letter to James Madison*, December 20, 1787]

Social Liberty
John Stuart Mill:

L26 "Protection, therefore, against the tyranny of the magistrate is not enough: there needs protection against the tyranny of the prevailing opinion and feeling; against the tendency of society to impose, by other means than civil penalties, its own ideas and practices as rules of conduct on those who dissent from them ...

The object of this Essay is to assert one very simple principle ... that the sole end for which mankind are warranted, individually or collectively, in interfering with the liberty of action of any of their number, is self-protection.... The only part of the conduct of any one, for which he is amenable to society, is that which concerns others. In the part which merely concerns himself, his independence is, of right, absolute. Over himself, over his own body and mind, the individual is sovereign....

This then, is the appropriate region of human liberty. It comprises, first, the inward domain of consciousness; demanding liberty of conscience in the most comprehensive sense; liberty of thought and feeling; absolute freedom of opinion and sentiment on all subjects, practical or speculative, scientific, moral, or theological.... Secondly, the principle requires liberty of tastes and pursuits; of framing the plan of our life to suit our own character; of doing as we like, subject to such consequences as may follow: without impediment from our fellow-creatures, so long as what we do does not harm them, even though they should think our conduct foolish, perverse, or wrong. Thirdly, from this liberty of each individual, follows the liberty, within the same limits, of combination among individuals; freedom to unite, for any purpose not involving harm to others: the persons combining supposed to be of full age, and not forced or deceived."

(*On Liberty*, I)

Isolationism
Thomas Jefferson:

L27 "I am for preserving to the States the powers not yielded by them to the Union, & to the legislature of the Union its constitutional share in the division of powers ... I am for free commerce with all nations; political connection with none; & little or no diplomatic establishment. And I am not for linking ourselves by new treaties with the quarrels of Europe; entering that field of slaughter to preserve their balance, or joining in the confederacy of kings to war against the principles of liberty."
[*letter to Elbridge Gerry*, January 26, 1799]

Liberty, Reason, and Science
John Locke:

L28 "[T]he *freedom* then of man and liberty of acting according to his own will, is *grounded on* his having *Reason*, which is able to instruct him in that Law he is to govern himself by, and make him know how far he is left to the freedom of his own will."
(*Second Treatise*, §63)

Thomas Jefferson:

L29 "I am for freedom of religion, & against all manoeuvres to bring about a legal ascendancy of one sect over another; for freedom of the press ... for encouraging the progress of science in all its branches; and not for raising a hue and cry against the sacred name of philosophy ..."
[*letter to Elbridge Gerry*, January 26, 1799]

In short, the liberal **perspective** is that the world consists of rational, self-interested *individuals*, who are essentially prior to political society, and by nature exist free and equal. The **ideal** for which liberalism strives is the preservation and enhancement of individual *liberty* within a system of enforceable rights under a government committed to the rule of law. Within such a framework, individuals will be able to cultivate their own particular good with security and at peace with others. The **program** of liberalism, at least initially, was to secure its ideal through *reform* of traditional institutions or their actual replacement with rationally designed instruments of accountable, *limited government*.

B. CONSERVATISM

THE CONTEXT

Conservatism seems the counterpart of liberalism — its natural opposite as day is to night, or winter is to summer. But it is sometimes possible for liberals to be conservative, or for conservatives really to be liberals. In the early 1990s in Russia, for example, "liberals" led by Boris Yeltsin pressed for the kind of economic system favoured by North American "conservatives" — though similar to the economic vision of "liberals" in early nineteenth–century Britain. This sort of contradiction begins to dissolve if we realize that conservatism is even more bound to the context of place and time than other ideologies. While it is true that liberalism arose in a particular context (reaction against feudal absolutism), the liberal creed of beliefs remains consistent and coherent removed from that context. This is not so obviously true with conservatism, which might better be understood initially as a **disposition** to preserve what exists, to resist change, and/or to support the traditional ways of a community or society (see C1). The content of conservatism will thus depend on what already exists, what is traditional or prevalent in the community. (Those who would go further — i.e. bring back what is going or gone — may be termed *radical conservatives* or (more pejoratively) *reactionaries*.) In a society where liberal values have become well established or entrenched, conservatism may well seek to preserve liberalism from reform or radical change; in an authoritarian dictatorship, conservatism may support clearly illiberal ideas. The original conservatives, those who sought to preserve the traditional institutions and values of their society in the face of the liberal revolution, need to be distinguished from those conservatives with whom we are familiar today. These initial conservatives can be identified by their British name — Tories (a term also sometimes used by liberals to de-

Conservatism As Disposition
Michael Oakshott:

C1 "To be a conservative is to be disposed to think and behave in certain manners; it is to prefer certain kinds of conduct and certain conditions of human circumstances to others; it is to be disposed to make certain kinds of choices....

To be conservative, then, is to prefer the familiar to the unknown, to prefer the tried to the untried, fact to mystery, the actual to the possible, the limited to the unbounded, the near to the distant, the sufficient to the superabundant, the convenient to the perfect, present laughter to utopian bliss. Familiar relationships and loyalties will be preferred to the allure of more profitable attachments; to acquire and to enlarge will be less important than to keep, to cultivate and to enjoy; the grief of loss will be more acute than the excitement of novelty or promise. It is to be equal to one's own fortune, to live at the level of one's own means, to be content with the want of greater perfection which belongs alike to oneself and one's circumstances."
("On Being Conservative")

scribe their opponents in the early days of the American republic). As a specific reaction against liberalism, tory conservatism (or toryism) may share only a little with other conservative movements, especially those with which students are likely to be familiar today.

TRADITION AND COMMUNITY

If, generally speaking, liberalism is the ideology of the individual, conservatism is an ideology of the community, and toryism the ideology of an idealized hierarchical community resembling late feudal society. In contrast to liberals, tories see the organic, hierarchical organization of society as natural; indeed, whatever its organization, society or community is natural in the same way that family is. For conservatism, however, humans are *always* found within a social whole; what is artificial is the distinction liberals make between the state of nature and civil society. The whole is greater than the sum of its parts, and individuals cannot be understood apart from their social existence. The primary unit then is not the individual, but the group or even the whole. In Edmund Burke's famous phrase, there is a "partnership not only between those who are living, but

Definitions of Conservatism
F. J. C. Hearnshaw:

C2 "If I were called upon to enumerate in summary fashion and tabular form the general principles of conservatism, particularly as it exists and displays itself in the world of modern national states, I should be disposed to say that conservatism stands for (1) reverence for the past, (2) the organic conception of society, (3) communal unity, (4) constitutional continuity, (5) opposition to revolution, (6) cautious or evolutionary reform, (7) the religious basis of the state, (8) the divine source of legitimate authority, (9) the priority of duties to rights, (10) the prime importance of individual and communal character, (11) loyalty, (12) common sense, realism and practicality." (*Conservatism in England*)

Samuel P. Huntington [*This author provides three distinct definitions of conservatism; the first of which corresponds to our tory conservatism, and the last our general characterization of conservatism.*]:

C3 "*First*, the *aristocratic* theory defines conservatism as the ideology of a single specific and unique historical movement: the reaction of the feudal-aristocratic-agrarian classes to the French Revolution, liberalism, and the rise of the bourgeoisie.... Conservatism thus becomes indissolubly associated with feudalism, status, the *ancien regime*, landed interests, medievalism, and nobility; it becomes irreconcilably opposed to the middle class, labour, commercialism, industrialism, democracy, liberalism, and individualism....

Second, the *autonomous* definition of conservatism holds that conservatism is not necessarily connected with the interests of any particular group, nor, indeed, is its appearance dependent upon any specific historical configuration of social forces. Conservatism is an autonomous system of ideas which are generally valid. It is defined in terms of universal values such as justice, order, balance, moderation....

Third, the *situational* definition views conservatism as the ideology arising out of a distinct but recurring type of historical situation in which a fundamental challenge is directed at established institutions and in which the supporters of those institutions employ the conservative ideology in their defense. Thus, conservatism is that system of ideas employed to justify any established social order, no matter where or when it exists, against any fundamental challenge to its nature or being, no matter from what quarter." ("Conservatism as an Ideology," *American Political Science Review*, 1958) between those who are living, those who are dead, and those who are to be born" (see C9). Insofar as the tory values the well-being of individuals, this is seen to be a byproduct of adherence to duty and maintenance of the strength of the community. Tories value that which contributes to the coherence, cohesion, and continuance of this community: its traditions, conventions, time-honoured institutions, structures, and practices (see C4). This way of putting matters, though, is very liberal, as if the conservative attachment to institutions and practices were merely instrumental: evaluating them rationally as means to an end. Rather, the conservative views these institutions (such as monarchy, the Church) or practices (traditional morality, deference to authority, performance of duty) as inseparable from a way of life handed down by history (see C5). The primary task of the state is to preserve the integrity of the community (which includes its institutions, practices, and values). In contrast to the abstract, often ahistorical character of liberalism, conservatism (especially the tory variety) venerates history and custom (see C2-C3).

ORGANIC HIERARCHY

Now, whereas the abstract (because conceived or imagined apart from their actual social situation) individuals of liberal thought are at least initially equal by nature, toryism takes the opposite position: individuals are necessarily (as history and experience demonstrate) unequal by nature. It is therefore not surprising if individuals are ordered and structured in society; on this view the hierarchical organization of society simply reflects the reality of different individual capacities, and is essential to the community's survival. (In some tory minds these innate capacities are largely inherited, are "in the blood." In the classic "nature versus nurture" debate, the conservative sides with "nature," the liberal with "nurture.") Thus the aristocracy of feudal society is a natural governing class that has emerged through history on the basis of its superior endowments (see C8). Central to this vision is the recognition that such a natural inequality establishes mutual obligations between the superior and the inferior. The aristocracy holds a privileged position at the head of society, but it also has responsibility for the welfare of the less fortunate; it is privileged in its possession of political power, but also obliged to exercise that power responsibly in the general interest. Admittedly, this is paternalistic, but it is not a callous celebration of inequality that acknowledges no social obligations. On the contrary, it is essential that **each** individual, whatever their rank or station, perform the duties and responsibilities associated with that situation. This is because each individual — from monarch to slave — is but part of a larger whole *and* serves a larger or nobler purpose. Thus, in contrast to the liberal emphasis on freedom or liberty,

Chivalry
Edmund Burke:

C4 "But the age of chivalry is gone. That of sophisters, economists, and calculators has succeeded, and the glory of Europe is extinguished forever. Never, never more shall we behold that generous loyalty to rank and sex, that proud submission, that dignified obedience, that subordination of the heart which kept alive, even in servitude itself, the spirit of an exalted freedom. The unbought grace of life, the cheap defense of nations, the nurse of manly sentiment and heroic enterprise, is gone!"
(Reflections on the Revolution in France)

Loyalty to the Constitution
Edmund Burke:

C5 "This Constitution in former days used to be the admiration and the envy of the world: it was the pattern for politicians, the theme of the eloquent, the meditation of the philosopher, in every part of the world. As to Englishmen, it was their pride, their consolation. By it they lived, for it they were ready to die. Its defects, if it had any, were partly covered by partiality, and partly borne by prudence.... I look with filial reverence on the constitution of my country, and never will cut it in pieces, and put it into the kettle of any magician, in order to boil it, with the puddle of their compounds, into youth and vigour. On the contrary, I will drive away such pretenders; I will nurse its venerable age, and with lenient arts extend a parent's breath."
(Speech on Reform of Representation of the Commons in Parliament)

Prescription
Edmund Burke:

C6 "Prescription is the most solid of titles, not only to property, but, which is to secure that property, to government. They harmonize with each other, and give mutual aid to one another. It is accompanied with another ground of authority in the constitution of the human mind, presumption. It is a presumption in favour of any settled scheme of government against any untried project, that a nation has long existed and flourished under it. It is a better presumption even of the *choice* of a nation,—far better than any sudden and temporary arrangement by actual election.... Nor is prescription of government formed upon blind, unmeaning prejudices. For man is a most unwise and a most wise being. The individual is foolish; the multitude, for the moment is foolish, when they act without deliberation; but the species is wise, and, when time is given to it, as a species, it almost always acts right." (Speech on Reform of Representation of the Commons in Parliament)

C7 "We know that *we* have made no discoveries, and we think that no discoveries are to be made, in morality, nor many in the great principles of government, nor in the ideas of liberty, which were understood long before we were born, altogether as well as they will be after the grave has heaped its mould upon our presumption and the silent tomb shall have imposed its law on our pert loquacity.... We fear God; we look up with awe to kings, with affection to parliaments, with duty to magistrates, with reverence to priests, and with respect to nobility ... instead of casting away all our old prejudices, we cherish them to a very considerable degree, and, to take more shame to ourselves,we cherish them because they are prejudices; and the longer they have lasted and the more generally they have prevailed, the more we cherish them. We are afraid to put men to live and trade each on his own private stock of reason, because we suspect that this stock in each man is small, and that the individuals would do better to avail themselves of the general bank and capital of nations and ages."
(*Reflections on the Revolution in France*)

Aristocracy
Edmund Burke:

C8 "A true natural aristocracy is not a separate interest in the state, or separable from it. It is an essential integrant part of any large body rightly constituted. It is formed out of a class of legitimate presumptions, which, taken as generalities, must be admitted for actual truths. To be bred in a place of estimation; to see nothing low and sordid from one's infancy; to be taught to respect one's self; to be habituated to the censorial inspection of the public eye; to look early to public opinion; to stand upon such elevated ground as to be enabled to take a large view of the wide-spread and infinitely diversified combinations of men and affairs in a large society; to have leisure to read, to

reflect, to converse; to be enabled to draw the court and attention of the wise and learned, wherever they are to be found; to be habituated in armies to command and to obey; to be taught to despise banter in the pursuit of honour and duty; to be formed to the greatest degree of vigilance, foresight, and circumspection, in a state of things in which no fault is committed with impunity and the slightest mistakes draw on the most ruinous consequences; to be led to a guarded and regulated conduct, from a sense that you are considered as an instructor of your fellow-citizens in their highest concerns, and that you act as a reconciler between God and man; to be employed as an administrator of law and justice, and to be thereby amongst the first benefactors to mankind; to be a professor of high science, or of liberal and ingenuous art; to be amongst rich traders, who from their success are presumed to have sharp and vigorous understandings, and to possess the virtues of diligence, order, constancy, and regularity, and to have cultivated an habitual regard to commutative justice: these are the circumstances of men that form what I should call a *natural* aristocracy, without which there is no nation."
(*Appeal from the New to the Old Whigs*)

toryism stresses order, stability, adherence to duty. Privilege is necessary and right (See C9-C11).

STRONG AUTHORITY

There is an ambivalence to the tory stance regarding power and authority. On the one hand, strong authority is necessary and good insofar as it sustains the organic structure of the community. On the other hand, inasmuch as the community is sustained through custom, convention, and tradition, the active scope or role for government is ideally quite small. In this way, tories favour a strong, but relatively inactive state (besides, a state too busy will inevitably bring unnecessary change). Thus tory conservatism is comfortable with the absolute state if its authority is exercised by the right people. Tories are fond of traditional institutions such as hereditary monarchy, and of legislative assemblies so long as they are aristocratic, or controlled by the privileged classes. Tories would, though, if consistent, worry about a "proper balance" between the monarch and the aristocracy; in this regard, the emergence of absolute monarchs who built their power at the expense of the traditional nobility would have been troubling to tory conservatives. On the other hand, toryism was *articulated* largely in reaction to the liberal attack on both aristocracy and absolute

The Organic Conception of Society
Edmund Burke:

C9 "Society is indeed a contract.... It is a partnership in all science; a partnership in all art; a partnership in every virtue and in all perfection. As the ends of such a partnership cannot be obtained in many generations, it becomes a partnership not only between those who are living, but between those who are living, those who are dead, and those who are to be born. Each contract of each particular state is but a clause in the great primeval contract of eternal society, linking the lower with the higher natures, connecting the visible and invisible world, according to a fixed compact sanctioned by the inviolable oath which holds all physical and all moral natures, each in their appointed place."
(Reflections on the Revolution in France)

C10 "Nothing is more certain than that our manners, our civilization, and all the good things which are connected with manners and with civilization have, in this European world of ours, depended for ages upon two principles ... I mean the spirit of a gentleman and the spirit of religion. The nobility and the clergy, the one by profession, the other by patronage, kept learning in existence, even in the midst of arms and confusions, and whilst governments were rather in their causes than formed. Learning paid back what it received to nobility and to priesthood, and paid it with usury, by enlarging their ideas and by furnishing their minds."
(Reflections on the Revolution in France)

G.W.F. Hegel:

C11 "In summary, the vitality of the State in individuals is what we call Morality. The State, its laws, its institutions are the rights of the citizens; its nature, its soil, its mountains, air and waters are their land, their country, their external property. The history of the State are their deeds, and what their ancestors have accomplished belongs to them and lives in their memory. Everything is their possession just as they are possessed by it, for it constitutes their substance and being.

Their minds are full of it and their wills are their willing of these laws and of their country. It is this temporal totality which is One Being, the spirit of One People. To it the individuals belong; each individual is the son of his people and, at the same time, insofar as his state is in development, the son of his age. No one remains behind it, no one can leap ahead of it." *(Reason in History, 66)*

Undemocracy
Edmund Burke:

C12 "Society requires not only that the passions of individuals should be subjected, but that even in the mass and body, as well as in the individuals, the inclinations of men should frequently be thwarted, their will controlled, and their passions brought into subjection. This can only be done *by a power out of themselves*, and not, in the exercise of its function, subject to that will and to those passions which it is its office to bridle and subdue. In this sense the restraints on men, as well as their liberties, are to be reckoned among their rights." (*Reflections on the Revolution in France*)

Conservatism and Religion
Edmund Burke:

C13 "We know, and what is better, we feel inwardly, that religion is the basis of civil society and the source of all good and of all comfort.... On these ideas, instead of quarrelling with establishments, as some do who have made a philosophy and a religion of their hostility to such institutions, we cleave closely to them. We are resolved to keep an established democracy, each in the degree it exists, and in no greater." (*Reflections on the Revolution in France*)

G.W.F. Hegel:

C14 "[T]he world is not abandoned to chance and external accident but controlled by *Providence*.... The truth that a Providence, that is to say, a divine Providence, presides over the events of the world corresponds to our principle; for divine Providence is wisdom endowed with infinite power which realizes its own aim, that is, the absolute, rational, final purpose of the world." (*Reason in History*, 14-5) monarchy, and defended both. It is when government becomes more democratic or representative of the non-privileged classes that tories become more supportive of the limited state. These conservatives are more likely to support constitutionalism than democracy (see C12). The ultimate source of authority for tories is often transcendent, such as in God, or the "natural order," in contrast to the popular authority grounding liberalism.

MARKET SCEPTICS

The foundation of the traditional aristocracy was the feudal relation between landlord and tenant. Medieval society was basically agrarian, with peasants working the land for themselves, but also for the lord, to whom they owed a debt of produce or labour, and often also for the Church. In economics then, tories were (at least initially) suspicious of the market, which undermined feudal relations in a variety of ways. Market society brought with it a fluidity and a pace of change which tended to dissolve traditional values, tastes and ways of life. Peasants were drawn to the cities to become labourers, a new business class emerged to challenge the aristocracy, the authority of custom was challenged, overthrown, or simply ignored. The secure identification of an individual with a place, a particular occupation, a clearly recognized set of duties and obligations, and a sound knowledge of one's inferiors and superiors —all this was challenged by market society. Small wonder that tories first resisted its triumph. In many cases, though, members of the landed aristocracy realized that there was no incompatibility between an aristocracy of birth and an aristocracy of wealth, and that wealth grounded in land could be supplemented with wealth made in commerce and manufacture. Toryism eventually made its peace with the market economy, but in doing so, the conservatism it represented started down the road to liberalism. Tory antipathy to markets survives in the insistence sometimes found in conservatism that markets serve the good of the community, an insistence that is more in tune with economic nationalism than *laissez-faire*.

ESTABLISHED VALUES

One of the strongest elements of toryism is its support of traditional values: religious, moral, and social. The religious and moral beliefs and practices of a society are regarded as part and parcel of its necessary structure; to challenge or reject them is to challenge the value or integrity of the community itself. Tories, then, will generally be closely allied with the church (particularly if it is an officially sanctioned or established church) and above all, convinced of the importance of religion (see C13-C14). Traditional moral values and practices will

Right Action
G.W.F. Hegel:

C15 "If men are to act, they must not only intend the good but must know whether this or that particular course is good. What special course of action is good or not, right or wrong, is determined, for the ordinary circumstances of private life, by the laws and customs of a state. It is not too difficult to know them.... Each individual has his position; he knows, on the whole, what a lawful and honourable course of conduct is. To assert in ordinary private relations that it is difficult to choose the right and good, and to regard it as a mark of an exalted morality to find difficulties and raise scruples on that score indicates an evil and perverse will."
(*Reason in History*, 37)

Cautious Attitude Towards Change
Edmund Burke:

C16 "Your constitution, it is true, whilst you were out of possession, suffered waste and dilapidation; but you possessed in some parts the walls and, in all, the foundations of a noble and venerable castle. You might have repaired those walls; you might have build on those old foundations. Your constitution was suspended before it was perfected, but you had the elements of a constitution very nearly as good as could be wished.... Those opposed and conflicting interests which you considered as so great a blemish in your old and in our present constitution interpose a salutary check to all precipitate resolutions. They render deliberation a matter, not of choice, but of necessity; they make all change a subject of *compromise*, which naturally begets moderation; they produce *temperaments* preventing the sore evil of harsh, crude, unqualified reformations and rendering all the headlong exertions of arbitrary power, in the few or in the many, forever impracticable."
(*Reflections on the Revolution in France*)

C17 "The science of government being therefore so practical in itself and intended for such practical purposes—a matter which requires experience, and even more experience than any person can gain in his whole life, however sagacious and observing he may be—it is with infinite caution that any man ought to venture upon pulling down an edifice which has answered in any

tolerable degree for ages the common purposes of society, or on building it up again without having models and patterns of approved utility before his eyes."
(*Reflections on the Revolution in France*)

Michael Oakshott:

C18 "Further, he [the conservative] is aware that not all innovation is, in fact, improvement; and he will think that to innovate without improving is either designed or inadvertent folly. Moreover, even when an innovation commends itself as a convincing improvement, he will look twice at its claims before accepting them. From his point of view, because every improvement involves change, the disruption entailed has always to be set against the bene-fit anticipated ... there is the chance that the benefits derived will be greater than those which were designed; and here is the risk that they will be off-set by changes for the worse."
("On Being Conservative")

C19 "What others plausibly identify as timidity, he recognizes in himself as rational prudence; what others interpret as inactivity, he recognizes as a dispo-sition to enjoy rather than to exploit. He is cautious, and he is disposed to indi-cate his assent or dissent, not in absolute, but in graduated terms. He eyes the situation in terms of its propensity to disrupt the familiarity of the features of his world."
("On Being Conservative")

---

also be central to these conservatives, not simply as individual beliefs, but rather as matters of public morality. Unlike the liberal, who may well share with the tory many beliefs about right and wrong but is willing to let individuals decide for themselves, the tory is not usually so tolerant, but advocates an active en-forcement of moral standards. If public opinion and censure are not enough to do this, then the state should be employed to uphold what is right (see C15). Whereas the liberal is concerned with rights, the conservative insists that indi-viduals must do what (the conservative knows) is right. Tolerance is not gener-ally a central feature of toryism.

If the liberal's individualism has implications for both domestic and foreign policy, so too the tory's sense of community results in a preference for the national interest. Local custom and preference are important, but if given too much reign, become divisive and injurious. Burke (see C26, Chapter Four) articulated clearly the need to set aside local feeling in order to ascertain the common good of the greater community. Similarly, it is the national interest that guides relations with other states, and this can manifest itself aggressively or defensively. In the former instance, the values of the nation are exported, or foreign lands are conquered to add to the glory, wealth, or security of the nation. (A liberal – Catholic or Protestant – could never justify a war fought on religious grounds, but a tory could.) Defensively, the national interest is the justification for policies designed to preserve the prosperity, character, or customs of the nation. An example of this would be protectionist economic policy.

THE WISDOM OF PREJUDICE

Just as our final point about liberalism was to stress its rationalism, our final observation about toryism is that it justifies itself on the basis of tradition. What has been handed down from generation to generation through history is regarded as right or worth preserving simply because it has withstood "the test of time." (Whether the phrase "the test of time" really says anything significant is another matter.) It is a temptation (to which liberals often succumb) to see this traditionalism as simply the irrational veneration of history. It may with more insight be seen as symptomatic of a cautious attitude towards the powers of reason. The liberal is confident that we can design institutions and programs to change the world in ways that will solve our problems; the conservative is not so sure. What passing "the test of time" may mean on this view is methods or practices that have succeeded, have worked, whatever their limitations. The conservative is reluctant to throw these away for something new and untested, unproven. This is what Burke meant by "a presumption in favour of any settled scheme of government against any untried project, that a nation has long existed and flourished under it [any settled scheme]." (C6, see also C16-C19)

IN SUMMARY

It bears repeating that while all tories are conservatives, not all conservatives are tories. Conservatism almost always seeks to preserve (or restore) a certain *status quo*, and the *status quo* of original toryism was the hierarchical, aristocratic society of the seventeenth and eighteenth centuries. There are few today who advocate restoring that society, and toryism in this original sense can be said to have largely vanished. But in a more general sense, toryism lives on as a strain within contemporary conservatism which emphasizes the collective over the individual, views hierarchy as natural or inevitable, and believes that the most fortunate in society have obligations towards or responsibilities for the welfare of the least advantaged. The closest thing to this today may be found within European Christian Democracy (see Chapter Three). It is also clear in the passages presented above, that the conservative disposition is grounded in many instances in a relatively pessimistic or even negative view of human nature. While this is a point we will elaborate more fully in the next chapter, it is worth noting here as a point of consistency between original and later conservatisms.

C. SOCIALISM

THE CONTEXT

If toryism was a reaction against liberalism on behalf of a vanishing *status quo*, socialism was a reaction against the world created by successful liberalism. Some early socialists, it is true, were reacting with liberals against aristocratic society, but obviously with a different vision and emphasis. The most significant socialist thinkers though, were motivated by a distaste for liberal society, particularly for the consequences of the market economy so central to the liberal vision. Socialism was *the* ideology of the nineteenth century, gaining significance after the effects of the Industrial Revolution had become obvious, and after the liberal revolution had succeeded in dissolving feudal society in most of Europe.

UTOPIANS AND MARXISTS

Some note should be made of a distinction made by Karl Marx, who contrasted his own "scientific" socialism to the "utopian" socialism of previous (and contemporary) thinkers such as Owen, Saint-Simon, Fourier, and Proudhon. To group these thinkers (and many others Marx included with them) under one banner is to obscure a great host of significant differences between them (see S1) but nonetheless, there is a validity to Marx's distinction, and it was Marxism, which, at the end of the nineteenth century, had become the most successful and influential socialism. The fundamental difference is that so-called "utopian" socialists believed that socialism would be achieved by a moral revolution, a transformation in what people believed and acted upon; the "scientific" socialism of Marx and Engels saw socialism as the eventual outcome of material factors, the product of economic and social transformations embedded within the nature of capitalist society. In this latter view, the revolution

Socialist Ideals
Leszek Kolakowski [*speaking of the ideas found in the works of Utopian so-cialists which anticipated ideas of Marx*]:

S1 "As regards the socialist future ... we may enumerate the following ideals:
The abolition of private ownership of the means of production.
A planned economy on a national or world scale, subordinated to social needs and eliminating competition, anarchy, and crises.
The right to work, as a basic human entitlement.
The abolition of class divisions and social antagonisms.
The whole-hearted, voluntary cooperation of associated producers.
Free education of children at the public expense, including technical training.
The abolition of the division of labour and the degrading consequences of specialization; instead, the all-round development of the individual, and free opportunity for the use of human skills in every direction.
Abolition of the difference between town and country, while permitting indus-try to concentrate as at present.
Political power to be replaced by economic administration; no more exploita-tion of man by man, or rule of one man over another.
Gradual effacement of national differences.
Complete equality of rights and opportunities as between men and women.
The arts and sciences to flourish in complete freedom.
Socialism as a boon to humanity as a whole; the exploitation of the proletar-iat as the chief factor tending to bring about socialism. "
(1978: I, 221)

would depend upon "objective" conditions, not the good intentions of indi-viduals.

EQUALITY IN COMMUNITY

Like liberals and contrary to tories, socialists begin with the proposition that humans are fundamentally equal; unlike liberals and in agreement with tories, socialists see humans as having an essentially social or communal nature. Social-ists oppose the inegalitarian beliefs of tories and the individualism of liberals (see S2). In the latter case, socialists also disagree about the nature of equality or in-equality which is present in society, and which is acceptable or not. Liberals oppose the inherited or traditional inequalities of the hierarchical feudal condition; they are concerned to ensure that neither laws nor regulations deny individuals the same chances or opportunity to achieve their goals, protect their self-interest, or obtain well-being. Inequalities which result from differences in individual effort, or from how individuals exploit the equal opportunity provided them, are not problematic to most liberals, and quite acceptable or "natural" to many. Early liberals also accepted a wide range of existing structural inequalities: in asserting that all had "equal opportunity," these liberals were blind to those disadvantages of poverty, social class, and gender, that most of the population laboured under. To the socialist, the inequalities to which the liberal did not object were simply unacceptable. There can be no equality of opportunity in a class-ridden society, and individuals everywhere owe their outcomes as much to chance, inheritance, unequal opportunities, and structural factors as to individual effort.

As Kolakowski points out (1978:I, 222), within socialism the "utopians" were more concerned with equality, or with present inequality as indicated by the poverty of the working class; Marx, by contrast, stressed the alienation of wage labourers (see S3), a condition not addressed merely by eliminating poverty. This points to an enduring divide within socialism between those concerned with the *distribution* of economic goods (market allocations) and those concerned with the *ownership* of the means of economic production (private property capitalism) (see S4–S5).

Not accidentally, the utopians were often most concerned with designing and detailing their utopia (best of all worlds); some even tried, on a small scale, to establish model communities which would show the way to others (see S6-S7). Scientific socialism, by contrast, focused analysis on the conditions of alienation *within* capitalist society, and looked within capitalism for the conditions or causes of its transformation. In this last sense, the scientific socialism of Marx and Engels was most intrigued by the possibilities inherent in the economic system, rather than, as with the utopians, focused upon its effects (see S8).

CLASS

The socialist might even agree with the liberal that in *abstract models,* the market is impartial and rewards individuals, but in practice, the socialist argues, the market is partial to those with resources and rewards classes of individuals privileged in terms of assets like capital, or information, or education. The error of the liberal is precisely that she *abstracts* from social reality. The grounding of the liberal perspective in individualism obscures the reality of other categories, such

A Manifesto of Community and Equality
François Babeuf:

S2 "1. Nature has given every man an equal right to the enjoyment of all its goods.

2. The purpose of society is to defend this equality ... and to increase, through universal cooperation, the common enjoyment of the goods of nature.

3. Nature has imposed upon everyone the obligation to work; no one has ever shirked this duty without having thereby committed a crime.

4. All work and the enjoyment of its fruits must be in common.

5. Oppression exists when one person exhausts himself through toil and still lacks everything, while another swims in abundance without doing any work at all.

6. No one has ever appropriated the fruits of the earth or of industry exclusively for himself without having thereby committed a crime.

7. In a true society, there must be neither rich nor poor.

8. No one may, by accumulation of all the available means of education, deprive another of the instruction necessary for his well-being: instruction must be common to all...."

(From the doctrine of Babeuf)

Alienation
Karl Marx:

S3 "The bourgeoisie, wherever it has got the upper hand, has put an end to all feudal, patriarchal, idyllic relations. It has pitilessly torn asunder the motley feudal ties that bound man to his 'natural superiors,' and has left no other nexus between man and man than naked self-interest, than callous 'cash payment'.... It has resolved personal worth into exchange value, and in place of the numberless indefeasible chartered freedoms, has set up that single, unconscionable freedom—Free Trade. In one word, for exploitation, veiled by religious and political illusions, it has substituted naked, shameless, direct, brutal exploitation."

(from the Manifesto of the Communist Party)

as class. The social science of the socialist is concerned with how individuals are privileged or disabled by their position within the social structure, a structure seen largely in economic or political-economic terms. What matters about individuals is their social relations, and, following Marx, the socialist sees these as class relations (see S9).

From the socialist perspective, the liberal revolution managed to replace an aristocracy of birth with an aristocracy of wealth. A privileged elite founded on aristocratic tradition and birth-lines gave way to a privileged elite founded on economic power (see S10). Even worse, though, the reciprocal obligations that bound feudal lord to peasant and were at least a meagre compensation for the structural inequality of medieval society, also vanished; the liberal allows such obligations to lapse in the belief that individuals are authors of their own fate. This informs the classic liberal view that the socialist deplores: the poor or underprivileged have only themselves to blame, and it is the responsibility of neither the privileged or well-off to look out for those less advantaged.

STRONG DEMOCRACY

While socialism is ultimately concerned with creating a society in which all individuals are genuinely equal, its concern in the present world is to eliminate what it sees as exploitation or subjugation of the least privileged classes in society; in seeking to do so, it gains little affection from those most advantageously positioned in society. Ideally, then, for the socialist the state is an instrument to be used on behalf of the exploited or underprivileged classes against the advantaged classes. Like the tory, but for different reasons, the socialist believes in a strong state, not the limited, minimal state of classic liberalism. The socialist tends to be wary of rights, then, because they are more effectively employed by those with resources than by those without, often to thwart the fundamental social change which socialists believe is necessary, and because they privilege individuals against the collectivity. Unlike the tories, though, who are concerned that a strong state be in the right hands, socialists are (in theory at least) strong supporters of democracy; instead of rights which an elite minority can use to prevent the state from acting, socialists favour a strong state controlled by the majority. After all, the socialist reasons, those less advantaged are usually the majority rather than the minority. At the same time, successful social and political transformation should diminish the need for state activity (see S11). Socialists are in theory even more radically disposed towards democracy than liberals, then, with important exceptions that we will note in Chapter Three.

Property Is Theft
Pierre Proudhon:

S4 "If I were asked to answer the following question: *What is slavery?* and I should answer in one word, *It is murder*, my meaning would be understood at once. No extended argument would be required to show that the power to take from a man his thought, his will, his personality, is a power of life and death; and that to enslave a man is to kill him. Why, then, to this other question: *What is property?* may I not likewise answer, *It is theft*, without the certainty of being misunderstood; the second proposition being no other than a transformation of the first?"
(*What is Property?*)

Louis Blanqui:

S5 "A few individuals have seized upon the common earth by ruse or by violence, and, claiming possession of it, have established by laws that it is to be their property forever, and that this right of property is to be the basis of the social constitution ...

This right of property logically extended itself from the soil to other instruments, namely the accumulated products of labour, designated by the generic term, capital. Now, since capital, which is sterile by itself, bears fruit only through manual labour, and furthermore, since it is the material that preeminently requires the application of social forces in order for it to be worked, the majority excluded from the possession of it is condemned to forced labour, to the profit of the possessing minority....

Only association, substituted for individual property ownership, will bring about the reign of justice through equality. This is why the men of the future ardently desire to work out the principles of association and present them to the world."
(from *Critique Sociales*)

Socialist Utopias
Robert Owen:

S6 "Facts prove, ...
First,—That character is universally formed *for*, and not *by*, the individual.
Second,—That *any* habits and sentiments may be given to mankind.
Third,—That the affections are *not* under the control of the individual.
Fourth,—That every individual may be trained to produce far more than he
can consume, while there is a sufficiency of soil left for him to cultivate.
Fifth,—That nature has provided means by which population may be at all
times maintained in the proper state to give the greatest happiness to every
individual, without one check of vice or misery.
Sixth,—That any community may be arranged ... in such a manner as not
only to withdraw vice, poverty, and, in a great degree, misery, from the
world, but also to place *every* individual under circumstances in which he
shall enjoy more permanent happiness than can be given to *any* individual under the principles which have hitherto regulated society.
Seventh,—That all the assumed fundamental principles on which society has
hitherto been founded are erroneous ... And—
Eighth,—That the change which would follow the abandonment of those erroneous maxims which bring misery into the world, and the adoption of principles of truth, unfolding a system which shall remove and for ever exclude
that misery, may be effected without the slightest injury to any human being." (An Address to the Inhabitants of New Lanark)

Charles Fourier:

S7 "Associative labour, in order to exert a strong attraction upon people,
will have to differ in every particular from the repulsive conditions which render it so odious in the existing state of things. It is necessary, in order that it
become attractive, that associative labour fulfil the following seven conditions:
1. That every labourer be a partner, remunerated by dividends and not by
wages.
2. That every one, man, woman, or child, be remunerated in proportion to
three faculties, *capital, labour,* and *talent*.
3. That the industrial sessions be varied about eight times a day, it being impossible to sustain enthusiasm longer than an hour and a half or two hours in
the exercise of agricultural or manufacturing labour.

4. That they be carried on by bands of friends, united spontaneously, interested and stimulated by very active rivalries.
5. That the workshops and husbandry offer the labourer the allurements of elegance and cleanliness.
6. That the division of labour be carried to the last degree, so that each sex and age may devote itself to duties that are suited to it.
7. That in this distribution, each one, man, woman, or child, be in full enjoyment of the right to labour or the right to engage in such branch of labour as they may please to select, provided they give proof of integrity and ability. Finally, that, in this new order, people possess a guarantee of well-being, of a minimum sufficient for the present and the future, and that this guarantee free them from all uneasiness concerning themselves and their families."
[from *Theorié de l'Unité Universelle*, vol II]

The Productive Power Of Capitalism
Karl Marx and Friedrich Engels:

S8 "The bourgeoisie, during its rule of scarce one hundred years, has created more massive and more colossal productive forces than have all preceding generations together.... what earlier century had even a presentiment that such productive forces slumbered in the lap of social labour?"
(from *the Manifesto of the Communist Party*)

THE END OF CAPITALISM

The most important task of the state, for socialists, is to regulate, to reform, even to replace the private property market economy of liberalism because of the inequality or alienation it creates. It is precisely the economic liberty or market autonomy which the liberal values, that the socialist says is responsible for the inequality of capitalist society, and for the consequent absence of genuine freedom for all those underprivileged in that society. In the place of private property, the pure socialist argues for collective or public ownership of the means of production, distribution, and exchange which capitalism employs (i.e. industry, transportation, financial institutions, etc.). In the place of market autonomy and the (mal)distribution it creates, the socialist calls for central planning, and redistribution on rational, egalitarian principles. These are of course the most contentious parts of the socialist position. Within socialism, consider-

Class Antagonisms

S9 "The history of all hitherto existing society is the history of class struggles. Freedom and slave, patrician and plebeian, lord and serf, guild-master and journeyman, in a word, oppressor and oppressed, stood in constant opposition to one another, carried on an uninterrupted, now hidden, now open fight, a fight that each time ended, either in a revolutionary reconstitution of society at large, or in the common ruin of the contending classes....

The modern bourgeois society that has sprouted from the ruins of feudal society has not done away with class antagonisms. It has but established new classes, new conditions of oppression, new forms of struggle in place of the old ones.

Our epoch, the epoch of the bourgeoisie, possesses, however, this distinctive feature: It has simplified the class antagonisms. Society as a whole is more and more splitting up into two great hostile camps, into two great classes directly facing each other—bourgeoisie and proletariat."
(from *the Manifesto of the Communist Party*)

---

able difference arose about the degree of emphasis that should be put on collective ownership, and about those forms of democracy associated with liberal individualism. These and other differences lie behind the distinctions between communists or **Marxists**, after the nineteenth-century German philosopher Karl Marx, and socialists of a less radical variety, committed to at least some elements of liberal democracy, who called themselves **democratic socialists**. But this too, anticipates the discussion in Chapter Three.

SOCIALIST ETHICS

On moral questions, socialism is less straightforward than either liberalism or toryism. It shares with liberalism a distrust of *traditional* morality, but does not share the celebration of individual choice. Some strains of socialism were very much grounded in Christian movements, and were likely to share the moral positions of these religious sects (see S12); other strains (like Marxism) which were agnostic or atheist, were suspicious of the moral positions of religious adherents. Similarly, the social scientific disposition of much socialist thought has directed it away from speculation concerning ethical questions. The collectivist dimension of socialism means that when and where it is able to reach a moral

The Rule of the Bourgeoisie

S10 "Each step in the development of the bourgeoisie was accompanied by a corresponding political advance of that class ... the bourgeoisie has at last, since the establishment of modern industry and of the world market, conquered for itself, in the modern representative state, exclusive political sway. The executive of the modern state is but a committee for managing the common affairs of the whole bourgeoisie."
(from *the Manifesto of the Communist Party*)

Strong Government
Louis Blanc:

S11 "But if it is necessary to become engaged in a program of social reform, it is no less necessary to pursue one of political reform. For it the first is the *end*, the second is the *means*....

For once it is admitted that a man must have the *power* to develop and exercise his faculties in order to be really free, the upshot is that society owes every one of its members both instruction, without which the human mind *cannot* grow, and the instruments of labour, without which human activity *cannot* achieve its fullest development. Now, how will society be made to give suitable instruction and the necessary instruments of labour to every one of its members, if not by the intervention of the state? It is therefore in the name of freedom that we are asking for the rehabilitation of the principle of authority. We want a strong government because, in the regime of inequality within which we are still vegetating, there are weak persons who need a social force to protect them....

If the dearest hope of our hearts is not deceived, a day will come when a strong and active government will no longer be needed, because there will no longer be inferior and subordinate classes in society."
(*Organization of Labour*)

"New" Christianity
Claude Henri Saint-Simon:

S12 "The entire moral doctrine of the New Christianity will be derived directly from this principle: *All men must behave as brothers toward one another*: and this principle,which belongs to primitive Christianity, will undergo a *transfiguration*, by which it will be presented as the principle that today must be the aim of all religious activity.

This regenerated principle will be presented in the following form: *Religion must direct society toward the over-all goal of the most rapid possible amelioration of the condition of the poorest class.*"
(*The New Christianity*)

---

judgement, socialism tends to promote and enforce this judgement with a vigour comparable to that of the defenders of traditional morality.

Most obviously, socialism shares with toryism a collectivist dimension; individuals matter **because** they are part of something larger: the human species, or a common humanity. An essential difference here is that socialists partake of the optimistic nineteenth–century notion that human nature is perfectible, while toryism is pessimistic about human potential (except for those of a "noble" nature). Both tories and socialists see traditional society in terms of hierarchically arranged social classes; for the tory such hierarchy is proper, while for the socialist such an arrangement is oppressive and unjust.

With liberalism and against toryism, socialism is generally rationalist, sharing the Enlightenment confidence that humans can rationally fashion and control their lives in a myriad of beneficial ways. As noted though, the rationalism of socialists is more empirically grounded in social analysis, and less likely than Enlightenment liberalism to rely on abstract models. In Marxist versions, particularly, socialism presents a more historically–conditioned analysis than liberalism; recognition of the relevance of history is something shared with toryism.

IN SUMMARY

What distinguishes socialism from both rival visions is its thorough grounding in equality. Its perspective is shaped by perception of inequality in the world, its belief in the essentially antagonistic division of society into classes, and its championing of the interests of the disadvantaged classes within a private property, market economy. The ideal is a condition of equality and harmony in which class differences have been eliminated. The program of this ideology of rational egalitarian collectivism is to acquire (by democratic means or otherwise) the political power necessary to transform capitalist society.

CONCLUSION

The starkest contrasts come from portraying the ideologies simply as we have just done (although they may seem at first glance anything but simple). A summary of the main points is provided in Table 2.1, and this should be recognized for the caricature that it is; ideologies are much more complex than any table can convey. It is also worth repeating that we have discussed ideologies here in their initial form, as they were bred in contexts far removed from our historical present, and therefore, far removed from the everyday experience of contemporary readers. Nonetheless, the ideologies that we are likely to recognize today often do bear some relation, or trace some lineage to these original expositions. It may well seem strange to talk of a liberalism that does not embrace democracy, or of a conservatism that is suspicious of capitalism, but that is how matters once stood. Many features of our own society such as a general public education, the absence of child labour, a minimum wage, and formal equality between the sexes, were radical ideas that one hundred fifty years ago *only* socialists espoused. As matters change, ideology changes too.

In reality, the picture long ago became much more complicated. It might be more useful, for example, to understand liberalism and socialism as each the source of a family of ideologies with certain fundamental principles in common, but often divided over other, sometimes crucial points. Our frame of reference is the last two centuries, or roughly from 1789 (the French Revolution) to the contemporary age. In that time, one ideological current — toryism — has largely evaporated, or to the extent that it has survived has been absorbed within liberalism. This is a testimony to the success of the Liberal Revolution in western society, so thorough in its transformation of society that there are few if any today who believe that a return to an organic hierarchical aristocratic society is possible, let alone desirable.

There are some, no doubt, who also believe that socialism is a spent ideological current, and the most obvious reason for thinking so is the collapse of communist regimes in the former Soviet Union and Eastern Europe. As we will see, though, communism (whether Russian or Chinese or Albanian) is only one member of the socialist family of ideologies, and for many, the black sheep of the family. It is clearly premature to conclude that all socialism is as exhausted as communism, however much this seems obvious to North American students. We need only note that socialist parties are part of the government, or

Table 2.1

	Socialism	Liberalism	Toryism
Social Vision	fully egalitarian collectivist	formally egalitarian individualist	hierarchical organic
Key Values	equality fraternity	liberty security	order stability
Dispositions: intellectual moral	rationalist conformist/ tolerant	rationalist tolerant	traditional conformist
Politics	unlimited state democracy class relations	limited state representative gov't individual rights	absolute state monarchy/aristocrasy natural law
Economics	market regulation redistribution public ownership	market autonomy private property	premarket economy land rent

form the main opposition in almost all countries of Europe today, as well as in Japan, Australia, and New Zealand.

In short, before speculating further about the future of ideologies, we need to examine the development and sophistication of liberalism and socialism, as well as what it means to be a conservative in today's world.

NOTES: THE SOURCES OF FIRST GENERATION IDEOLOGIES

A: LIBERALISM

Thomas Hobbes (1588–1679) Perhaps the greatest of English liberals (there is little in liberalism that cannot be traced back to his thought), Hobbes was regarded as a tory because of his argument for an absolute sovereign, and his stated preference for monarchy over parliament. Nonetheless, this (purely pragmatic) nod to monarchy was his only conservative feature. A thorough rationalist and empiricist, Hobbes rejected all tradition and custom, had little or no sense of community, and expressed succinctly and consistently the liberal notion that the state is an artificial instrument designed to provide security for individuals within a framework of laws and liberties. His greatest work, *Leviathan*, appeared in 1651.

John Locke (1632–1704) More commonly acknowledged and appreciated than Hobbes, Locke articulated many of the touchstones of liberal ideology — limited, representative government; no taxation without representation; consent of the majority; the right to life, liberty, and property; the right to revolution against tyranny, etc. — in his *Second Treatise on Government*, which was written in anticipation of the Glorious Revolution of 1688, but published in 1689. At various times a tutor, physician, diplomat, and secretary to Lord Shaftesbury, Locke also held governmental posts. As a philosopher, Locke made significant contributions in other areas, primarily epistemology; students of politics should also see his *Letter on Toleration* (1689).

Charles Secondat, Baron de Montesquieu (1679–1755) His fame lies with one of the great works of political philosophy — the *Spirit of the Laws* (1748) — which few have ever read from cover to cover: as Plamenatz has put it: "No book so well written, and with so much that is excellent in it, was ever so liable to weary the reader." (1963: I,254) Regarded as some by the father of sociology, Montesquieu's political significance was to argue for the doctrine of the separation of powers, or alternatively, of mixed government, an argument based on consideration of the experience of governments around the world and through the ages.

Adam Smith (1723–1790) The father of economic liberalism, most remembered today for his *The Wealth of Nations* (1776), Smith was famous first for his *Theory of Moral Sentiments* (1759), a theory of ethics based on the operation of sympathy. Smith, of course, did not invent the notion that capitalism should be given free reign by minimizing government regulation of market activity, he simply articulated it with a clarity, power, and consistency not seen hitherto (and rarely since). Central to his theory is what has become known as the doctrine of the "invisible hand" (see Chapter Four).

Thomas Jefferson (1743-1826) Author of the Declaration of Independence, Jefferson was as much a republican as a liberal, an ardent democrat, and champion of the small landholder. He was also the third President of the United States (1801-1809). Jefferson advocated states' rights, religious freedom, isolationism, and looked forward to the inevitable demise of slavery. Most of his work lies scattered in letters, speeches, and state papers, his one book, *Notes on the State of Virginia*, appearing in 1785.

Jeremy Bentham (1748-1832) Bentham is the father of utilitarianism (although the term only appears in his works twice), a reformulation of liberalism that relies on neither an argument from a state of nature, nor on claims of abstract right. A utilitarian government seeks to maximize the greatest good (utility) of the greatest number. Utility is happiness, which consists of pleasure (and the absence of pain). One of the Philosophical Radicals, Bentham and his followers sought thorough reform of British institutions. His most celebrated work was *Introduction to the Principles of Morals and Legislation* (1789).

James Mill (1773-1836) James Mill was Bentham's closest disciple, and did much to put utilitarianism before the public in comprehensible form, particularly through his essays which appeared in journals and the Encyclopedia Britannica. The essay *On Government* (1820) is the best known of these. Mill also wrote a celebrated treatise on associationist psychology and a treatment of political economy that expounded the principles of laissez-faire.

John Stuart Mill (1806-1873) The son of James Mill, John Stuart was a philosophic giant of the nineteenth century, who made significant contributions to logic and political economy before turning his pen to political questions. His work *On Liberty* (1859) remains the classic text arguing for a minimum of interference with the fundamental freedoms of individuals, although it is sometimes overlooked that Mill's immediate concern was a threat posed not by government but by public opinion. Mill also championed the rights of women, argued for representative government, and made important revisions to utilitarian ethical theory.

B: CONSERVATISM

Edmund Burke (1729-1797) The writings and speeches of Burke often seem to be the fount from which all conservatism flows. Interestingly, Burke sat in the English Parliament as a Whig for almost thirty years, but he was both an aristocratic and a situational conservative (see C3). The key to Burke's apparent inconsistency (he could support the American revolution, and condemn the French revolution) is the evolutionary way in which England became liberal, so that parliamentary, representative government coexisted with a traditional monarchy, landed aristocracy, and absence of democracy. Burke supported all the fundamental institutions of his England. His most famous work is the *Reflections on the Revolution in France* (1790), written before, but anticipating those darkest periods of that upheaval that became known as The Terror.

Joseph de Maistre (1753-1821) and Louis de Bonald (1753-1840) De Maistre and Bonald were principal authors (in France) of the reaction to the French Revolution on behalf of traditional institutions and values. This feature of their thought (in step with that of Burke) is what has caused ultra-conservative thought to be called "reactionary," and we now think of reactionaries as those who would restore a way of life that has disappeared. Bonald and de Maistre championed the monarchy, aristocracy, the Church, and obedience to the authority of all three; they condemned liberal confidence in reason, and denied the validity of rights or any other limitations on the properly constituted authority of the state.

G.W.F. Hegel (1770-1831) If Burke was the apotheosis of the conservative politician, then Hegel was conservatism's high priest. Perhaps the last philosopher to attempt to grasp all of reality within one comprehensive system, Hegel became the official state philosopher of early nineteenth–century Prussia. Totalitarian systems of both the right and left have been traced to Hegel's objective idealism, and yet some have seen in him the strongest affirmation of rationalist liberalism. His most accessible work is *Reason in History* (1840), but his most important political work remains the *Philosophy of Right* (1821).

C: SOCIALISM

François Babeuf (1760-1797), Claude Henri Saint-Simon (1760-1825), Charles Fourier (1772-1837), Robert Owen (1771-1858), Louis Blanqui (1805-1881), Pierre Joseph Proudhon (1809-1865), and Louis Blanc (1811-1882) These thinkers, diverse and complex in their own fashion, are among those included by Marx (and most everyone thereafter) in the category of "utopian" socialists. Saint-Simon and Fourier were certifiable eccentrics, the latter's vision of future perfection and harmony extending not only to all of humanity, but to nature as well (under human domination). Owen is regarded as the father of English socialism, a successful mill owner who attempted to create small scale versions of utopia, both in Scotland and America. Fourierist communities also were established in America in the middle of the nineteenth century, the most notable being Brook Farm. Blanqui invented the notion of the "dictatorship of the proletariat," which would later be taken over and transformed by Marx and Lenin. Proudhon's lasting legacy has been stronger with anarchism than socialism, and Blanc's reformist stance makes him a precursor of twentieth–century welfare state social democracy. Virtually every one of these thinkers (or his disciples) was subjected to ruthless criticism by Marx in his development and presentation of "scientific" socialism.

Karl Marx (1818-1883) and Friedrich Engels (1820-1895) Marx is undoubtedly the most influential figure in all of political ideology. Socialism has been dominated by Marxism (either directly, or in opposition to it), and both liberalism and conservatism have been shaped by their struggles against Marxism. Originally one of a group of philosophers known as the Young Hegelians (left-wing disciples of Hegel), Marx articulated a theory of historical materialism which developed socialist thought through an analysis of social productive forces and relations. Most of Marx's life was devoted to the study, analysis, and critique of capitalist economic theory and practice. Ironically, Friedrich Engels was the son of a wealthy textile manufacturer, and it was his wealth which supported Marx through much of his life. In addition to being Marx's patron and friend, Engels was his sometime collaborator, and after Marx's death, edited and published his remaining work. As a populizer of Marxism, Engels did much to identify this brand of socialism with "dialectical materialism," which combined Marx's insights about the material bases of history, with a quasi-Hegelian determinism about the laws of history.

SUGGESTED READING:

[Publishing information is not provided for texts in political thought which are either out of print, or widely available in contemporary editions.]
Burke, Edmund. (1790). *Reflections on the Revolution in France.*
——. (1791). *An Appeal from the New to the Old Whigs.*
Fried, Albert, and Ronald Sanders, eds. (1964). *Socialist Thought: A Documentary History.* Garden City, N.Y.: Anchor Books.

Hearnshaw, F.J.C. (1933). *Conservatism in England*. London and Basingstoke: Macmillan.

Hegel, G.W.F. (1820). *Reason in History*.

Hobbes, Thomas. (1651). *Leviathan*.

Huntington, Samuel P. (1957, June). "Conservatism as an Ideology." *APSR* 51, 454-73.

Jefferson, Thomas. Selections in Merrill D. Peterson, ed. (1975). *The Portable Thomas Jefferson*. New York: Viking Press.

Kolakowski, Leszek. (1978). *Main Currents of Marxism: The Founders*. Oxford: Oxford, University Press.

Locke, John. (1685). *Second Treatise on Government*.

———. (1666). *A Letter Concerning Toleration*.

Marx, Karl, and Friedrich Engels. (1976). *Collected Works*. New York: International Publishers.

Mill, James. (1820). *On Government*.

Mill, John Stuart. (1859). *On Liberty*.

———. (1869). *The Subjection of Women*.

———. (1861). *Utilitarianism*.

———. (1861). *Considerations on Representative Government*.

Oakeshott, Michael. (1962). *Rationalism in Politics*. London: Methuen.

Rousseau, Jean-Jacques. (1753). *Discourse on Inequality*.

———. (1762). *The Social Contract*.

Chapter Three

Ideologies: The Second Generation

ON NOVEMBER 9, 1994, Americans woke up having elected a Republican-controlled Congress for the first time in 42 years. The soon-to-be Speaker of the House, Newt Gingrich, proclaimed it a victory for his "Contract with America" (see C24). Was this, as many regarded, a triumph for American conservatism, or, a return to classic liberal values of a limited role for government, or, both? (To put the Republican victory in perspective, it should be noted that the low turnout — 38% — meant that only 22% of the total of registered voters actually voted Republican.) In the 1993 general election in Canada, the New Democratic Party fell from 43 to 9 seats, and to 7% of the popular vote. Was this the beginning of the end for democratic socialism on the northern half of the continent, had that demise already occurred and gone unnoticed, or is it still too soon to say?

Ideologies fall out of fashion when their vision no longer appeals, or when their perspective no longer makes sense of individuals' social and political realities. Contexts change, and an ideology that remains static risks —like all else that stays fixed in a time of flux —being left behind. The three ideologies examined in the previous chapter have, at least to this point in the twentieth century, survived, and they have survived because they have not remained static. They have developed because the contexts within which they exist and to which they respond have changed. In this chapter we will outline in broad form the principal moments of that development with a view to identifying the often problematic character of contemporary conservatism, liberalism, and socialism. Common to each of these ideologies is a context provided by the dominance of liberalism over the remnants of feudalism, a context of the successes and failures of triumphant liberalism. Liberal successes have challenged conservatism and socialism, while liberal failures have energized these rival systems and given liberals cause for self-reflection. In the background of these ideologies as we experience them today are also several ideas which gained special prominence in the nineteenth century.

One of these is the notion of human perfectability, or more specifically, that humanity is capable of a progressive development from a primitive or imperfect state of being to an ever more refined and elevated condition. This is seen to be true of individuals, each of whom represents a set of capacities or potentials susceptible of development. Just as importantly, it is true of the species which, from generation to generation, exhibits improvement. Human nature, then, is not the same in all times and places, nor is it a static given, but something of a work in progress (this was the century, after all, which discovered "evolution"; see L31). Both liberalism and socialism share, in their own way, in the belief in human progress. Conservatives, on the other hand, are more sceptical, doubting that all change is necessarily for the better, and certainly dubious that all (or any) individuals have a perfectible nature.

The nineteenth century was also the century of social science, giving birth to anthropology, sociology, psychology, economics, and political science as professional disciplines. A byproduct of this academic specialization is the common perception that individuals are very much the product of social institutions such as educational systems, economic and social class, kinship systems, and family structures (see L30). This particular idea had enormous significance for socialism, but was accorded relevance by conservatives and liberals only grudgingly, if at all. Opposing the socialist notion that humans are socially-determined in their destiny, conservatives argue that they are determined by nature (or by "their nature"), and liberals insist that nature and environment aside, individuals are self-made, or at least are capable of making their own destiny.

Finally, our first generation ideologies are confronted in the nineteenth century by an awareness of the sweep of history and by the emergence of nationalism. The rationalism of the Enlightenment (which was at the base of much liberal thought) tended to abstract from or "bracket-out" history, resting on the notion that a common humanity exists despite all differences of place and time. In the nineteenth century, social and political thought "rediscovered" history, an awareness very compatible with the notion of progress or development noted above (L30). In its most extreme form, the awareness of history expressed itself as a belief in necessary laws governing human history and development, a belief we might call **historicism**. Thinkers as diverse as Collingwood and Marx were historicists, and historicism is a tendency more associated with conservatism or socialism than with liberalism.

Enlightenment rationalism abstracted not only from time, but also from place, tending to treat all individuals, regardless of nationality or culture, as members of a common humanity. Both liberalism and socialism drew on this idea, but the nineteenth century was a time in which nationalism exploded in much of the world as an awareness, promotion, and celebration of an exclusive particular identity. As we will note below, there is a strongly conservative element in the nationalist disposition, but as a sense of identity, nationalism cuts across, or perhaps precedes ideological divisions, as liberal and socialist cosmopolitanists have often found to their chagrin.

These are some of the fundamental developments — social, political, and intellectual — which have transformed the ideologies as initially formulated into variants we are more likely to recognize today.

A. LIBERALISM REFORMS ITSELF

In the late eighteenth and early nineteenth centuries, thinkers such as Adam Smith and James Mill articulated the ideas which embodied liberalism: limited, representative government, and a minimal state embodying the economic principle of **laissez-faire**. By the middle of the twentieth century Americans identified liberalism with an activist if not interventionist state, epitomized by Roosevelt's New Deal and Johnson's Great Society programs, which provided considerable government support for and extension of individual entitlements, especially to the underprivileged. In Canada also, government supports and transfers, regulation of the marketplace, and even limited state ownership of companies were associated with liberalism. Those advocating more individual initiative and less government interference were known as conservatives (see next section). (The choice between describing state involvement in economic matters as activist or interventionist is itself something of an ideological decision. To describe government activity as "interference" is to accept the "*laissez-faire*" view that markets should operate "unhindered"; conversely, to talk about state "participation" in the economy implies acceptance of the reformed liberal or social democratic view that there is a role for government in managing and regulating market transactions. By government "activity" we hope to convey a neutral usage, leaving the matter for our readers to judge.) Clearly liberalism was transformed in the century and a half from James Mill to John Rawls.

THE VISION REMAINS UNCHANGED

The short explanation of this transformation, perhaps, is that liberalism reacted to its own successes and shortcomings. It responded to the competition provided by socialism, to the demise of feudal society and with it (by and large) toryism, and to the pressures of a democratic political process that it, liberalism, helped to democratize. The vision of liberalism did not alter fundamentally:

Reform Liberalism
John Dewey:

L30 "The history of social reforms in the nineteenth century is almost one with the history of liberal social thought. It is not, then, from ingratitude that I shall emphasize its defects, for recognition of them is essential to an intelligent statement of the elements of liberal philosophy for the present and any nearby future. The fundamental defect was lack of perception of historic relativity. This lack is expressed in the conception of the individual as something given, complete in itself, and of liberty as a ready-made possession of the individual, only needing the removal of external restrictions in order to manifest itself.

... an individual is nothing fixed, given ready-made. It is something achieved, and achieved not in isolation, but with the aid and support of conditions, cultural and physical, including in 'cultural' economic, legal, and political institutions as well as science and art. Liberalism knows that social conditions may restrict, distort, and almost prevent the development of individuality. It therefore takes an active interest in the working of social institutions that have a bearing, positive or negative, upon the growth of individuals who shall be rugged in fact and not merely in abstract theory. It is as much interested in the positive construction of favourable institutions, legal, political, and economic, as it is in the work of removing abuses and overt oppressions ...

The two things essential, then, to thorough-going social liberalism are, first, realistic study of existing conditions in their movement, and, secondly, leading ideas, in the form of policies for dealing with these conditions in the interest of development of increased individuality and liberty."
(*"The Future of Liberalism"*, 1935)

---

liberals continued (and continue) to seek a society in which individual well-being is maximized through the enlightened pursuit of self-interest within a progressively broadening and secure sphere of individual liberty. Over time, though, the breadth and scope of liberals' concerns have altered.

On the one hand, with each success in securing individual liberty, liberalism has not halted but moved on to fresh concerns. A modern liberal's concerns with racial and gender equality, with rights for gays and lesbians, for the continued absence of prayer in schools, and for the public provision of goods such as education and health care — these would have struck the liberals from whom we quoted in the last chapter as radical, perhaps outrageous, demands. Nonetheless, what the modern liberal demands is grounded on the same principles with which the classic liberal demanded representative government, the protection of property, or religious freedom. The modern liberal pursues these principles farther and has the luxury of doing so because the classic liberal demands were by and large met.

At the same time, as liberals succeeded in implementing their political and economic agenda, they often came to the recognition that their liberal vision was as yet incompletely realized. Representative, liberal government and a thriving private property, market economy did not suffice to ensure liberty and well-being for all. This recognition led to two strategies: the reform of political and economic institutions and the reform of traditional social institutions as they touched upon issues such as education, the status of women and children, sexuality, and other areas of social and personal liberty. Like others we will call these modern (twentieth century) liberals "reform liberals," in contrast to the "classic liberals" of the eighteenth and early nineteenth centuries. (Although J.S. Mill died in 1873, his writings are both the culmination of classic liberalism, and the foundation for the reform liberalism that followed.)

A NEW PERSPECTIVE

While the liberal vision remains largely intact, the liberal perspective has changed greatly, partly because the context has changed, and partly because new ideas have considerable influence.

When the *status quo* was the rigid, relatively authoritarian structures of feudal society, liberalism tended to emphasize the negative role of the state in restricting individual freedom. While liberals recognized that some restriction of the ability of individuals to act is necessary for social peace and security, they sought to minimize these restrictions, especially where they were fetters on economic and social progress. By the nineteenth century, in many nations, liberalism had become the new *status quo*, and yet many individuals were not appreciably better off, or more free, than they had been (or would have been) in medieval society. In the immediate aftermath of the Industrial Revolution, many of those in the lowest strata of society were clearly worse off. While the liberal revolution had brought political and economic liberty, it had not brought these freedoms — or their benefits — to all. This had two consequences for liberalism.

One was the recognition that the state (or government) is not the only institution (more correctly, set of institutions) that restricts the freedom of individuals. The institutions of civil society — the capitalist economy, the family, social

Liberalism and Democracy
John Dewey:

L31 "The foundation of democracy is faith in the capacities of human nature; faith in human intelligence and in the power of pooled and cooperative experience. It is not belief that these things are complete but that if given a show they will grow and be able to generate progressively the knowledge and wisdom needed to guide collective action. Every autocratic and authoritarian scheme of social action rests on a belief that the needed intelligence is confined to a superior few, who because of inherent natural gifts are endowed with the ability and the right to control the conduct of others; laying down principles and rules and directing the ways in which they are carried out."
("Democracy and Educational Administration," 1937)

Property and Power
John Dewey:

L32 "That the control of the means of production by the few in legal possession operates as a standing agency of coercion of the many, may need emphasis in statement, but is surely evident to one who is willing to observe and honestly report the existing scene. It is foolish to regard the political state as the only agency now endowed with coercive power. Its exercise of this power is pale in contrast with that exercised by concentrated and organized property interests."
(*Liberalism and Social Action*, 1963)

Equality of Opportunity
John Dewey:

L33 "Belief in equality is an element of the democratic credo. It is not, however, belief in equality of natural endowments. Those who proclaimed the idea of equality did not suppose they were enunciating a psychological doctrine, but a legal and political one. All individuals are entitled to equality of treatment by law and in its administration. Each one is affected equally in

quality if not in quantity by the institutions under which he lives and has an equal right to express his judgment, although the weight of his judgment may not be equal in amount when it enters into the pooled result to that of others. In short, each one is equally an individual and entitled to equal opportunity of development of his own capacities, be they large or small in range. Moreover, each has needs of his own, as significant to him as those of others are to them. The very fact of natural and psychological inequality is all the more reason for establishment by law of equality of opportunity, since otherwise the former becomes a means of oppression of the less gifted."
("Democracy and Educational Administration," 1937)

---

norms and attitudes — can also restrict individual liberty (see L32). As John Stuart Mill argued in *On Liberty* — and as we may often find true still today — personal liberty has as much or more to fear from public opinion and its pressures for conformity, as from the activities of the state. Secondly, it becomes possible to see liberty not only in the negative sense of an absence of restrictions, but in the positive sense of an ability to do this or that. For example, it may be legally possible for anyone to acquire property, but if the economic system does not provide any opportunity for those born in poverty to escape that condition, are they any more free than if they were legally barred from ownership?

In the nineteenth century, some liberals came to see that individuals are denied freedom in the positive sense by the laws and institutions of a purportedly liberal society. At the same time, liberals increasingly accepted the notion of progressive humanity, and with it the imperative to remove restrictions or impediments to that progress. (The term "progressive" can be understood simply to mean "changing" or "developing," without the accompanying belief (usually held by liberals and socialists) that this development is "for the better." I will generally use "progressive" to mean advocating change or newer ideas, and oppose it to "traditional," which stresses continuity and time-honoured truths.) The result of these developments was a shift in liberalism from emphasizing the need for greater freedom from the state to an emphasis on the need for greater equality in the enjoyment of liberty.

As noted in the previous chapter, liberalism has always had an egalitarian component rooted in the identity of the abstract individuals with which liberal thought begins. This abstract identity informs the notion of the "rule of law" and other liberal beliefs about fair and impartial treatment by public authority. If society and government were to provide the same opportunity for all individuals, then any differences in condition which resulted would be attributable

Liberal Equality
John Rawls:

L34 "The first statement of the two principles reads as follows.

First: each person is to have an equal right to the most extensive basic liberty compatible with a similar liberty for others.

Second: social and economic inequalities are to be arranged so that they are both (a) reasonably expected to be to everyone's advantage, and (b) attached to positions and offices open to all....

By way of general comment, these principles ... are to govern the assignment of rights and duties and to regulate the distribution of social and economic advantages. As their formulation suggests, these principles presuppose that the social structure can be divided into two more or less distinct parts, the first principle applying to the one, the second to the other. They distinguish between those aspects of the social system that define and secure the equal liberties of citizenship and those that specify and establish social and economic inequalities. The basic liberties of citizens are, roughly speaking, political liberty (the right to vote and to be eligible for public office) together with freedom of speech and assembly; liberty of conscience and freedom of thought; freedom of the person along with the right to hold (personal) property; and freedom from arbitrary arrest and seizure as defined by the rule of law. These liberties are all required to be equal by the first principle, since citizens of a just society are to have the same basic rights.

The second principle applies, in the first approximation, to the distribution of income and wealth and to the design of organizations that make use of differences in authority and responsibility, or chains of command. While the distribution of wealth and income need not be equal, it must be to everyone's advantage, and at the same time, positions of authority and offices of command must be accessible to all. One applies the second principle by holding positions open, and then, subject to this constraint, arranges social and economic inequalities so that everyone benefits."
(*Two Principles of Justice*, 1971)

to individual skill and effort, in short, to what individuals made of the opportunities provided them. The equality that liberals desire, then, is equality of opportunity, a notion captured by metaphors like "a level playing field" or "starting the race on an even footing." The liberal can accept that there will be winners and losers in the great competition of life, but she also wants none of the competitors to have special advantages (see L33).

To enhance a positive enjoyment of liberty, to promote equality of opportunity, and to reform any number of institutions that diminish individual freedom, liberalism changed its posture toward the state. Instead of viewing government as the primary challenge to individual liberty, as it certainly was in the medieval absolutist state, liberals came to believe that the state in a liberal society can function to preserve and enhance liberty, to reform the institutions of civil society, and to provide opportunity for those disadvantaged by their ascribed social position. From the stance of *laissez-faire* and the minimal state (see Chapter Five), liberals moved to acceptance of an activist state, a government much larger than what liberalism originally envisaged.

A REVISED PROGRAM

In short, then, a variety of practical problems associated with continued inequality and the lack of freedom provided the incentive for reform of liberalism — reform which took three main directions:

• the incorporation of political democracy,

• an expansion of rights claims by individuals, and

• the abandonment of *laissez-faire* political economy.

One of the earliest and most significant revisions of liberalism was an incorporation of political democracy. Early liberal thinkers such as Locke had advocated representative government but had expected that the representatives would be drawn from and selected by the property-owning classes. For an aristocracy of birth, early liberals would have substituted an aristocracy of wealth by defining political rights in terms of a certain level of property ownership. This had the effect of raising the social status of a considerable number of individuals who had acquired wealth through successful activity in a market economy, but it was a far cry from establishing a broadly-based democracy. The Industrial Revolution had created a large class of urban workers, who, owning no

Reform Liberalism and Rights
Franklin Delano Roosevelt:

L35 "This Republic had its beginning, and grew to its present strength, under the protection of certain inalienable political rights—among them the right of free speech, free press, free worship, trial by jury, freedom from unreasonable searches and seizures. They were our rights to life and liberty.

As our Nation has grown in size and stature, however—as our industrial economy expanded—these political rights proved inadequate to assure us equality in the pursuit of happiness.

We have come to a clear realization of the fact that true individual freedom cannot exist without economic security and independence. 'Necessitous men are not free men.' People who are hungry and out of a job are the stuff of which dictatorships are made.

In our day these economic truths have become accepted as self-evident. We have accepted, so to speak, a second Bill of Rights under which a new basis of security and prosperity can be established for all—regardless of station, race, or creed. Among these are:

The right to a useful and remunerative job in the industries or ships or farms or mines of the Nation;

The right to earn enough to provide adequate food and clothing and recreation;

The right of every farmer to raise and sell his products at a return which will give him and his family a decent living;

The right of every businessman, large and small, to trade in an atmosphere of freedom from unfair competition and domination by monopolies at home or abroad;

The right of every family to a decent home;

The right to adequate medical care and the opportunity to achieve and enjoy good health;

The right to adequate protection from the economic fears of old age, sickness, accident, and unemployment;

The right to a good education.

All of these rights spell security. And after this war is won we must be prepared to move forward, in the implementation of these rights, to new goals of human happiness and well-being."

(Message to the Congress on the State of the Union, January 11, 1944) property, had no political rights. It was this class (by and large) which socialism claimed to represent and to whom it appealed for support. Partly for reasons of principle and partly for the pragmatic purpose of heading off the socialists, liberals came to support extending the franchise (the right to vote) first to male members of the working class and, much later, to women of all social classes.

One reason for liberal reluctance to extend democracy was a conflict between the belief in rational government, and the apparent irrationality or nonrationality of the bulk of the population. We should remember that liberalism emerged in an age before general education, when the majority of people were unschooled and illiterate. If it is safe to say that public participation in politics presupposes a public educated or informed about politics, then those who believe most sincerely in democracy must also be strongly concerned with the quality of education received by citizens. As the general level of education and literacy improves, the fears about democracy subside. A classic example of the difficulty here is provided by John Stuart Mill's reflections. Driven by his liberal principles to conclude that democracy is the best form of government, Mill nonetheless would have given more votes to those whose occupation reflected the greatest mental skill or education. He also would have restricted the work of the elected legislature to ratifying decisions made by a non-elected group of experts.

A second dimension of liberal reform was an expansion of rights claims on behalf of individuals. **Rights** may be understood as *entitlements individuals claim from the state or other individuals*. Entitlements may be moral or legal (see further on rights in Chapter Four); in the latter case the state is legally obliged to respect or enforce entitlements. Although it is not always the case, rights are usually about protections for something individuals value (like their lives, freedoms, properties, etc.). The extension of entitlements to individuals previously unprotected from the state or other individuals is a significant (and ongoing) development within liberalism. For example, early liberals were much concerned with establishing and protecting the rights of property owners. This was very beneficial to those who owned property, but offered little benefit to those who were propertyless, and indeed often left them more vulnerable to the actions of those with property. A primary means for reformist liberals to expand the sphere of personal liberty was to bring new categories of rights under the protective umbrella of the state. The extension of legal and political rights to women in the first decades of this century, the civil rights movement in the United States in the 1960s, and the addition of the Charter of Rights and Freedoms to the Canadian constitution in 1982 offer clear examples of reform liberalism in practice (see L35).

The third and perhaps most significant area of liberal reform was the abandonment of *laissez-faire* political economy, and participation in the development of the twentieth–century welfare state. From the start, liberalism sought, in part, to justify the inequality associated with capitalism by arguing that those who are least advantaged in liberal society are better off than they would have been prior to liberalism, or might be under any other social arrangements. Advocates of the market economy, such as Adam Smith, firmly believed that if competition and market mechanisms were allowed to work unfettered by government regulation, the condition of the working class would be improved; over the long term wages would rise, prices would fall, and all would become wealthier. Similarly, liberal economists could argue that the tremendous economic growth created by capitalism more than compensated for any inequality by providing better than any other system might for those at the bottom of the economy. In practice, though, both of these arguments were suspect. In the first place, for a number of reasons, the liberal economy in reality did not work as beneficially for the labouring classes or the unemployed as theory promised. Secondly, socialism claimed to offer a political economy which would improve the conditions of the least advantaged, employing the productive capacity of market society without reproducing its attendant inequality.

Abandoning the minimal state, reformist liberals looked to an activist state to overcome the weaknesses of *laissez-faire*, to moderate the inequalities and inequities of the market economy, and to act positively to enhance the actual liberty of all in society, but particularly of those currently disadvantaged by the existing social arrangements (see L34). A wide variety of tools was developed and employed by liberals in power, including increasing regulation of economic life, actual intervention in the economy, and progressive application of levers of economic management, all culminating in the twentieth–century welfare state (see Chapter Five). Despite the scope and extent of these departures from *laissez-faire*, this reformed liberalism remained committed to the market and to private property. For this reason, despite what its critics have sometimes alleged, the activist state of reformed liberalism falls far short of the interventionist state of socialism. In this regard, too, it is notable that the liberal welfare state has usually been much less comprehensive and extensive than the welfare state constructed by social democrats or socialists (see below).

IN SUMMARY

Once feudal society and its ideas became history, liberalism turned on itself the impulse to reform institutions and other social arrangements on a rational basis consistent with individual liberty, or rather, applied this impulse to the society it had been instrumental in creating. Sometimes grudgingly, liberals recognized the ways that institutions and privilege can favour some individuals or groups, leading to inequality in the way liberty is enjoyed. Equality of opportunity became the goal of extending the benefits of liberty to all, with the intention that each should be able to make the most of his/her capacities, talents, or interests. The legitimate role of the state was transformed from that of sentinel, providing the order and security within which individuals work and play, to that of guardian, educator, and advocate — intervening and reorganizing liberal society on behalf of those excluded from the workshop or the playground. Lest this sound too paternalistic, we should also stress the increasingly democratic temper of liberalism which seeks to involve individuals and groups in a more meaningful way in the very political process by which liberty is enhanced and secured.

B. LIBERAL CONSERVATISM

The point has been made already that the content of conservatism is to a great degree dependent on the context: what is it that conservatives wish to "conserve"? If conservatism is a defense of the *status quo* against the efforts of those who would implement serious reform or change, then there can be as many different conservatisms as there are *status quos*. If conservatism is captured in the phrase "what is, is right," then it is also difficult to imagine any state of affairs, once existing, which conservatism could not justify. These observations are consistent with the view of *situational* conservatism identified in the last chapter. If, then, at some time in the eighteenth and nineteenth century in most of

Conservative Liberalism
Michael Oakeshott:

C19 "I do not think it is necessarily connected with any particular beliefs about the universe, about the world in general or about human conduct in general. What it is tied to is certain beliefs about the activity of governing and the instruments of government, and it is in terms of beliefs on these topics, and not on others, that it can be made to appear intelligible. And, to state my view briefly before elaborating it, what makes a conservative disposition in politics intelligible is nothing to do with a natural law or a providential order, nothing to do with morals or religion; it is the observation of *our current manner of living combined with the belief ... that governing is a specific and limited activity*, namely the provision and custody of general rules of conduct, which are understood, not as plans for imposing substantive activities, but as *instruments enabling people to pursue the activities of their own choice with the minimum frustration*, and therefore something which it is appropriate to be conservative about."
("On being Conservative," 1962)

Europe and many of her present or former colonies, liberalism became the *status quo* as represented by the dominant political and economic institutions, *conservatism in such liberal societies should have a markedly liberal character.*

At the same time, in describing the tory conservatism which opposed liberalism, we encountered several ideas capable of surviving the demise of any fondness for feudalism. These were notions such as natural inequality, the importance of religion, the value of traditional morality, and a pessimism about human nature (what the conservative might claim is simply a "realism" about people). None of these is incompatible with the primary institutions of liberal society, in particular a constitutional, limited government and a private property market economy. Modern conservatism in liberal societies, then, has turned out to be, in almost every case, a mixture of (traditional) conservatism and liberalism. What makes this quite easily confusing is the variety of ways in which liberalism and conservatism may be combined. At the very least, all conservatives in modern liberal societies partake in the liberal consensus (see Chapter Four) that accords legitimacy to a private property market economy, the basic institutions of constitutional representative government, and to the rule of law. This consensus is so complete in some societies (like the United States) that it is no longer recognized by many people as specifically "liberal." What distinguishes conservatives from each other is how much of this liberal consensus they have come to share, and on the other hand, what they reject in the liberal catalogue of values.

CONSERVATIVE LIBERALS

Consider in the first instance, classic liberals who objected to the changes brought about by reform liberalism. Such liberals who wished to preserve the *status quo* in the face of reform would be conservative liberals. Such a liberal would support a *laissez-faire* economy and the associated notion of the minimal state. He would support representative government, be wary of extending popular democracy too far, and probably regard the American Bill of Rights (1789) as a code needing no expansion or supplementation. The moral values of the nineteenth century, stressing the virtues of the Christian family, would sit comfortably with him. Over time, this conservative liberal would be simply called a conservative, just as the reform liberal would be called a liberal. In fact, some of the most eloquent spokesmen of conservatism have been conservative liberals, such as Burke (who was a Whig and not a Tory) or Michael Oakshott (see C19).

LIBERAL CONSERVATIVES

A position very similar to that just outlined can be reached from a different angle. Start with a tory conservatism like that discussed in the previous chapter. Imagine then that as liberal political and economic institutions are entrenched, tories become reconciled to them, but do not abandon their own beliefs about human nature, order and stability, change, and natural inequality. Since the liberal institutions they come to accept are the as yet unreformed institutions of classic liberalism — *laissez-faire* and limited representative government — there is very little to distinguish these liberal conservatives (conservatives who adopt liberal institutions) from the conservative liberals (liberals with a conservative disposition). The picture, though, is more complicated than this.

MARKET TORIES AND CHRISTIAN DEMOCRACY

Two further variations on the conservative theme are quite similar, but may seem odd or curious to Americans. Consider again the "original" conservatives we called tories. Over time, most if not all tories made their peace with the economic side of liberalism; instead of clinging to notions of an agrarian, feudal economy, they accepted and adapted to the modern, industrial market

The Radical Right
"Alienation and the Radical Right":

C20 "The ideology of the radical right consists of ... six ... features discussed below ...

Individualism ...Only a determined campaign of anticollectivism holds any promise of rediscovering traditional American individualism.

Republicanism "This is a Republic, not a democracy—Let's keep it that way!" says a mail sticker popular in Birch Society circles. This nation is not, cannot be, a democracy, for the central credo of democracy is equality, which is contrary to the laws of nature and which science demonstrates to be a false premise in the light of human experience.... Only republicanism, or government for the people by a qualified elite, can save us from the ravages of immoral mob-rule.

Fundamentalism Americans are implored to return to divine and eternal truths, both biblical and secular....

Purification Conspiracy and betrayal—in the guise of social change—are felt to have reached ominous proportions.... The nation must be purified and redeemed....

Restoration The United States is presumed to have attained a Golden or Heroic Age, usually, though not invariably, located somewhere in the century preceding "that man" F.D.R.... Domestically, the golden age is sometimes equated with the *status quo*, though more frequently located in the past....

Unilateralism ...the complex of assumptions, policies and programs governing American foreign policy during the past several decades must be rejected. ... In short, the United States should act, rather than humbly react, and should do so in the spirit of justified unilateralism, unencumbered by false principles of diplomacy, expedience or multilateralism."
(Gilbert Abcarian and Sherman M. Stanage, 1965)

economy. The critical issue here is which dimensions of their tory conservatism did they bring with their new allegiance to liberal economics? One of the features distinguishing tories from liberals was their belief in natural inequality. The inequality associated with a market economy would pose no problem to tories adapting to liberal institutions. For a supposed "natural" aristocracy based on family and social class, the market economy substitutes an aristocracy based on wealth and economic class.

Aristocratic conservatives, though, also possessed a belief in organic community which complemented their belief in natural inequality. If the least advantaged somehow have "inferior" natures, then this is the lot nature has given them and not something attributable to their own failures or lack of effort. So too, by this logic, the "superior" individuals of noble character are not self-made, but naturally endowed with the abilities, temperament, intellect, or whatever it is that makes them "superior." In an organic conception of society, those naturally superior have an obligation towards their inferiors: to educate them, to present to them an example of proper conduct, and where possible to provide for those unable to provide for themselves. Tories who bring this sense of *noblesse oblige* [OED: "privilege entails responsibility" (1982:682)] to their adoption of liberal institutions will have a basis for agreeing to some of the measures brought in by reform liberalism, in particular, those features of the welfare state that are designed to provide social relief to the least advantaged in society. It is important to understand the difference here: reform liberals reform the market economy in order to enhance the equality of opportunity for individuals; market tories (as we might call them) reform the market economy because they employ a collectivist (albeit inegalitarian) understanding of market society. In addition, there are many other issues on which reform liberals and market tories will disagree.

As noted, the idea of a market tory, or of bringing a collectivist understanding to the individualist institutions of liberal society, may seem odd to Americans, but this is precisely where the notion of national differences (see Chapter Eight) is relevant. The observation has been made on any number of occasions that the United States is a nation of liberal ideology, ranging from radical liberalism at one end of the spectrum to conservative liberalism at the other. Louis Hartz, Seymour Lipset, and others have seen this as a result of the "cleansing" effect of the American Revolution and the War of Independence. Tory conservatives present in the American colonies would, of course, have supported the English Crown. The victory of the colonials over the English meant that tories fled the colonies, back to Britain, or north to the British North American colonies that would later become Canada. This had two results: in the United States, the political culture was uniformly liberal, and differ-

The Neo-conservative as Economic Liberal

Keith Joseph (*a former Secretary of State under Margaret Thatcher*):

C21 "I would explain that, if allowed to, the market will provide a constantly rising set of minimum standards—including rising minimum standards of income. I would explain that there is now very little, if any, primary poverty in this country—that is, households with too little income, if reasonably managed, to pay for sufficient necessities, as currently conceived. Some special groups, such as widows and disabled, have too little income in general for their special needs.

But though there is little, if any, primary poverty, there is in this country a substantial amount of secondary poverty: discomfort, shortage and squalor. It exists in homes where there is an inability to put what money there is to good use. The fact is that whether among the elderly or among two-parent or one-parent families there are copers and non-copers. No one knows how in a free society to teach every non-coper how to cope. What is known is that in many cases extra money does not end squalor....

The fact is that it is only from the increasing efficiency of the free enterprise system that higher wages can be paid out of which the tax base will rise, thus supporting both higher earnings for those at work and more benefits for those who are dependent."

(*Stranded on the Middle Ground: Reflections on Circumstances and Politics*, 1976)

---

ences which emerged were different varieties of liberalism. In Canada, as Horowitz and others following him have argued, there was a tory strain of conservatism which survived, and eventually contributed to the phenomena of market tories (what Horowitz calls "red Tories"): conservatives who are economic liberals, but support measures of the welfare state designed to provide relief or opportunity to the least advantaged. These market tories then, are conservatives willing to let the state play a larger role in the economy than that acceptable to the conservatives we discussed above. In this author's view, market toryism in Canada is an ideological current that is drying up, if not already spent.

A more powerful and convincing view of market toryism can be found in European Christian democracy, another phenomenon that will need explanation for North American students. Recall that feudal society involved a close, albeit fractious, relationship between the state and the Roman Church. Liberalism, influenced by the rationalist Enlightenment and by Protestantism, argued for a separation between church and state. Free-thinkers, dissenters, and non-believers were typically liberals. Particularly in those countries which remained predominantly Roman Catholic, liberalism was seen to be the enemy of religion and the Church, and was opposed to any official position for the Church in civic life. Moreover, many Church adherents identified liberalism and its modern ways with materialism, urbanization, and secularization — in short, with features believed to undermine the faith and the institutions in which it is most at home, the family and the local community. Christian Democratic parties were formed to oppose liberal parties and defend the Church and its values. (Although Christian Democratic parties are Protestant in Scandinavia, and the large German party appeals to both Protestants and Catholics, most Christian Democratic movements have succeeded in predominantly Catholic nations. As Mény points out, in countries where *all* parties profess allegiance to the church, such as Ireland and Spain, Christian Democracy does not exist (1993:66).)

Not surprisingly, Christian democratic ideology has tended to support traditional Church positions on social and moral matters: opposition to abortion, civil divorce, and contraception; support for the traditional family; and deference to legitimate public authorities. In many cases, Christian Democratic ideology has been influenced by official doctrines published as papal encyclicals which have articulated the Church's position on most social and political issues. On many of these issues, Christian democrats and other (described in Europe as "secular") conservatives will be in essential agreement. Similarly, a cautious attitude about democracy and pessimism about human nature are also common ground between Christian democrats and secular conservatives, who diverge on two points. One is the role of the Church in education, Christian democrats supporting denominational schools in opposition to the liberal demand for secular education. American conservatives are divided themselves on this point, some regarding even the (comparatively mild) notion of prayer in schools as a violation of the traditional American constitutional division between church and state. The major difference, though, between European Christian and secular conservatives has tended to concern the role of the state in the economy. Whereas Europe's secular conservatives (like American conservatives) are usually economic liberals advocating a minimal state, Christian democracy has believed that economics should take second place to social concerns and, for this reason, has in the past supported state policies to protect or give relief to the poor or working classes, even when this has constituted what liberals would call "interference" in the marketplace. Interestingly, Pope Leo XIII wrote the following in his encyclical *Rerum Novarum* (1891): "The public administration must duly and solicitously provide for the welfare and comfort of the working

A Conservative Reflects on Democracy
David Frum:

C22 "In a democratic culture, feeling yourself separate from the people is distressing, even frightening: Can there be a stronger temptation than the desire to please the crowd, to say only what it wants to hear? Conservatives are fighting harder against gays in the military than against the Clinton health plan because they know that on the former issue the crowd will be with them and fear that on the latter, the crowd will not....

The early 1990s are in some ways more conducive to conservatism than the 1980s were.... Far more than in the 1980s, governors and mayors face voters who profess to prefer budget cuts to tax increases. But those same voters continue to expect lavishly equipped suburban high schools, subsidized tuition at state colleges, toll-free highways, and environmental improvements at others' expense. What could be more tempting to a politician than to teach voters to blame taxes and regulations not on the requirements of the middle class but on the inordinate demands of the poor? What could be more politically reckless than to attack bloated education, highway, and farm budgets, which largely benefit the middle class? Unfortunately, the refusal to take that apparently reckless course dooms all other conservative hopes to futility....

... conservative intellectuals should learn to care a little less about the electoral prospects of the Republican Party, indulge less in policy cleverness and ethnic demagoguery, and do what intellectuals of all descriptions are obliged to do—practice honesty and pay the price."
(*Dead Right*, 1994)

---

classes; otherwise that law of justice will be violated which ordains that each man shall have his due." The advanced welfare states of Western Europe have often been the product of a consensus (or compromise) between social democracy on the left and Christian democracy on the right.

In short, the conservatives in this section — market tories and Christian democrats — share much with other conservatives. If anything, they are more traditional than liberal conservatives about moral and social issues, but differ from other conservatives most in their support for state economic policies closer to those of reform liberalism, that is, for a state active in the provision of welfare.

Explaining Conservative Diversity
William Harbour:

C23 "Any analysis of Conservative thought which tries to force Conservatism into an ideological strait jacket would miss the strong anti-ideological
cast of Conservative thinking. The student of Conservative thought confronts
a significant methodological problem. One must for the sake of clarity provide an outline of the subject, which requires systematic analysis. But Conservatism is generally critical of philosophical system building. The form of analysis may unintentionally suggest a systematic characteristic which the subject
mater does not possess."
(*The Foundations of Conservative Thought*, 1982)

THE RELIGIOUS RIGHT

While Christian Democracy may be foreign to North American students, the
association of religious adherence and conservatism will not be. In almost any
culture, in normal circumstances, adherence to the dominant religion will be
somewhat conservative, preserving traditional values and ways of life. The degree to which a society or its politics have been secularized will have a bearing
on the link between religion and politics. From the arrival of the Pilgrims at
Plymouth Rock, American civil society has been profoundly religious, but almost as deeply rooted is the principle that the state (political life) be secular; that
there be no link between the government and religious institutions. The religious right (sometimes linked to, or called, the radical right or the new right; see
C20) in the United States would alter this long-standing relationship of official
religious neutrality. Like other conservatives, the religious right supports traditional moral values, grounded in this case in a fundamentalist reading of Christian scripture. These conservatives would like to see prayer in schools; believe
in a strong law and order state (including capital punishment); and generally
oppose abortion, feminism, rights for gays and lesbians, sex education in
schools, and whatever else they identify with "secular humanism," a generic label for all the ills of modern society. What takes these conservatives further than
others who might share part or all of the same concerns is their determination
to use the state to further their religious agenda or to dismantle the laws which
contradict it. The religious right in the United States has been closely associated
with tele-evangelists, and with organizations like the Moral Majority, which
later became the Liberty Federation. At the same time, unlike Christian

"Contract with America"
Associated Press:

C24 Republicans signed a policy blueprint in September that they called a Contract with America promising that within the first 100 days of Congress, the House of Representatives would vote on:

- A balanced-budget amendment to the Constitution and a legislative line-item veto;

- An anticrime package that would include limits on death-penalty appeals and more money for prisons and law enforcement;

- Welfare reform limiting recipients to two years of eligibility;

- Enforcement of child-support laws, tax incentives for adoption and an elderly-dependent-care tax credit;

- A $500-a-child tax credit;

- A prohibition on U.S. troops being placed under United Nations command and restoration of the essential parts of national security financing;

- Allowing Social Security recipients between 65 and 70 an income of $30,000 a year, up from the $11,000 limit, before any retirement benefits are lost;

- Cutting the tax rate on capital gains and regulatory relief for business;

- A limit on punitive damages in lawsuits and allowing judges to order losers to pay the litigation costs for both sides;

- Term limits for members of Congress."

Democrats, Christian conservatives in the United States embrace the market economy unreservedly, and are uneasy about the activist, interventionist state. This is consistent with the more individualistic, anti-statist character of American political culture and also with the fundamentalist Protestant character of much American religious conservatism (as opposed to the predominantly Catholic character of Christian Democracy).

FISCAL CONSERVATISM

In the modern Western world, then, all conservatives are marked by a belief in the private property market economy and by and large agree on a laissez-faire, minimal state approach to this economy (see C21-2). As the end of the century approaches, they are concerned to reduce the size and scale of government operations and eliminate government deficits. In this sense, then, they are all **fiscal conservatives**. The one exception to this is that conservatism — mainly European Christian Democracy — which continues to value social welfare enough to justify government regulation of, or activity in, the market. Christian Democracy shares with other conservatisms a belief in traditional social and moral values. On this dimension, though, conservative ideology covers a wide ground from very traditional to surprisingly progressive positions. In each case what is at stake is the degree of activity by the state and the nature of that activity. For example, with respect to social questions like morality, crime, education, or political empowerment, the spectrum ranges from strong state activity to preserve or promote "traditional" values, to a minimal state involvement on such questions, to strong state activity for change (progress) on these issues.

Accordingly, two contemporary labels reflect rather different varieties of the mingling of conservatism and liberalism that we have observed. A term that has become rather familiar in recent years is **neo-conservative**, which actually was coined to describe disgruntled liberals who had gone over to conservatism. What these erstwhile liberals object to, primarily, is what they perceive as the overly tolerant character of reform liberalism, its relativism, or lack of fidelity to moral principles. (Neo-conservatives are *not* great admirers of "political correctness," among other things.) Neo-conservatives call for a return to political and social morality; at the same time they are fiscal conservatives concerned about the growth of the state and the apparently associated rise of deficits. There is also at the same time, a current called **neo-liberalism**. Here fiscal conservatism is married to the progressive social and political positions of the reform liberals. Neo-liberals express concern about government spending, particularly deficits, but are more likely to seek the reform of social programs than their outright elimination. Similarly, neo-liberals would shift the strategy of the state from the provision of relief for those unemployed and marginalized to fostering the economic growth and social change which will eliminate unemployment and marginalization. It may well be that we will look back on the 1990s as the decade when formerly reform liberals became neo-liberals under the pressure provided by the effects of years of accumulated government deficits.

Clearly then, conservatism comes in any number of flavours today, although generally speaking, increasingly common to all versions is a belief in "fiscal responsibility," a general adherence to economic liberalism, and a strong commitment to moral principles, usually (but not always) of a traditional character and usually (but not always) linked to Christianity (see C23).

C. SOCIALIST SCHISMS

Near the beginning of this century, Vladimir Lenin (the most influential socialist after Karl Marx) published a small book entitled *What Is To Be Done* (1902), which concerned the nature of the transformation from a capitalist to a socialist society — what path should socialist theory and practice take? As the end of the century approaches, the question more likely to be raised is whether or not socialism is dead. Writing at the end of his life, the dean of American socialism, Michael Harrington, observed of the world's successful democratic socialist parties that "none of them has a precise sense of what socialism means, even if they have often proved to be more humane and efficient trustees of capitalism than the capitalists themselves." (1990:1-2) Although socialism was born and nourished in the conditions of the nineteenth century, it is the twentieth century which has witnessed its rise and (at least apparent) fall. This has also been the century in which socialism has become a family of ideologies, united on some fundamentals, but seriously divided over others.

As noted in the previous chapter, modern socialism is "scientific" rather than "utopian" — that is to say, it is based on the analysis and critique of contemporary liberal society rather than on a detailed vision of a post-capitalist society (i.e. a utopia). A consequence of this is that socialists are generally fuzziest about what the triumph of socialism would mean. Their vision remains expressed either negatively in terms of the absence of features associated with liberal capitalism — the end of alienation, the absence of exploitation, etc. — or is expressed positively in term of generalities: the realization of equality, democracy, community, freedom. The development of and divisions within socialism, then, have not been about ultimate ends but largely about means, about the program necessary to transform the capitalist society.

The Revolution
Vladimir Lenin:

S13 "... the theory of Marx and Engels of the inevitability of a violent revolution refers to the bourgeois state. The latter *cannot* be superseded by the proletarian state (the dictatorship of the proletariat) through the process of 'withering away,' but, as a general rule, only through a violent revolution.... The
necessity of systematically imbuing the masses with *this* and precisely this
view of violent revolution lies at the root of the *entire* theory of Marx and
Engels....

The supersession of the bourgeois state by the proletarian state is impossible without a violent revolution. The abolition of the proletarian state, i.e. of
the state in general, is impossible except through the process of 'withering
away.'"
(*State and Revolution*, 1917)

REVOLUTION OR REFORM?

At the time Lenin wrote the book noted above, all socialists were agreed that
capitalism required a radical, thorough transformation, but they disagreed
about whether it could be achieved gradually through reform or required sudden, drastic change through a revolution. If the latter, would this be a violent
or non-violent revolution? Closely related to positions concerning the nature
of the transformation was the further question of who should carry it out. Is socialist society necessarily the product of popular political action by the working
class, or is revolution to be brought about by an informed, dedicated elite?

Karl Marx had suggested that the revolution would occur in the most developed capitalist societies, where the working class would become conscious of
its exploitation and, acquiring revolutionary consciousness, would act to over-
throw capitalist institutions, economic and political. This was to be a two-stage
revolution: a political revolution by the working class to take control of the
state, and then a social revolution to eliminate capitalist relations of production,
hence creating a classless society. Until this social revolution had been completed, the state would remain a strong instrument of the working classes. Marx
called this period the "dictatorship of the proletariat," and identified this stage
as "socialism." Once the work of eliminating capitalist vestiges was complete,
the state could "wither away," and only then would society have reached the
stage of "communism" (see S13). Through most of his life, Marx seemed to be-

The Vanguard Party

S14 "The political struggle of Social Democracy is far more extensive and complex than the economic struggle of the workers against the employers and the government. Similarly (indeed for that reason), the organization of the revolutionary Social Democratic Party must inevitably be of *a kind different* from the organisation of the workers designed for this struggle. The workers' organization must in the first place be a trade union organisation; secondly, it must be as broad as possible; and thirdly, it must be as public as conditions will allow ... On the other hand, the organisation of the revolutionaries must consist first and foremost of people who make revolutionary activity their profession (for which reason I speak of the organisation of *revolutionaries*, meaning revolutionary Social Democrats). In view of this common characteristic of the members of such an organisation, *all distinctions as between workers and intellectuals*, not to speak of distinctions of trade and profession, in both categories, *must be effaced*. Such an organisation must perforce not be very extensive and must be as secret as possible.

... I assert: (1) that no revolutionary movement can endure without a stable organisation of leaders maintaining continuity; (2) that the broader the popular mass drawn spontaneously into the struggle, which forms the basis of the movement and participates in it, the more urgent the need for such an organisation, and the more solid this organisation must be ... (3) that such an organisation must consist chiefly of people professionally engaged in revolutionary activity; (4) that in an autocratic state, the more we *confine* the membership of such an organisation to people who are professionally engaged in revolutionary activity and who have been professionally trained in the art of combating the political police, the more difficult will it be to unearth the organisation; and (5) the *greater* will be the number of people from the working class and from the other social classes who will be able to join the movement and perform active work in it."
(*What Is to Be Done*, 1902)

lieve that the revolution would be a popular uprising by a working class grown conscious of its exploitation, having gained a "revolutionary consciousness." This seizure of the state could be violent, as the result of a sudden, drastic awakening by the proletariat and the passions involved in taking action against an exploitive order. Moreover, Marx anticipated that the forces with the most to lose in such a revolution would use whatever resources at their command to prevent the loss of economic and political power. Later in his career, Marx seemed to consider the possibility that the working class could accomplish the political task of seizing power by democratic means in those states where the franchise (right to vote) had been extended to the non-owning classes. At the time of Marx's death in 1883, the proletarian revolution had not occurred anywhere.

In 1889 the Second International was formed, an association of Marxist socialist parties from twenty-two countries. Pre-eminent among these was the German Socialist Party, within which a debate developed concerning the future course of socialism. In 1899, Eduard Bernstein published *Evolutionary Socialism* in which he argued that several of Marx's observations no longer held true and required revision to correspond to changing conditions. Capitalism was not on the verge of collapse, Bernstein observed, nor was the condition of workers continuing to deteriorate. Marx had failed to appreciate the possibilities of democratic reform within the capitalist state and that the state could be an instrument of regulation, reform, and redistribution and thereby improve the condition of the working classes. Hence Bernstein argued for a gradual transition to socialism through reform *within* the capitalist, democratic state (see S15). This non-violent transformation by political means Bernstein called "evolutionary" socialism. Opposing Bernstein and supporting Marxist orthodoxy was Karl Kautsky. Over the long haul, Bernstein's revisionism won out over Kautsky's orthodoxy among the socialist parties of the Second International. From this point, socialism clearly stood for a democratic, piecemeal approach to reforming and replacing capitalism. In Germany, the Socialist Party continued to grow, gaining political strength, receiving more than a third of the vote in the 1912 general election. Democratic socialism suffered a setback with the outbreak of the First World War which shattered international solidarity. Socialists in each country were expected to be good patriots and support the war effort rather than oppose it on behalf of the international interest of the working class. Socialists were divided on this question in countries like Germany, and socialism stalled in its march toward political power.

To Lenin, this was just another indication of the weakness of the evolutionary path to socialism. Taking some of Marx's observations about the nature of classes in capitalist society, Lenin pushed them further to argue that the workers in a capitalist society could at best only develop a trade union mentality and not the revolutionary consciousness necessary to promote and carry through radical change. The revolution of the working class would require the dynamic leadership of a committed core of revolutionaries, intellectuals grounded in Marxist theory, who would engage in agitation and propaganda. This core would be what Lenin called a "vanguard," to act and decide on behalf of the working class (the proletariat). The vanguard would be a party rigorously organized, se-

Evolutionary Socialism
Eduard Bernstein:

S15 "... No-one has questioned the necessity for the working classes to gain the control of government. The point at issue is between the theory of a social cataclysm and the question whether with the given social development in Germany and the present advanced state of its working classes in the towns and country, a sudden catastrophe would be desirable in the interest of the social democracy. I have denied it and deny it again, because in my judgment a greater security for lasting success lies in a steady advance than in the possibilities offered by a catastrophic crash.

... Whether the legislative or the revolutionary method is the more promising depends entirely on the nature of the measures and on their relation to different classes and customs of the people.

In general, one may say here that the revolutionary way (always in the sense of revolution by violence) does quicker work as far as it deals with removal of obstacles which a privileged minority places in the path of social progress: that its strength lies on its negative side.

Constitutional legislation works more slowly in this respect as a rule. Its path is usually that of compromise, not the prohibition, but the buying out of acquired rights. But it is stronger than the revolution scheme where prejudice and the limited horizon of the great mass of the people appear as hindrances to social progress, and it offers greater advantages where it is a question of the creation of permanent economic arrangements capable of lasting; in other words, it is best adapted to positive social-political work."
(*Evolutionary Socialism*, 1899)

lective about membership, and run on the principle of "democratic centralism" (see S14). In 1903 the Russian socialists split between the Bolshevik (majority) and Menshevik (minority) factions — the latter ironically supporting a mass party, the former deciding for the vanguard type of party that Lenin advocated. When Russia experienced a liberal revolution in 1917, it was the Bolsheviks under Lenin and Trotsky who eventually seized power and triumphed in the civil war which followed. In 1919, the Third International (Comintern) was formed. This was an association of communist parties worldwide, dedicated to promoting and defending the proletarian revolution internationally (in effect a network of parties faithful to and consistent with the communist ideology of the Soviet party).

Early in the twentieth century, then, it became possible to distinguish clearly between socialism and communism. Socialism is democratic, reformist, and peaceful; communism is authoritarian, revolutionary, and if necessary committed to violent struggle. These differences are significant and underpin others. When we say that communism is authoritarian there are two important senses in which this is so; it involves an anti-democratic concentration of power and a commitment to a total employment of the state on behalf of the revolution's ends. Consider the former: the vanguard party is not simply an elite acting on behalf of the proletariat rather than an organization of the (entire) proletariat, it is the *only* party permitted to exist, to organize, to solicit public support, and most importantly, to gain office. The distinction between party and government is completely obscured, if it can be said to exist at all in any meaningful sense. No opposition to the communist party or its positions is tolerated or regarded as legitimate. By contrast, democratic socialism accepts the legitimacy of opposition, the inevitability of plurality within contemporary society, and the challenge of competing for public support within electoral democracy. The state and government are and remain separate from the party, even if or when it succeeds in winning elections. It is clear, then, that **constitutionalism** is impossible within a communist system but remains as viable under democratic socialism as it does under liberal-conservatism.

Secondly, the communist party's monopoly on power goes hand in hand with a commitment to the total employment of the power of the state on behalf of the ends defined by communism. This complete exercise of the power of the state is often described as **totalitarianism.** There is no sphere of society in which the state is not seen to have a legitimate interest. The distinction between private and public, so central to liberal thought, is erased on the basis that it is bogus, and a barrier to the eradication of liberal capitalism. By contrast, in its commitment to peaceful, piecemeal reform, democratic socialism accepts implicitly, if not explicitly that there is a boundary between the public and the private, even if it might redraw or shift this line. Again the distinctions here are fine but crucial: the liberal claims there are spheres in which by right or by nature the state may not trespass, the communist says there are none such, and the democratic socialist says there are such to the extent that a genuine majority (which is inclusive of the working classes) has defined these spheres through democratic discourse and politics.

We should note that the denial of democracy and the totalitarian exercise of authority by the state under communism were usually justified as short-term expedients necessary to consolidate the revolution. As we observed, the politi-

Democratic Socialism
The Frankfurt Declaration (*produced at the 1951 meeting of the Socialist International, as summarized by Laidler*)**:**

S16 "1. Socialism does not require a rigidly uniform approach. Socialists are flexible about means but strive for the same goals—social justice, freedom, and world peace.
2. Socialism must be democratic and democracy can be realized only through socialism.
3. Socialism seeks the replacement of capitalism by a system based on a fair distribution of income and property.
4. The immediate aims of socialism are full employment, higher productivity, and social security.
5. Public ownership may include nationalization, creation of new public enterprises, or producers' and consumers' cooperatives.
6. Economic decision making should be decentralized whenever this is compatible with socialist planning.
7. Trade unions and cooperatives are necessary elements of democratic socialism.
8. Socialism seeks to abolish legal, political, and economic discrimination based on sex, regionalism, or racial and ethnic groupings."
(*History of Socialism*, 863-4)

cal revolution was to be followed by a social revolution which would reform fundamental institutions and structures of society on a socialist model. The political monopoly of the communist party was deemed necessary to prevent the disruption of the social transformation, either by those insufficiently grounded in socialist thought to understand what must be done, or by those remaining committed to bourgeois society (i.e. the owning classes). Once such opposition had ceased to exist, the state would wither away and the communist party would be inclusive of all. At such a point the party would cease to be a vanguard of the trained elite, having become instead an organization of all educated socialists (i.e. everyone). In practice of course the monopoly of power and its ruthless exercise were never relaxed in those countries that were communist until they ceased to be communist. It was not the realization of communism that allowed the authoritarian character of the state to relax, but the abandonment of communism. In communist regimes, much of the authority of the state was employed rooting out opposition and silencing dissent, rather than engineering the transformation of society to a socialist condition. Hence the association of communist regimes and "police states," etc. Instead of transforming the economy and perfecting the economic management implicit in the concept of a socialist mode of production, communist governments spent much of their energy coping with resistance to their programs and policies. The government that was to accomplish so much for "the people," often became the enemy of the people. Here the failure of communism to accept, as democratic socialism has, the plurality of modern society, is central.

At the end of the twentieth century, communism stands thoroughly discredited on the basis of its practice, and the always strong temptation to discredit socialism by trying to identify it with communism is stronger than ever for socialism's opponents. As we have indicated, there are real and significant distinctions obliterated by this identification, and one does not have to be a socialist to appreciate these points. Ironically, the world's largest nation (China) remains officially communist but has abandoned socialism in favour of a market economy and is engaged in the creation of a capitalist class. China remains "communist" primarily through the one-party monopoly of the power of the state and its ruthless exercise of that power against all opposition. Equally ironically, at this time of writing (1995), former communists form the government, or are partners in the government, of every formerly communist East European country except the Czech Republic. In almost every case, they do so as socialists or social democrats.

DEMOCRATIC SOCIALISM AND SOCIAL DEMOCRACY

The fundamental distinction between socialism and communism was originally rooted in differences over democracy and about a revolutionary or reformist strategy of change. Both believed in the replacement of a private property market economy with a socialized (collective or public ownership) economy under the direction of the state. Over time, though, socialism has also increasingly made its peace with the private ownership of property. Democratic socialism has long ceased to call for the total collectivization of property in the hands of the state, or otherwise (see S16). In the twentieth century, democratic socialism has at most supported the nationalization (appropriation and control by the state) of key industries or sectors of the economy such as transportation or banking. Various elected socialist governments (France, Britain) have nationalized private corporations in areas like coal-mining or steel production without attempting to replace the market as the primary means of allocation of resources and without having any designs on private property at large. Such par-

Abandoning The Class Struggle

S17 "In Britain itself the class structure has been transformed. Our society is no longer split into two distinct classes with a chasm between them. Today power is based on function as well as on ownership of wealth. Managers, administrators, even trade union officials, hold key positions, and privilege has clothed itself in new forms. The composition of the labour movement has also shifted. The organised manual workers are still the hard core, but other under-privileged groups are now embraced as well, and there are many middle-class adherents. The very nature of the Labour Party has changed to reflect these new circumstances. It is no longer a 'class' party in the old sense, representing manual workers only; it is a national party in which many diverse interests find a home....

For European socialists in the nineteenth century the position seemed simple. Capitalism was to be overthrown; something known as socialism would naturally replace it. A straight choice was proclaimed between two clear-cut antithetical systems—destroy the one and the other would supersede it.

Today we know that this is a myth. There are not two distinct and opposing systems, only an infinite series of gradations. No one defines British society today as 'socialism,' yet it is also not nineteenth century capitalism. All the changes we have seen in our lifetime—full employment, planning, controls, housing programs, social security, the national health service, progressive taxation—have produced a structure to which no ready-made label can be tagged. It may be said that these changes are a part of the transition to socialism. But have any of us knowledge of a system of institutions which would mark the end of the transition? And if we had, would there be any agreement on their nature?...

The class struggle is no more a fixed pattern of action for the achievement of socialism than socialism itself is a fixed set of institutions. It is true that those who suffer from the class structure are more likely to fight against it than those to whom it brings advantages. But members of the privileged classes have also played an important part in the struggle for a better society; and some of the underprivileged have, at times, rebelled only in order to gain new privileges for themselves. Classes cannot be divided off into sheep and goats. Even if they could, to pit class against class in the end leads to a naked struggle for power and advantage, destroying the very values which socialists wish most to uphold."
(Socialism: A New Statement of Principles, 1958)

tial nationalization has been the extreme edge of democratic socialism in recent decades and a policy increasingly unlikely to be employed, even by parties which have done so in the past. By and large socialism no longer seeks to substitute public or collective ownership for private ownership of property. Socialists continue to be wary about the influence and power of corporate property and, by the same token, supportive of genuine collective ventures such as cooperatives or worker-owned businesses, but they are no longer committed to eliminating private corporations or to restructuring the entire economy on an alternative basis. The last large-scale nationalization in a Western nation was that undertaken by a Socialist government in France after 1981; by mid-decade the Socialists had begun privatising. At the time of writing, the British Labour leader Tony Blair is engaged in an effort to modify the section of his party's charter which commits it to widespread public (i.e. state) ownership of the economy (see S18-9).

The retreat of socialism from radical positions to accommodation with private property and the market means that it is increasingly difficult to distinguish socialism from social democracy. (This may seem an extremely fine distinction to North Americans, but in several European countries socialist and social democratic movements have existed quite distinct from each other.) **Social democracy** differs from socialism in two primary ways: firstly, it sees itself (like liberalism) as a movement that cuts across class lines, appealing to the interests of all in society, in the name of social justice or fairness. In this respect social democracy rejects the class-based politics of Marxism and has often been inspired by and appealed to a radical interpretation of the Christian social gospel of fraternal equality.

Secondly, social democracy tends to rely more upon regulation and redistribution at the time while socialism presses for nationalization or alternatives to the market economy. In other words, social democrats are less concerned with transforming capitalism than with adjusting or compensating for its outcomes. The culmination of social democracy is the fully developed welfare state, and the epitome of this has been the egalitarian society constructed and presided over by the Swedish Social Democratic Party. Table 3.1 attempts to capture some of the key differences between the different ideologies of the left.

As socialism has in practice moved closer to the positions of social democracy, the distinctions we have made may seem like differences in emphasis rather than fundamental distinctions (see S17). Indeed, as we move from communism to socialism to social democracy, we come to a point at which we approach reform liberalism. The telling distinction here comes down to the perception of the fundamental relationship of the individual to society and to other individuals. What marks the communist, socialist, and social democrat from

Clause Four

Old Clause Four:

S18 "To secure for the workers by hand and by brain the full fruits of their industry and the most equitable distribution thereof that may be possible upon the basis of the common ownership of the means of production, distribution and exchange, and the best obtainable system of popular administration and control of each industry or service."

New proposed clause four:

S19 "1. The Labour Party is a democratic socialist party. It believes that by the strength of our common endeavour, we achieve more than we achieve alone so as to create for each of us the means to realise our true potential and for all of us a community in which power, wealth and opportunity are in the hands of the many not the few, where the rights we enjoy reflect the duties we owe, and where we live together, freely, in a spirit of solidarity, tolerance and respect.

2. To these ends we work for:

- a dynamic economy, serving the public interest, in which the enterprise of the market and the rigour of competition are joined with the forces of partnership and cooperation to produce the wealth the nation needs and the opportunity for all to work and prosper, with a thriving private sector and high quality public services, where those undertakings essential to the common good are either owned by the public or accountable to them;

- a just society, which judges its strength by the condition of the weak as much as the strong, provides security against fear, and justice at work; which nurtures families, promotes equality of opportunity and delivers people from the tyranny of poverty, prejudice and the abuse of power.

- an open democracy, in which government is held to account by the people; decisions are taken as far as practicable by the communities they affect; ;and where fundamental human rights are guaranteed;

- a healthy environment, which we protect, enhance and hold in trust for future generations.

3. Labour is committed to the defence and the security of the British people, and to cooperating in European institutions, the United Nations, the Commonwealth and other international bodies to secure peace, freedom, democracy, economic security and environmental protection for all.

4. Labour will work in pursuit of these aims with trade unions, cooperative societies and other affiliated organisations, and also with voluntary organisations, consumer groups and other representative bodies.

5. On the basis of these principles, Labour seeks the trust of the people to govern."
(from *The Economist*, March 18th 1995)

Table 3.1

	Socialism	Social Democracy	Communism
strategies for change	evolutionary	evolutionary	revolutionary
ownership of property	mainly private	state control of key enterprises /sectors	state control of all productive property
allocation of resources	regulated market redistribution	regulated market redistribution	command economy limited markets
democracy	pluralist	mass working-class party	one party totalitarian state

liberals, however reformed or progressive these liberals may be, is a primary emphasis on the whole and on the collective basis of individual experience.

CONCLUSION

Stepping back and looking at the larger landscape reveals that in the past two centuries the ideological horizon has become narrower, and less clearly defined. The relatively clear and distinct portraits that we were able to draw in the first generation of ideologies depended on sharp features that have softened considerably once we reach the second generation. The common element eroding these distinctions is the pervasive success of liberalism, a success confirmed (not denied!) by the fact that few of those who are liberals call themselves such today. Toryism, a conservatism celebrating an organic hierarchical community, has all but vanished and certainly attracts very few in undiluted form. Similarly, the most extreme variations within socialism (and this is not confined to communism) have become *passé*. Liberalism's rivals on both the right and left have accommodated themselves to liberal society to a large, if still varying, degree. Within the ideologies of the Western world, then, there has been considerable convergence, which expresses itself as a consensus of values, *within which it is still possible for there to be quite polarized and passionate differences*, usually about the policies and programs which best reflect or realize those values. Before examining the ideologies that fall outside, or would reconstruct this consensus, we need to examine its key elements more closely.

SUGGESTED READING:

[Publishing information is not provided for texts in political thought which are either out of print, or widely available in contemporary editions.]

Avineri, Shlomo. (1968). *The Social and Political Thought of Karl Marx*. Cambridge: Cambridge University Press.

Bell, Daniel, and Irving Kristol, eds. (1981). *The Crisis in Economic Theory*. New York: Basic Books.

Berlin, Isaiah. (1969). *Four Essays on Liberty*. Oxford: Oxford University Press.

Buckley, William F., ed. (1970). *Did You Ever See A Dream Walking? American Conservative Thought in the Twentieth Century*. Indianapolis: Bobbs-Merrill.

Cunningham, Frank. (1987). *Democratic Theory and Socialism*. Cambridge: Cambridge University Press.

Dewey, John. (1935). *Liberalism and Social Action*. New York: G.B. Putnam's Sons.

Gutman, Amy. (1980). *Liberal Equality*. Cambridge: Cambridge University Press.

Harrington, Michael. (1989). *Socialism*. New York: Penguin Books.

Hayek, Friedrich A. (1957). *The Road to Serfdom*. Chicago: University of Chicago Press.

Kristol, Irving. (1983). *Reflections of a Neoconservative*. New York: Basic Books.

Lenin, V.I. (1902). *What Is To Be Done?*

McLellan, David. (1983). *Marxism after Marx*. London, Macmillan.

Minogue, Kenneth. (1963). *The Liberal Mind*. New York: Vintage Books.

Nisbet, Robert. (1986). *Conservatism: Dream and Reality*. Minneapolis: University of Minnesota Press.

Pateman, Carole. (1978). *The Relevance of Liberalism*. Boulder, Colo.: Westview Press.

Sandel, Michael, ed. (1984). *Liberalism and its Critics*. New York: New York University Press.

Shaw, George Bernard, ed. (1958). *The Fabian Essays in Socialism*. London: Allen & Unwin.

Smith, Adam. (1776). *The Wealth of Nations*.

Stockman, David A. (1987). *The Triumph of Politics: The Inside Story of the Reagan Revolution*. New York: Avon Books.

Taylor, Charles. (1991). *The Malaise of Modernity*. Concord, Ontario: House of Anansi.

Watkins, Frederick. (1957). *The Political Tradition of the West*. Cambridge, Mass.: Harvard University Press.

Chapter Four

Towards Consensus: Ideology in an Age of Justice and Democracy

"So liberalism ... had arrived at the very center of society." (see L36)

IF OUR DESCRIPTIONS OF THE SECOND GENERATION of liberalism, conservatism, and socialism are at all accurate, then one conclusion is inescapable: development has been in the direction of consensus. One may conclude either that conservatism and socialism have been converging on the liberal center, or that liberalism has managed to colonize both of its rivals. Whether the presence of liberal ideas within the conservative and socialist camps is to be regarded as a contamination or a healthy infusion, depends, of course, on one's perspective, but the presence is undeniable. So, we noted that liberalism was itself influenced by the contact with its rivals, albeit more by socialism than by tory conservatism — and here too whether this indicates a pollution or an enrichment is itself an ideological judgement. Each of the ideologies, then, has become less distinct from its rivals than was once the case. On many fundamental or basic questions, there is no longer much to distinguish these ideologies, although on specifics their disagreements may seem as sharp as ever. For example, once upon a time toryism, liberalism, and socialism presented radically different visions of the economic system: liberals advocating an unfettered market economy, and conservatives and socialists rejecting it from very opposite perspectives. Today, conservatives, liberals, and (most) socialists alike accept the inevitability (if not desirability) of the market economy — *this much* is no longer much debated, although adherents of these ideologies still contest strenuously the economic policy that the state should pursue within the context of a market economy. The survival of the modern welfare state may today be very much a matter of debate; the survival of capitalism is not.

The capitalist market is but one institution around which a certain ideological consensus has emerged in the modern period; there are others, perhaps even more fundamental, which we will examine in this chapter. The relationship between institutions and ideologies is a difficult one, a give and take that is continuous. We call this a liberal age, or say that liberalism is the dominant ideology, because our primary political and economic institutions are more obviously informed by liberalism than by other, rival ideologies. At the same time, institutions transmit or reinforce ideas, values, and beliefs; the convergence that we began to observe in the previous chapter is in part a result of conservatism and socialism adapting to a world of liberal institutions.

To some degree, institutions survive because they educate us to accept or believe in them; to some degree they survive because of sheer inertia — it is easier to live with them than to replace them. And in some measure, we must admit that institutions last because they work, because they perform a necessary role or function in our society. We may (because of our beliefs) reject this role, or believe other institutions could perform it better, but for the moment a given institution is in place and is working in its own fashion, and this gives it an advantage over any hypothetical or ideal institution. One of the failures of socialism to supplant the private property economy has been the inability of socialist or communist governments to put into practice an alternative economic system that can be as productive or organize production as efficiently as the market. This is why socialists, without abandoning their beliefs in equality and fraternity and without relinquishing their critique of the class relations in a market economy, have nonetheless accepted the apparent indispensability of that institution.

Another example is provided by democracy. Once democratic institutions are securely in place and scarce positions of power and authority are determined through competition in a democratic political process, it is difficult for any anti-democratic ideology to survive. If one rejects democracy, then one rejects the judgement of the voters, and voters in turn, quite sensibly, will (usually) reject anti-democratic parties and politicians. In a democracy, all ideologies become democratic because the context for political success requires such an adaptation. The interesting possibility also arises, though, that ideologies become democratic in their rhetoric while remaining undemocratic in their intent or their actual policies. Such a discrepancy between appearance and reality can result in public cynicism or distrust of ideologies or of those who espouse them. The point remains that ideologies can be shaped by the institutional context within which they operate, and this is consistent with our opening observation that ideologies are context-driven sets of beliefs.

One of the most fundamental political beliefs is about the source of the power exercised by governments, considering "source" in a special way — what is it that *justifies* this use of power or makes it right? In fact, we usually acknowledge that power is justified by using a different term — **authority**. Authority is the **legitimate** use of power, and implies our consent, our **obligation**. One of the oldest and most basic political questions, then, is what is it that secures our consent, obliges us, confers authority?

The sociologist Max Weber suggested that three grounds of legitimacy are present in different societies. The first of these is **traditional** legitimacy, that is, rule which is justified on the basis of its long history and an "habitual orientation to conform." (1958: 79) It is custom, the fact that things have always been done this specific way which makes them right. Secondly, Weber spoke of **charismatic** legitimacy, based on the belief that the rulers possess extraordinary personal qualities which in turn justify their privileged position of power. This is more than the view that such individuals are gifted; it is the claim that they are *uniquely* gifted, as asserted by all who have claimed to be divinely chosen or appointed. Finally, Weber defined **legal-rational** authority, in which legitimacy derives from "belief in the validity of legal statute and functional 'competence' based on rationally created **rules**." (1958: 79) Where authority is sanctioned by its basis in law and assumed through a rule-governed process such as an election, its legitimacy is said to be legal-rational.

Legal-rational authority grounds the claims to obligation of most contemporary states. (In the past, states or their rulers frequently claimed authority on traditional or charismatic grounds.) To say, though, that a society possesses legal-rational authority is to describe an aspect of its politics, not to justify it. Within the legal-rational state, justification (the theory explaining obligation) typically makes reference to more specific concepts; in fact almost all states claim that their decisions are "just," and (or) that what they do reflects the popular will. In short, within legal-rational states today, justification of authority rests on two concepts: **justice** or (and) **democracy**. It is around these ideas and the institutions which embody them, that the ideological consensus we have been describing has coalesced.

A: JUSTICE

Our political tradition is rich in terms of the understandings of justice which have been presented, acted upon, or put forward for consideration. One of the first great political texts, Plato's *Republic*, is concerned with answering the question "what is justice?" Loosely stated, justice is a set of normative principles concerning politics or, more specifically, addressing the relationship between the state and its individuals, as well as those relationships between individuals in which the state or society has taken an interest. Thus much of the content of justice deals with the exercise of authority or power by the state, and what individuals have a right to claim or expect from the state. In virtually any society, justice is also concerned with certain kinds of relations between individuals. Criminal and civil law concern classes of actions which individuals perpetrate against others. It is entirely possible that what is an issue of private morality in one society, such as adultery or personal insult, may be regarded as a public issue subject to authoritative sanctions in another society. In the latter case, this may indicate a moral consensus which the state has been entrusted with enforcing, or which the state has taken upon itself to enforce. Whichever is the case, the exercise of the power or authority of the state makes the issue a matter of justice.

So far, we have addressed justice in only the broadest and most general sense. More commonly, discussions of justice concern specific principles. Should rewards be distributed on the basis of merit or of need? Should discriminations be made on the basis of race, language, or creed? Is ignorance of the law an excuse from its sanctions? Should individuals accused of crime be required to prove their innocence, or the accusers required to prove the guilt of the accused? Answers to these questions assume or draw upon specific principles of justice, and each is susceptible to a variety of answers. Different historical periods will favour distinct principles of justice and so, too, will different ideologies.

In the hierarchical, organic structure of feudal society, the duties and responsibilities of individuals were closely linked to their specific "station"—their place within the social structure. Justice in such a society was largely concerned with maintaining the integrity of the social structure by ensuring that individuals carried out the duties and responsibilities assigned to them by custom, tradition, and law. The focus of justice was the contribution made by individuals to the functioning, stability, or well-being of the community at large. The liberal revolution inverted this; the central question became the contribution of the community at large (in the form of the state) to the well-being and security of individuals. Thus in Hobbes's theory, the state is justified on the basis of its contribution to individual welfare by providing security through a framework of laws, within which individuals may peacefully pursue their self-interest and thereby prosper. In presenting this justification of the state, Hobbes was saying not only that this is why the state comes into being (Hobbes was aware this may not be *historically* true), but also and more importantly that this is why the state **should** exist — that this is the **purpose** for which it should exist. The security and well-being of individual citizens should guide the state in its exercise of power and authority. This notion, stated by Hobbes with greater clarity and consistency than anyone before him, runs through all the liberal thinkers who follow him and is perhaps the most fundamental conception behind liberal justice.

As the ideology of the modern period, liberalism proposed principles of justice about which a large measure of consensus has emerged; they are embedded in many of the public institutions of Western society. Common to these principles was a reaction against the often arbitrary, personal character of authority in an age of monarchy and aristocratic privilege. With these principles, liberals sought a regular, rational authority exercised through impersonal instruments such as law. This authority can be seen as satisfying the demands of both Enlightenment rationality and an emerging market economy. These liberal principles of justice are the **rule of law**, respect for individual **rights**, and **equality**. This is the historical order in which these three principles were articulated and received recognition, an order reflected in the degree of consensus attached to each. While it is rare to hear the rule of law disputed as a valid regulative principle, a small (but decreasing) number do challenge the "rightness" of individual rights, and there is yet considerable disagreement about the validity of equality as a principle of justice — and much uncertainty about what kind of equality might be just.

Even when consensus is reached about the *principles* of justice, debate may persist about whether or not policies, or laws, or actions conform to those principles. It is one thing to articulate the elements contained in the principle of the rule of law, another still to determine whether or not specific legal practices or legislative procedures meet these standards. People who agree that justice demands equality may disagree completely, for example, on whether affirmative action is consistent with or contrary to the principle of equality. A further difficulty concerns how we determine in any given situation *which* principle of justice to apply. Should individual rights be our prime consideration, even when the exercise of those rights leads to inequality, or should the claims of equality justify setting aside or overlooking individual rights? Should restitution or deterrence be the principle guiding criminal sanctions? Should welfare be treated as a matter of individual right or as a question of the proper distribution of social utility? A consensus within ideologies about the fundamental principles of justice may still permit considerable controversy concerning their application.

The Rule of Law
Thomas Hobbes:

L37 "Civil Law, is to every Subject, those Rules, which the Commonwealth has Commanded him, by Word, Writing, or other sufficient Sign of the Will, to make use of, for the Distinction of Right, and Wrong; that is to say, of what is contrary, and what is not contrary to the Rule.... Laws are the Rules of Just, and Unjust; nothing being reputed Unjust, that is not contrary to some Law. Likewise, that none can make Laws but the Commonwealth; because our Subjection is to the Commonwealth only ... "
(*Leviathan*, Chapter 26)

John Locke:

L38 "And so whoever has the legislative or supreme power of any commonwealth, is bound to govern by established *standing laws*, promulgated and known to the people, and not by extemporary decrees; by *indifferent* and upright *judges* ..."
(IX, 131)

THE RULE OF LAW

Law has, of course, been with us for many more centuries than liberal society. The *Concise Oxford English Dictionary* describes law as "[the] body of enacted or customary rules recognized by a community as binding," or "one of these rules"; on this basis, we might observe that all political communities or societies possess law [1982:568]. Even if (like Hobbes) we reserve the term law for those rules that are made binding through the enforcement of coercive sanctions, we will have to admit that there has been law as long as there have been states (since the state is distinguished by the centralization of authority necessary to make and enforce rules or decisions upon the community). The rule of law, then, has nothing to do with the presence or absence of law; it is rather a principle governing the nature or use of law. The rule of law places certain requirements upon lawmakers and demands certain qualities of law itself.

Through much of the middle ages a rudimentary framework of law prescribed penalties for particular harms and means for establishing innocence or guilt. By modern standards this framework was extremely narrow in scope, and its dictates could be — and frequently were — overridden on the authority of a nobleman or monarch. The fact that rulers used the instrument of law did not hide the fact that their decisions often reflected purely personal criteria and dispositions. The rule of men was in this way personal, irregular, particular, and arbitrary.

In contrast to such arbitrary rule or government, the ideal of a rule of law came to represent something impersonal, regular, universal, rule-governed, and thus more predictable. The **rule of law** is the principle that obliges everyone, including those in power, to obey formal, public, neutral rules of behaviour. In theory, the rule of law requires that citizens be governed by consistent, publicly known, impartial rules **and** that those who exercise authority do so by publicly known, impartial, and consistent rules. In practice, implementing the principle of the rule of law means establishing **procedures** by which authority is exercised. Consequently we can identify the "rule of law" as a norm of **procedural justice**, and the norm of procedural justice which has come to command general consensus within Western political culture. There are at least five elements that we can identify as requirements of the rule of law:

- **Legal culpability**. One is punished only for breaking a law and is subject to uniform, known sanctions. Simply displeasing or annoying those in authority should not be grounds for punitive action.

- **Public law**. The law must be publicly known; it is unjust to find anyone responsible for breaking a rule of which they were kept ignorant. This places two obligations: one on the state, to publish all laws, and another on citizens, to inform themselves of laws that apply to them. For this reason it is also a commonplace that "ignorance of the law is no excuse from its penalties."

- **Valid law**. Hobbes tells us that it is not enough for the law to be published; there must be a sign that indicates it is actually the sovereign's will. This sign could be use of a royal seal or stamp, or the use of official state letterhead, but in the final analysis we know the law is genuine and not counterfeit because it is made according to **known and accepted procedures**. This is one function performed by the **legislative stages** through which all legislative proposals must pass. It follows from this that law will be made by legislatures.

- **Universality**. It must be possible to enforce or apply the law to everyone, including those who exercise power and/or authority. Lawmakers and law-enforcers must be no less subject to the law than ordinary citizens. Thus we accept the notion that a president may be impeached, a prime minister prosecuted, or a judge arrested.

- **Impartiality**. All individuals stand equal before the law, and on this basis only relevant criteria such as guilt or innocence should be applied. The personal prejudices or interests of judges should never play a role in proceedings, nor should individuals be judged on the basis of their personal attributes. This is the idea that lies behind the image that "justice is blind." That is to say, if justice is impartial, it takes no notice of irrelevant differences such as race, religious creed, age, gender, etc., but rather treats all individuals as identical abstract legal personalities. In this sense it might be said that the state does not need to know *who* we are, only *that* we are. Before the state, all individuals stand equal as abstract legal entities or *persons*.

If these five elements seem extremely obvious, this is in part because they have become firmly imbedded in our legal and political practice, and in part because we have lost acquaintance with states where the exercise of authority conforms to different criteria. This dominance of the rule of law as a regulative principle of procedural justice is part of what it means to say that we live in a society where authority has a legal-rational basis.

Four institutional conditions also seem to be necessary accessories to the rule of law:

- A **constitution**. A constitution is a body of fundamental laws concerning the exercise of authority and the relation between the state and the people. Some such body of rules is necessary if the requirement of universality is to be met.

- An **independent judiciary**. It is essential, if impartiality is to be maintained and if rulers are also to be subject to the law, that judges be free from the influence or power wielded by officials of the state. Judges must be able to decide cases on the basis of the issues at hand, not out of concern for the wishes of third parties who take an interest. Neither should the state or its officials be able to influence proceedings to which they are a party, either as accused or defendant.

- A **public legislature**. Aristotle believed that the virtue of law is that it is dispassionate, not distracted by personal passions and feeling. For this very reason, though, he thought it necessary that law emerge from a consensus of the wise and just individuals in a society. In modern times, law has become an instrument produced by the collective effort of legislators operating within a set of rules or procedures. A body of people needs rules and procedures to operate effectively, and such rules can provide for greater fairness, openness, and even flexibility than might otherwise be the case. The establishment of such rules and procedures also allows for debate, reflection, and reconsideration of proposed laws. In order to meet the requirements of validity and publicity, it is necessary that law-making itself occur in public. Only in this way can citizens have any certainty that good and correct procedures have in fact been followed.

- **Civilian control of the police and military**. The state is commonly identified as that body which has a monopoly of coercion: that is, only the state may legally *force* behaviour or actions, and only the state may *use* force to punish violations of the law. The body which employs force to uphold the law within the state is the police, and the body which employs force to defend the state against foreign aggression or encroachment is the military. It is noteworthy that two cases where the rule of law is violated are captured by the terms "police state," and "military dictatorship." These terms indicate the collapse of the distinction between law-makers and law-enforcers. There are a variety of reasons why it is generally accepted in liberal cultures that those who enforce the law should not make the law, but rather serve or be answerable to those who do make the law. Some of these reasons have to do with democracy, or our notions about rights (i.e. the concern that there should be limits on the legitimate use of force), and some have to do with our idea of law as impartial, public, and predictable.

In summary, then, the rule of law involves the articulation and establishment of legal-rational principles governing the exercise of authority and power, and the development of procedures and rules conforming to those principles. The rule of law is thus a set of regulative concepts, existing as standards by which we can measure the performance of the state and its officials and providing a basis for increasing the likelihood that citizens will receive fair, impartial, and consistent treatment whenever authority is exercised. At the same time, since Aristotle's time there has also been a concern that authorities have the flexibility to deal with individual cases as they merit and not be hampered in this fashion by rigid rules. We see this concern addressed in the discretion given to magistrates in sentencing, to political or formal executives to pardon or commute sentences, and in other ways in which officials are granted discretion in the exercise of their power. Most often though, this leeway or flexibility is itself today something prescribed and confined by laws.

Almost without exception, the ideologies we have been examining have embraced the rule of law and do not currently challenge it in theory nor, with any consistent vigour, in practice. There are two small qualifications we might make.

First of all, traditionalists or tories take a conservative approach to law, in some circumstances preferring customs, conventions, or traditions to the *positive law* that is made by legislatures. The ascendence of the rule of law also can be seen from this perspective as undermining the authority of other forms of rules, like rules of morality or societal conventions. On the other side of this same issue, liberal rationalists like Hobbes and Bentham would have done away with convention and custom altogether; constitutional conventions (so important to British parliamentary government) and common law (the judge-made law prevailing in Anglo-American legal systems) both violate a strict reading of the principles of the rule of law.

Secondly, we need to recall that the purpose of the rule of law is to protect individuals from arbitrary authority. It is possible to see these procedural checks as impediments to action by the state on behalf of the common good, or the nation, or some other collective identity. For example, traditional conservatives will be concerned to protect the integrity of the community from internal threats or external danger, and on this basis, be tempted to relax the rule of law when dealing with criminals, spies, or other "enemies of the people (state)." On the other hand, revolutionary socialists (i.e. communists or Marxists) will see the rule of law (like other liberal institutions) as an instrument primarily employed to protect capitalist society and the owning class. Obviously, a revolution against the existing social order requires a willingness to set aside, at least temporarily, the rule of law. The ideological mainstream, on the other hand, that consists of liberal conservatism, reform liberalism, and democratic socialism, has come virtually to take the rule of law for granted.

RIGHTS

The rule of law is a **procedural** rather than a **substantive** principle. That is to say it deals with **how** the law is made or applied, rather than with **what** the law concerns. The rule of law is concerned with the recipe, but not the quality of ingredients or the taste of the meal that emerges; with the rules of a sport, but not with the game itself. For this reason the rule of law provides no guarantee, in and of itself, that citizens receive justice: it is still quite possible to make bad laws using proper procedures. By analogy, an election is a procedure by which citizens determine who will gain positions of authority, and it has been argued that an election is a better procedure for determining the ruling class than any

Rights

Thomas Jefferson (*conveying to Madison his view of the draft of the American constitution*):

L39 "... I will now add what I do not like. First the omission of a bill of rights providing clearly and without the aid of sophisms for freedom of religion, freedom of the press, protection against standing armies, restriction against monopolies, the eternal and unremitting force of the habeas corpus laws, and trials by jury in all matters of fact triable by the laws of the land and not by the law of Nations. " (letter to James Madison, Dec. 20, 1787)

Thomas Paine

L40 "Natural rights are those which appertain to man in right of his existence. Of this kind are all the intellectual rights, or rights of the mind, and also all those rights of acting as an individual for his own comfort and happiness, which are not injurious to the natural rights of others. Civil rights are those which appertain to man in right of his being a member of society. Every civil right has for its foundation, some natural right pre-existing in the individual, but to the enjoyment of which his individual power is not, in all cases, sufficiently competent. Of this kind are all those which relate to security and protection....

The natural rights which he retains, are all those in which the *power* to execute is as perfect in the individual as the right itself. Among this class, as is before mentioned, are all the intellectual rights, or rights of the mind: consequently, religion is one of those rights. The natural rights which are not retained, are all those in which, though the right is perfect in the individual, the power to execute them is defective. They answer not his purpose. A man, by natural right, has a right to judge in his own cause; and so far as the right of mind is concerned, he never surrenders it: but what availeth it him to judge, if he has not power to redress? He therefore deposits this right in the common stock of society, and takes the arm of society, of which he is part, in preference and in addition to his own. Society *grants* him nothing. Every man is a proprietor in society, and draws on the capital as a matter of right.

... From these premises, two or three certain conclusions will follow.

First, that every civil right grows out of a natural right; or, in other words, is a natural right exchanged.

Secondly, that civil power, properly considered as such, is made up of the aggregate of that class of the natural rights of man, which becomes defective in the individual in point of power, and answers not his purpose; but when collected to a focus, becomes competent to the purpose of every one.

Thirdly, that the power produced from the aggregate of natural rights, imperfect in power in the individual, cannot be applied to invade the natural rights which are retained in the individual, and in which the power to execute is as perfect as the right itself."
(*The Rights of Man*, 1791/2)

Edmund Burke:

C25 "Government is not made in virtue of natural rights, which may and do exist in total independence of it, and exist in much greater clearness and in a much greater degree of abstract perfection; but their abstract perfection is their practical defect. By having a right to everything they want everything. Government is a contrivance of human wisdom to provide for human *wants*. Men have a right that these wants should be provided for by this wisdom. Among these wants is to be reckoned the want, out of civil society, of a sufficient restraint upon their passions. Society requires not only that the passions of individuals should be subjected, but that even in the mass and body, as well as in the individuals, the inclinations of men should frequently be thwarted, their will controlled, and their passions brought into subjection. This can only be done *by a power out of themselves*, and not, in the exercise of its function, subject to that will and to those passions which it is its office to bridle and subdue. In this sense the restraints on men, as well as their liberties, are to be reckoned among their rights."
(*Reflections on the Revolution in France*)

other alternative. Elections, however, do not guarantee good government. For the most part, the rule of law is silent concerning the **content** of the law. Does the law ban all abortions or permit all abortions? Does it forbid religious practice or allow the private ownership of semi-automatic weapons? Does it permit pollution of the environment or limit public nudity? None of these questions, or an infinite number of others, can be answered on the basis of the principle of the rule of law.

Rights, however, are very much about the *content* of the law. They are *entitlements which citizens can claim against the state and other individuals* and which therefore confine the content of the law within certain established limits. Rights are an attempt to remove or at least reduce the possibility that the government will make unjust laws or exercise power legally but unjustly. Rights state that there are certain subjects about which the government may not legislate, certain freedoms which the government may not abridge, or certain actions which the state may not take.

If nothing else, the story of justice in the twentieth century narrates the triumph of **rights**. Almost every issue that receives attention is presented by at least one of the interested parties as a question of rights. For some, the centrality of rights to modern political discourse represents a triumph of certain kinds of individualism on one hand and the decline of community on the other. Respect for individual **rights** is a specifically modern and very liberal notion, the liberal counterpart to medieval **Right**. In feudal communities, individuals enjoyed rights and could claim redress for entitlements denied, but in such communities this person's right or that person's right would be legitimate because of its agreement with *"the Right,"* the objective moral order upon which the community was agreed and which governed its relations. "Rights" in the medieval context were not the properties of individuals, but enjoyed by individuals by virtue of their membership in a moral community, by virtue of their collective participation in "what is right." An individual who was not of the community could not be said to have rights – for this reason there was no difficulty with the idea of foreigners as slaves. At the same time, rights were particular. Because feudal communities were inegalitarian, highly differentiated structures, the rights of each individual would depend on their "station" – e.g. as peasant, soldier, nobleman, or priest. Just as rights served to establish the proper place of the individual within the community, so too did **duties.** If my right is what I am morally entitled to as peasant, king, or artisan, then my duty is what I am obliged to do as peasant, king, or artisan. Individuals' rights and duties were inseparable halves of the communal whole embodied in the notion of *Right*.

In liberal theory, by contrast, individuals have **rights** (or claim redress for denied entitlements) as inalienable individual properties. Rights are claims which you or I make and which some other party such as the state or another individual is required to respect. What justifies these claims is no longer a shared notion of "what is right," for none may exist, but rather their legal definition. Rights are legal entities, embodied in law, whether statute or common, or in the device of an entrenched constitutional code. [Rights are commonly enumerated in a "code." When such a code is placed in the constitution it is said to be "entrenched," because amendment is thereby made more difficult. A rights code may also be embodied in ordinary statute, but then is easily amended, repealed, or added to by subsequent legislative activity. An entrenched rights code (e.g., in Canada the *Charter of Rights and Freedoms*, in the United States the *Bill of Rights*) typically takes precedence over any statute codes (for example, those codes applied by provincial Human Rights Commissions) which must then conform to the entrenched code.] Because these rights are the property of individuals **per se**, and not as members of a community, they are universal rather than particular, at least in theory. The abstract individual created by the notion of an impartial rule of law is also the bearer of rights. This separation of rights from community is what informs declarations of the "Rights of Man," or the United Nations' universal declaration of human rights. Finally, because rights have become legal (and political) rather than moral claims, they are no longer seen to be contingent upon or tied to the performance of duties.

The liberal argument that **rights** are inalienable properties of individuals which other parties (including the state) must respect, and the enshrinement of individual rights in entrenched codes, tend to obscure the political nature of rights. Consider the question, "to what rights are you entitled?" One answer is to talk about what you *should* receive, and this returns us to notions about "what is right"; in this way of talking, rights are **moral entitlements**. It is also possible to talk about what each of us is entitled to *in fact*, which requires reference to the law which defines or entrenches entitlements. This will vary from polity to polity, each with its own definition of legal entitlements. For example, the American constitution appears to give citizens the right to bear arms; Canadians know they have no such entitlement (note that neither position is the same as saying that citizens should bear arms, that it is not right for citizens to bear arms, etc.) The rights actually enjoyed are defined by law, and law is itself a political act, the result of humans legislating. As such, rights exist only so long as the legislation that defines them remains in force, and even entrenched rights codes can be changed through subsequent political actions. In this way, in fact, we enjoy rights in our capacity as members of a polity. The status of the rights we enjoy will ultimately depend upon the political decisions made within our state, and thus upon the distribution of the power to make such decisions.

We will subsequently consider rights to be legal entitlements enjoyed by individuals with respect to other parties consisting of other individuals or the state. The **objects** of rights are of basically three kinds:

- Freedoms: These are negative entitlements for they require the other party to refrain from interference with individual action or behaviour. Typical examples of such are freedom of expression, freedom of association, freedom of religion, etc.

- Protections: These too are negative entitlements which require some party (usually the state) to protect us from harm that others might inflict, intentionally or otherwise. Examples of such are human rights codes, environmental protection legislation, labour laws, property rights.

- Benefits: These involve positive entitlement to specific goods, services, or resources. Examples of this are minority language services, social assistance payments, alimony, social benefits such as health services, and education.

The institutional requirements for rights are by and large satisfied by conditions of the rule of law: the need for an independent judiciary, of an impartial legal system, and of respect for the principle of constitutionalism. Rights are usually enumerated in law, either in the ordinary statutes or bills issued by the legislature, or in special sections of the constitutional law. The American Bill of Rights, the Canadian Charter of Rights and Freedoms, and the first nineteen articles of the German Basic Law are examples of the latter. Placing a code of rights in the constitution "entrenches" it: makes it more difficult to alter given the greater difficulty (usually) involved in changing constitutional law than ordinary legislation. This entrenchment makes rights more "secure," which can be a blessing or a curse depending on the content of the rights and one's perspective or social situation. An entrenched rights code also becomes a basis for *judicial review* where the courts have the ability to strike down legislation or executive acts as unconstitutional.

Ideologically, there is less consensus about rights than there is about the rule of law. Traditional tory conservatives will object not so much to rights, but to two aspects of the liberal presentation of rights. Firstly, rights tend to be articulated simply as claims or entitlements of individuals in the absence of any corresponding duties or obligations. From a tory perspective all rights are connected with responsibilities, and whoever fails to perform the latter should forfeit the former. Secondly, liberals present rights as universal: each of us is a bearer of the same rights. For tories, who believe in the rightness of hierarchy and the naturalness of inequality, rights should at least be differentiated according to ranks or stations in society.

Radical socialists will also be suspicious of rights, albeit for two very different reasons. The first is that rights are claimed by individuals, and, particularly when they serve as the basis for judicial review, they can be used to block or veto the decisions made or supported by a democratic majority. In the contest — when there is a contest — between liberty (which favours individuals) and democracy (which is an expression of the collective), socialism gives the nod to democracy. Secondly, radical socialists argue that rights are not as universal as liberals claim; they are, rather, only *abstractly* universal. Consider, for example, property rights (with which of course, socialists are most concerned): while the liberal says, correctly, that each individual has a right to property, meaning that the state will protect each in their legitimate possessions, the socialist says, correctly, that this right is only meaningful if one possesses something worth protecting. For the mass of propertyless workers, property rights provide no benefit and, on the contrary, only perpetuate the misery of the working class by keeping the owning classes secure and in a privileged position in any confrontation with labour. In short, the socialist is concerned that rights make those with a disproportionate share of scarce resources more secure and thwart any progressive redistribution or reorganization.

Despite the tory and radical socialist arguments against rights, as we have seen elsewhere, so too here most conservatives and socialists have made their peace with rights and have even incorporated the language of rights in their programs. In a liberal society, all mainstream ideologies place a value on individual rights, but they differ in the emphasis they place on those rights, on the kinds of rights they value, or the content of the rights they seek to have recognized.

If we recall the division of rights into *freedoms*, *protections*, and *benefits*, then we can also see that each ideology might place a different emphasis on these kinds of rights. Conservatives and liberals will be more likely to emphasize protections and freedoms while reform liberals and social democrats may emphasize benefits. Secondly, each ideology will see the purpose of rights differently. Conservatives will see rights as means of preserving the *status quo*, or of maintaining individuals as they are, and therefore will favour those rights — whether freedoms, benefits, or protections — which do this. Conservatives will value property rights, the right to bear arms, and some fundamental freedoms, for example. Reform liberals will see rights having a further purpose, namely to empower or enable individuals to develop their capacities and pursue their interests to the fullest. They will favour those rights which create new opportunities for people or provide them with the means of self-realization: for example, education benefits, civil rights, welfare benefits, freedom of expression and religion. Democratic socialists will see rights as an avenue for transforming society, and their emphasis will be on those protections which help the disadvantaged rather than the advantaged — progressive labour laws rather than property rights — and on benefits similarly targeting the least well-off — social assistance, unemployment benefits, subsidized daycare, university education, and health care. Finally, we may expect to find some difference between ideologies in terms of *who* are the bearers of rights. Conservative liberals, taking the more classically liberal position, will tend to see individuals, simply as persons, as bearers of rights. This is the view of abstract universality, which states that each of us is entitled to make the same claims, and this perspective will oppose the tendency of reform liberalism to privilege groups as bearers of special claims to right. As noted, reform liberals will want to extend rights to those disadvantaged or disenfranchised by the *status quo* or traditional ways of thinking. While accepting the notion in theory of abstractly universal rights, the modern liberal will in practice seek to extend the protections or benefits afforded by rights to groups previously (or inadequately) unrecognized or unprotected: women, children, gays and lesbians, people of colour, immigrants, refugees, the homeless, etc. Socialists will also work with reform or radical liberals for many of these latter causes, especially given the identification of socialism with the disadvantaged and downtrodden. There are times, though, when the claims of some of these newly empowered groups conflict (or appear to conflict) with the claims of socialism's traditional constituency: the working class. Ultimately, socialism would be comfortable with identical rights for all, but only once the structures of inequality present in modern society have been replaced with egalitarian, collective alternatives. In the presence of inequality, equal rights protect the advantaged.

EQUALITY

The discussion of rights moves us in the direction of equality, the final and least settled norm of liberal justice. In our discussion in the previous chapter, we noted the development — however uneven and incomplete — of the idea of equality within liberalism in the late nineteenth and early twentieth centuries. In part this was a reaction to socialism, the ideology for which equality is the fundamental value, but there is also an egalitarian current in liberalism which is not socialist, just as there have been eloquent advocates of equality (such as Rousseau) who were not socialists. The liberal embrace of equality involved movement from a naive belief among early liberals in an equality of opportunity that required no state assistance to the recognition that anything approaching a "level playing field" requires state activity as a levelling agent. Eventually, that is, liberalism moved from focusing on individuals as abstract units to considering the distribution of values or goods between or among individuals within the community or society in which we find them. Most generally, **wealth, power** (or authority), and **status** are the usual values with which distributional justice is concerned. Perhaps in our own society we could also include other goods like **education** or **health care**. In short, attention within liberal democracies has increasingly turned to principles of **social justice,** one of which is equality. Concern within liberal democracies for social justice has found concrete expression in a wide variety of measures, from progressive income tax, to selective grants for post-secondary education, to affirmative action hiring programs.

Behind the concern for social justice stands the observation that individuals are not by and large the authors of their own fate, but determine their own outcomes only within the opportunities and with the advantages that the particular circumstances of their birth and life afford them. The distribution of these opportunities and advantages is in large part the outcome of social arrangements and institutions ultimately resting on (or tolerated by) the authority of the state. It is not enough, then, for authority to be exercised within the rule of law and in respect of rights; the state is obliged — or so the argument goes — to do what it can to ensure a just distribution of social goods and benefits. What then constitutes a just distribution? About this there is considerable debate. It is not at all obvious to everyone that an equal distribution is the most just distribution, nor do those who do endorse equality necessarily agree about what it means.

We should also observe that in reality, patterns of distribution are mainly the result of social customs and individual transactions in which competing interests and judgements of utility are worked out *and thus* justice is not primarily or often a central consideration. Moreover, patterns of distribution are reinforced and maintained by institutions and social structures to which individuals become habituated, having little say or control over these institutions or structures. Inequalities are passed on from generation to generation and it is simply not true to say that at any moment in time, the people of a society have freely chosen the patterns of distribution which prevail. It is possible to argue, however, that only such consent could make these patterns of distribution "right" or "just." In this view, social justice requires democracy, whether in order to preserve or maintain a condition of equality, whether to work towards the transformation of an inegalitarian society into one more consistent with equality, or whether simply to ensure that the inegalitarian distributions in society are the product not of custom, coercion, or ignorance, but rather of universal, informed consent.

Of the three principles of justice that have emerged since the liberal revolution, equality is the most recent, and the one to which allegiance is yet most tenuous. We would not expect conservatives, or even conservative liberals for that matter, to embrace equality, given that one of the fundamental beliefs of conservatism is in the inevitable (if not desirable) inequality of human natures. For the conservative it is our very real differences in capacity, in desert, and in motivation, which justify hierarchy and privilege and which cast suspicion on democracy. Liberals, on the other hand, regard individuals as identical *insofar as they are individuals* and, accordingly, look to an equality of individuality. The imperatives of this kind of equality can be satisfied, by and large, by a thorough application of the principle of the rule of law and by respect for the rights of individuals. This equality of official treatment or regard is the only notion of equality that we would expect conservative liberals to accept. Conservative liberals will object when reform liberals go further, and seek a radical extension of rights to various categories of individuals. As noted above, reform liberals seek in this fashion to create an equality of opportunity for individuals currently or historically disadvantaged by social institutions and structures. On this basis, radical liberals have supported affirmative action programs which intentionally reserve scarce positions (hence opportunity) for individuals who are members of an historically disadvantaged group (women, people of colour, the physically or mentally disabled). These programs are necessary, liberals argue, not only to redress historic injustices, but because the implementation of policies against discrimination will not be sufficient to counter biases that are imbedded in institutions and systems. Only when organizations and institutions have become properly representative of all groups in society will such special programs become superfluous. Affirmative action programs have been attacked by liberalism's opponents on both the right and the left. Conservatives may resent them as an attack on the privilege and hierarchy they believe is necessary for social order and stability. More commonly, conservative liberals (and even some reform liberals) argue that affirmative action is *reverse discrimination*, and as such the righting of one injustice by a second. It represents an unequal treatment of individuals no better than the previous discrimination that it seeks to overturn. In this way, both the advocates and the opponents of affirmative action claim to be doing what equality demands. Democratic socialists have often joined liberals in supporting affirmative action and in most cases certainly agree with the goal of ending historical inequalities and injustices. The socialist may, though, have reservations about affirmative action in that it tends to promote and preserve thinking about individuals in terms of the categories that separate them, like race, gender, language, sexual orientation, etc. The socialist is not only an egalitarian, but a collectivist who wishes to promote and affirm community, our commonality.

As an egalitarian, the socialist is also more thoroughgoing than the liberal. The latter is concerned with equality of opportunity, with ensuring that each of us has the chance to succeed, to develop our capacities and promote our own interests. From this perspective, the inequalities which result from our development, competition, or pursuit of interest are quite acceptable so long as we began on an equal footing. The socialist goes further, seeking a society in which there is an equality of condition. The socialist's critic points out how uninteresting a society of identical individuals would be, and the socialist replies that this is not what she means or intends. Socialism believes, like liberalism, that we can be different and equal, but it is much less tolerant about the ways in which our difference can be compatible with equality. To put the matter somewhat simplistically, liberalism argues that we should not be punished or rewarded on the basis of differences over which we have no control, like the differences for which nature is responsible: our colour, sex, physical or intellectual endowment, etc; but that we are legitimately distinguished for what we make of ourselves and our opportunities through our personal effort or application. Socialism is less convinced, firstly, that we should be rewarded with a disproportionate share of scarce social goods for our achievements and, secondly, that our achievements are as much "our own doing" as liberals think. Most socialist theories of distribution, then, have less to do with achievement, and more to do with need, or effort, or both of these.

B: DEMOCRACY

We live in a democratic age, but democracy remains a problematic variable in our modern political experience. Increasingly, the modern state must be democratic to be legitimate; yet, at the same time, the impression persists that often our institutions present a democratic facade behind which a largely undemocratic politics persists. Our political culture is effectively democratic; it is no accident that the ideologies which are elitist and anti-democratic — fascism and communism — remain at the margins. To some degree, as noted earlier, the unanimous voice for democracy within our political culture is institutionally constrained. In a democratic system all parties speak for democracy, but often with different degrees of conviction and with various understandings of what is required to merit the adjective "democratic." The actual state of democracy in the modern age (the present time included) represents a compromise or trade-off between the logic for democracy and the social and cultural impediments to its actualization. Like justice, though, democracy has become a major condition of contemporary legal-rational authority and, for this reason, if no other, a central element in the ideological consensus we have been examining. (Strong arguments can also be made that democracy is a condition of justice: not a sufficient condition, but in many cases a necessary condition.)

DEMOCRACY DEFINED

Democracy literally means "rule of the many." It was contrasted in classical literature with the "rule of the few" (aristocracy) and the "rule of one" (monarchy). Today, "democracy" is more often understood as the "rule of the *people*," inviting comparison with Abraham Lincoln's famous phrase about a govern-

Democracy
William Cobbett:

L41 "Our rights in society are numerous; the right of enjoying life and property; the right of exerting our physical and mental powers in an innocent manner; but, the great right of all, and without which there is, in fact, no right, is, the right of taking a part in the making of the laws by which we are governed. This right is founded in that law of nature ... it springs out of the very principle of civil society; for what compact, what agreement, what common assent, can possibly be imagined by which men would give up all the rights of nature, all the free enjoyment of their bodies and their minds, in order to subject themselves to rules and laws, in the making of which they should have nothing to say, and which should be enforced upon them without their assent? The great right, therefore, of every man, the right of rights, is the right of having a share in the making of the laws, to which the good of the whole makes it his duty to submit."
(*Advice to a Citizen*, 1829)

John Stuart Mill:

L42 "From these accumulated considerations it is evident that the only government which can fully satisfy all the exigencies of the social state is one in which the whole people participate; that any participation, even in the smallest public function, is useful; that the participation should everywhere be as great as the general degree of improvement of the community will allow; and that nothing less can be ultimately desirable than the admission of all to a share in the sovereign power of the state. But since all cannot, in a community exceeding a single small town, participate personally in any but some very minor portions of the public business, it follows that the ideal type of a perfect government must be representative."
(*Considerations on Representative Government*, 1861)

ment "of the people, by the people, and for the people." (Gettysburg Address) Democracy is a form of **popular sovereignty**, which is the idea that the authority of the state derives from the people who are governed. What distinguishes democracy is its insistence that the authority of the state not only *derives* from the public, but ultimately *rests* with the public in one fashion or another. At some point in time, in some way, the people must actually be involved in the exercise of the authority of the state, or those who exercise the authority of the state must be accountable to the people. Democracy is subversive of authority in that it insists that power ultimately belongs to the ruled, not the rulers.

How do the people rule in a democracy? Ruling is the exercise of power and authority, so democracy involves public participation in the exercise of power and authority. Originally, when societies were smaller and the scope of government was much less than it has become today, it was possible to think about "the people" exercising authority themselves. As communities became larger, more fragmented, and the tasks of the state became more complex, the **direct** participation of the people in government became increasingly impractical, and democracy came to mean the popular choice of delegates or representatives who govern *on behalf of* the people. In classical times, people understood by "democracy" the direct participation of all citizens (male property-owners) in the task of government; since the liberal revolution, democracy has been generally understood as a form of **representative** government in which people choose their rulers. In contemporary democracies, much comes down to the quality of that "choice" which citizens have. Moreover, as Rousseau (the first major Western thinker to embrace democracy fully) recognized, if people choose representatives to rule them, there must be some means by which the people keep their representatives accountable. In short, then, in direct democracy, the people exercise authority and power personally; in representative democracy, the people choose delegates to exercise authority and power on their behalf — an exercise for which these delegates are answerable to the people at some subsequent point in time.

Obviously, modern liberal democracies are examples of representative democracy, but there are also moments of direct democracy within these states, primarily through referendums and initiatives. Here the decision-making undertaken by elected representatives is supplemented by occasional direct participation by the citizenry, direct participation which may be more or less binding on the government.

The greatest opportunities for democracy thus seem to lie with the legislative function, which is sometimes exercised directly today through referendums and initiatives, but most often is carried out indirectly by elected repre-

Representative Autonomy
Edmund Burke:

C26 "Certainly, Gentlemen, it ought to be the happiness and glory of a representative to live in the strictest union, the closest correspondence, and the
most unreserved communication with his constituents. Their wishes ought to
have great weight with him; their opinions high respect; their business unre-
mitted attention. It is his duty to sacrifice his repose, his pleasure, his satisfac-
tions, to theirs—and above all, ever, and in all cases, to prefer their interest to
his own.

But his unbiased opinions, his mature judgement, his enlightened conscience, he ought not to sacrifice to you, to any man, or to any set of men living. These he does not derive from your pleasure—no, nor from the law and
the constitution. They are a trust from Providence, for the abuse of which he is
deeply answerable. Your representative owes you, not his industry only, but
his judgement; and he betrays, instead of serving you, if he sacrifices it to your
opinion.

... government and legislation are matters of reason and judgement, and
not of inclination; and what sort of reason is that in which the deliberation precedes the discussion, in which one set of men deliberate and another decide,
and where those who form the conclusion are perhaps three hundred miles
distant from those who hear the arguments?

To deliver an opinion is the right of all men; that of constituents is a
weighty and respectable opinion, which a representative ought always to re-
joice to hear, and which he ought always most seriously to consider. But
authoritative instructions, **mandates** issued, which a member is bound blindly
and implicitly to obey, to vote, and to argue for, though contrary to the clear-
est conviction of his judgement and conscience; these are things utterly unknown to the laws of this land, and which arise from a fundamental mistake of
the whole order and tenor of our constitution.

Parliament is not a **congress** of ambassadors from different and hostile interests, which interests each must maintain, as an agent and advocate, against
other agents and advocates; but Parliament is a **deliberative** assembly of **one**
nation, with **one** interest, that of the whole—where not local purposes, not local prejudices, ought to guide, but the general good, resulting from the general reason of the whole. You choose a member, indeed; but when you have
chosen him, he is not a member of Bristol, but he is a member of **Parliament**. If
the local constituent should have an interest or should form a hasty opinion
evidently opposite to the real good of the rest of the community, the member

for that place ought to be as far as any other from any endeavour to give it effect. . . .Your faithful friend, your devoted servant, I shall be to the end of my life: a flatterer you do not wish for."
(*Speech to the Bristol Electors*, November 3, 1774)

Alexander Hamilton:

C27 "The republican principle demands that the deliberate sense of the community should govern the conduct of those to whom they intrust the management of their affairs; but it does not require an unqualified complaisance to every sudden breeze of passion, or to every transient impulse which the people may receive from the arts of men, who flatter their prejudices to betray their interests. It is a just observation that the people commonly *intend* the PUBLIC GOOD. This often applies to their very errors. But their good sense would despise the adulator who should pretend that they always *reason right* about the *means* of promoting it. They know from experience that they sometimes err; and the wonder is that they so seldom err as they do ... When occasions present themselves, in which the interests of the people are at variance with their inclinations, it is the duty of the persons whom they have appointed to be the guardians of those interests, to withstand the temporary delusion, in order to give them time and opportunity for more cool and sedate reflection."
(*Federalist Paper # XIII*)

Jean Jacques Rousseau:

L43 "Thus the people's deputies are not, and could not be, its representatives; they are merely its agents; and they cannot decide anything finally. Any law which the people has not ratified in person is void; it is not law at all. The English people believes itself to be free; it is gravely mistaken; it is free only during the election of Members of Parliament; as soon as the Members are elected, the people is enslaved; it is nothing. In the brief moments of its freedom, the English people makes such a use of that freedom that it deserves to lose it."
(*The Social Contract*, 1762)

sentatives. The executive and judicial functions of the state have rarely been exercised directly by the body of citizens and certainly not in modern times. Even a thorough democrat like Rousseau suggested that these tasks should be carried out by delegates of the people. In modern times it has not been uncommon for members of the executive to be elected, but commonly this only applies to the chief executive (especially in presidential systems). Most democracies are parliamentary and members of the executive are elected only because of a fusion of powers; they are elected as legislators and subsequently join the cabinet (the political executive). Complicating the picture is the fact that, in the modern state, executive and judicial responsibilities are carried out by large bureaucracies staffed by professional public servants.

While the most immediate and involved participation of citizens in government is the direct democracy of referendums, even this is a limited activity. Unlike many cases where decision-making is the final act in a whole process of involving debate, discourse, and amendment, citizen voting in a referendum occurs quite apart from the process by which the question is formulated and brought forward for decision. The direct democracy of the referendum and initiative, and of course electing representatives, are examples of non-participatory democracy. **Participatory democracy**, which requires that citizens be involved in the discussion and informed debate which precedes decision-making, is the democracy of small societies, of town hall meetings, sometimes of the workplace, but is rarely presented as a viable option for today's large plural societies.

Clearly then, democracy is a characteristic which may be present in a political system in a variety of ways and in various degrees of intensity. At the very least, to qualify as democratic, a system must present its citizens with the opportunity of selecting political elites in competitive, periodic elections. This is the very least, and it is possible for democracy to entail much more. We could construct a continuum beginning with an absence of public input and ending with a maximum of public involvement. Actual political systems or states fall somewhere on that continuum to the degree that they reflect these democratic elements. It should also be noted that most of the systems we characterize as democratic do not go very far beyond the minimum of periodic elections.

DISTRUST OF DEMOCRACY

It is easy for citizens who have grown up within a democratic political system to take it for granted. Historically though, the allegiance to democracy is rather recent. The relative youth of contemporary democracy is perhaps obscured by our knowledge that a democracy existed in ancient Athens, one that was in some senses more direct and participatory than today's democracy. In addition to the fact that Athenian democracy was limited to a small body of citizens (who were property-owning males), we might note that the democratic period in Athens was but a passing phase, and one denounced by many. Neither Aristotle nor Plato (the greatest Athenian philosophers) were democrats, and it seems that few among the educated classes mourned the passing of democracy in ancient Greece. The early critics of democracy had at least two concerns. First of all, democracy was seen to be inherently **unstable**, to be something which could easily degenerate into demagoguery and tyranny. (The term *demagogue* indicates someone who incites the crowd by playing upon its fears, vanity, or prejudice, and becomes its leader by such flattery or deceit.) In ancient experience, these leaders, originally acclaimed by the people, came to exercise power absolutely and without restraint, thus becoming *tyrants*. For the ancients, tyranny was the worst form of government, being roughly equivalent to (and receiving the same scorn that we today would reserve for) personal dictatorship. A second fear was that democracy involves a rule by the larger part of the people *against* the lesser part, or what we have called in more recent times, a "tyranny of the majority." Instead of being rule by all the people for the general welfare, democracy may become a rule by one class or group (albeit the largest) for its own interest, an interest which may involve exploiting or persecuting a minority.

Underlying these criticisms of democracy has very often been a relatively low opinion of "the people," that is to say, of ordinary citizens, who were assumed to be ignorant and irrational (supposed attributes which have informed elitist attitudes throughout the centuries). Accordingly, the argument runs, a certain amount of power must be kept in the hands of an enlightened elite to keep government from being usurped by a tyrant, or to shelter minority interests, or simply to protect the benefits and achievements of culture and civilization. We might point out that the fear of a "tyranny of the majority" has often been raised by a minority which is currently in positions economically, politically, or socially privileged — by a minority which is better off than the majority and which may well be so at the expense of the majority. Nonetheless, in large plural societies, the possibility of a majority (particularly of a religious, linguistic, or ethnic nature) oppressing a minority *is* a potential problem for fully participatory models of democracy. In those societies where the unequal exercise of power also ensures that the mass of the population remains poor and uneducated, the fears about democracy may well have considerable grounds. It is the effects of undemocracy here which make democracy dangerous. Not surprisingly, then, democracy remained a suspect form of government from the time of Aristotle until the late eighteenth century when thinkers like Rousseau began to make a strong case for its legitimacy. It was a few generations later before reforms began to make representative liberal governments into representative liberal democratic governments. The dangers of democracy were less apparent once the general population began to be neither poor nor ignorant. Certainly the success of democracy in the United States in the nineteenth century did much to recommend it to other liberal nations.

THE DEMOCRATIC FRANCHISE AND REPRESENTATIVE AUTONOMY

When democracy came to representative government, it involved extending the franchise (the right to vote for representatives) from a small propertied class to virtually all adult citizens. This happened in stages, often in the face of much opposition and resistance, and was only completed in the twentieth century in most contemporary democracies. (These extensions involved eliminating property qualifications as a condition of the franchise, the recognition of women as persons equally entitled to political rights, the removal of restrictions based on racial, ethnic or religious grounds, and a lowering of age limits to present levels.) This did not alter the basic functioning of representative government; the same institutions, conventions and practises continued to operate as before, with representatives enjoying perhaps even more autonomy from the immediate demands of constituents as their constituencies became more pluralistic. Moreover, the significance of extending the franchise depends on the importance of the vote within the institutions of liberal representative government. Certainly, to gain the right to vote was significant for citizens previously denied that right, but significant as much for the symbolic importance attached to full citizenship as for any power gained. Undeniably, each expansion of the franchise required elected officials – singly or in parties – to be more responsive to that section of the electorate so enfranchised than they likely would otherwise have been. Nonetheless, one reason this act of voting fails to carry more weight is the relationship between the voters and their representatives.

Elected representatives serve as members of a legislature: members of Congress in the United States and members of a legislature constituted on the parliamentary model in most Western democracies. In its original configuration – as an assembly of feudal lords – Parliament consisted of members with no legal obligations to their retainers (constituents), bound only by a moral obligation to consider the well-being of their constituents. So too, today, apart from the necessity of facing constituents in periodic elections, legislators typically have no legal responsibilities to their constituents. This absence of accountability for the period between elections can be called **representative autonomy**, and it is a feature of most contemporary democracies. The most eloquent defense of the autonomy of the elected representative is that provided by Edmund Burke in a 1776 letter to his constituents.

The autonomy Burke was advocating is not mere freedom or license: we say that the representative is "free" to follow his own judgement rather than that of his constituents, but we should note that as far as Burke was concerned, the representative is not free to do whatever he or she likes, but rather enjoys a freedom to use his or her reason to judge what is in the constituents' best interest. What Burke did not admit is that this creates a problem for constituents when the representative does not follow their opinions, judgements, etc. How does the constituent know whether or not the representative is making a thoughtful, informed decision about what is in their interest, or pursuing some other agenda — perhaps one of personal interest?

If we continue to regard democracy as "rule by the people," then critical examination suggests that liberal representative government, even with a universal franchise, barely qualifies as democracy. It does so only to the degree that citizens participate in the selection of rulers. We should acknowledge that this is often the extent of the participation which our liberal, representative democracy grants to its citizens. This also means that the justification of such a democracy comes down to the significance of a popular selection of political officials.

IDEOLOGY AND DEMOCRACY

As the discussion above may have indicated already, we should not expect tories and traditional conservatives to have been radical democrats. The inequality which these conservatives see as somehow imbedded in the "nature of things" is directly related to a view that there ought to be a hierarchy, a clear distinction between those who rule (who are naturally endowed with the capacities for ruling) and those who are ruled (who are not so favoured by nature). This argument that there is a difference in human natures that distinguishes those who should rule and those who should follow, can be traced back at least to Plato's *Republic*.

For liberals, on the other hand, the implicit egalitarian strain in the liberal philosophy of abstract individualism, coupled with the social contract approach which grounds government in the consent of the governed, produces a strong argument for democracy. The difficulty for most early liberals was the reality that most of "the people" were uneducated and poor; like tories, liberals concluded that democracy was too dangerous or radical a step. The difference here is that while tories argued that the people were necessarily (by nature) unfit to govern themselves, liberals could only argue that they were presently unfit (and potentially otherwise). Classic liberals were at least democrats in theory; in practise they were prepared to go further than tories in extending the franchise of representative government. It wasn't until reform liberalism emerged that democracy became an acceptable notion (outside the United States of course) and here, too, reform liberalism reacted on one hand to the pressure of socialism (which proclaimed a workers' democracy) and to changing realities on the other: increasing general education and a rising standard of living removed the "revolutionary" potential of democracy.

It was precisely the degree to which democracy ceased to be a revolutionary development that caused the most radical socialists to cease to hope for a democratic (i.e. electoral) revolution and, following Lenin, to seek the dictatorship of a vanguard party. What became, and is today, the mainstream of socialism — democratic socialism and social democracy — remains fundamentally committed, in theory and practice, to maintaining and often extending opportunities for democratic decision-making.

IN SUMMARY

Our examination of political history and practise reveals an ambiguous commitment to democracy; the democracy we have is quite limited and, within the limited scope of electing representatives is often incomplete or compromised. At the same time our ideologies, our constitutions, and even our foreign policy rest on a formal commitment to democracy, however vaguely defined.

As we have indicated, there are two fundamental ways to be secure from arbitrary power. One is to constrain the use of power so that it cannot harm us and the second is to exercise that power ourselves. The latter is the end of democracy, the former is the aim of justice. Further, our commitment to democracy may be weak, or take second place, if justice appears to be doing the job of protecting our interests. This will be particularly true if justice seems more convenient or efficient than democracy. The critic of (more) democracy will point out, and often quite rightly, that democracy is expensive, that it slows down the work of government, that it is economically inefficient and tends to burden the marketplace, that it involves a commitment by citizens to activity that may not be attractive (or as attractive as other leisure pursuits), that it is simply too time-consuming, or that it presupposes a level of political knowledge and experience which citizens do not presently have (and which it would be too expensive to provide them with). It is best, on these grounds, to keep government small, manageable, economic, and in the hands of experts. Such an argument gains strength when it can be demonstrated that justice secures us from the arbitrary or injurious use of that power by governmental elites. Given the establishment of constitutionalism, of the rule of law, and in particular the entrenchment of individual rights in normal and constitutional law, it is tempting to conclude that democracy has become something of a luxury, perhaps something superfluous. According to this argument, governments may best be kept honest by an appeal to the courts when our rights have been infringed — a method that is more efficient and convenient for the community at large (although it may not be for the individuals who must make such appeals) than wholesale political participation.

On the other hand, this last view overlooks the relationship between democracy and justice. Who protects, interprets, and defines our rights, politicians or judges? Can rights be secure if those who protect, interpret, and define them are not accountable to the public? Democracy is a possible means of keeping those who safeguard the citizens' rights accountable to the citizens. Similarly, social justice involves a variety of difficult decisions about the distribution of social values, the criteria by which distribution should take place, and about what kinds of inequalities should be tolerated. Who should make these decisions? If social justice is an entitlement of the people, rather than a gift from rulers, then perhaps there is a function for democracy here that is not optional. Who should determine the character of the state's management of economic life? Here some argue that democracy is a potential means by which the state can be made responsive to the needs of all classes, not merely those of the economic elite or of the dominant economic class. Are they right? At the very least, justice issues point out the interest that citizens might have in democracy, regardless of whether it is convenient, easy, or efficient.

SUGGESTED READING:

[Publishing information is not provided for texts in political thought which are either out of print, or widely available in contemporary editions.]

Andrew, Edward. (1988). *Shylock's Rights*. Toronto: University of Toronto Press.
Barber, Benjamin R. (1984). *Strong Democracy: Participatory Politics for a New Age*. Berkeley: University of California Press.
Benn, S.I., and R.S. Peters. (1959). *Social Principles and the Democratic State*. London: Unwin.
Dahl, Robert. (1956). *A Preface to Democratic Theory*. Chicago: University of Chicago Press.
Dworkin, Ronald. (1977). *Taking Rights Seriously*. London: Duckworth.
Green, Phillip. (1981). *The Pursuit of Inequality*. New York: Pantheon.
Greene, Ian. (1989). *The Charter of Rights*. Toronto: James Lorimer.
Held, David. (1987). *Models of Democracy*. Cambridge: Polity Press.
Jones, A.H.M. (1986). *Athenian Democracy*. Baltimore: Johns Hopkins University Press.

MacIntyre, Alasdair. (1984). *After Virtue.* 2nd Edition, Notre Dame, Indiana: Notre Dame Press.

Macpherson, C.B. (1977). *The Life and Times of Liberal Democracy.* New York: Oxford University Press.

Mansfield, Jane. (1980). *Beyond Adversarial Democracy.* New York: Basic Books.

Parenti, Michael. (1978). *Power and the Powerless,* New York: St. Martin's Press.

Pateman, Carol. (1970). *Participation and Democratic Theory.* Cambridge: Cambridge University Press.

Rawls, John. (1971). *A Theory of Justice.* Cambridge, Massachussetts: Harvard University Press.

Rousseau, Jean-Jacques. (1762). *The Social Contract.*

Walzer, Michael. (1983). *Spheres of Justice: A Defense of Pluralism and Equality.* New York: Basic Books.

Chapter Five

Towards Consensus: The Political Economy of Market Society

AT THE OUTSET OF THE PREVIOUS CHAPTER we noted the convergence of the mainstream ideologies around the notion of a private property market economy. Economic policy, or political economy, is a fundamental dimension on which ideologies distinguish themselves. Convergence on this dimension is the last example we wish to discuss of institutional constraints or pressures which are exerted on ideologies. This is also one area in which, despite considerable convergence about some fundamental issues, there remain enormous, and sometime bitter differences between rival ideologies. It has become abundantly clear in the modern age, that, rightly or wrongly, citizens expect the state to take responsibility for the management of the economy and in a democratic age will give expression to their preferences through the political process. Rival ideological positions concerning the economic management function of the state remain crucial to contemporary politics. There are three fundamental questions at stake here in modern market societies: (a) What is the proper role of the state with respect to the market? (b) Who benefits most from a regulated or unregulated market? (c) Is the "efficient use of resources" (as the economist defines "efficient") the most appropriate criteria for judging public policies?

A MARKET ECONOMY DEFINED

The context of our discussion is the predominance of a private property market economy, and that label indicates two dimensions of economic life: how resources are allocated, and who owns the principal means of economic production. In our own society, resources are primarily allocated in one of two ways: by **private transactions** in which individuals purchase goods or services from others, or by the **authoritative transfer** of these from one to another by the state. In other words, resources are largely allocated either by the market or by the authority of government. The market is simply the aggregation of individual transactions, or the purchase and sale by individuals of **goods, services, and labour**. In a completely "free" or unregulated market resource allocation occurs through **non-authoritative relations**: through private exchanges governed only by the "natural" laws of the market (i.e. supply and demand). Almost all societies beyond a minimal level of development have had a market (i.e. private exchanges), but a market economy exists only where the bulk of production occurs for the purpose of market activity (as opposed, for example, to economies where production occurs for immediate consumption or for authoritative allocation).

A related, but separate issue is the matter of ownership in an economy; is it something vested in individuals or is it somehow shared, as in a co-operative, or through the common membership of citizens in a state which in turn holds property? Ownership is twofold: on the one hand it reflects the title to possession of the goods, services, and labour which are exchanged (or not) in the marketplace. In this respect almost everyone owns something. More crucial, though, is the question of who owns the processes of production by which the objects of exchange are created. The distinction here is generally between private property, where the means of production are owned by (some of) the individuals in society, and public property, where ownership is held by the state, on behalf of the people. (There remain other possibilities, such as co-operatives.)

In contemporary Western societies which rely on markets for allocation, the production of goods is generally associated with private property. Modern market economies are consumer societies in which most individuals procure the means of life through purchases. (And, as levels of disposable income have risen, the quantity and quality of goods consumed has become concerned with much more than the provision of mere necessities.) In addition, most individuals in a modern market economy are also employees who sell their labour to a corporation, to a government institution, or to other individuals. There is thus a modern market in labour as well as in goods, products, or raw materials. In this way the market is central to the life of virtually everyone in modern society.

The modern market economy servicing a consumer society and organizing the largest part of socially productive labour did not come about all at once. It is the result of several centuries of development, of the emergence and development of technology, of the organization and employment of labour by capital, and of many other processes and techniques which had to be invented, learned, used, and perfected. Moreover, all this didn't "just happen"; particular markets may emerge spontaneously, but not market society. It was the result of countless laws, policies, and programs implemented by governments, and was often secured through much struggle among competing interests over the shape of these policies or laws.

The growth and dominance of the market required a revolutionary transformation of the economic system that had governed medieval society, an economic revolution that had profound political consequences. In short, the new market economy required two developments: (a) that individuals be removed from the structures of medieval society in order to be "free" to be active in the market (consumers and/or buyers or sellers of labour); and (b) that political authority be exercised in ways consistent with, and supportive of, the needs of the market. These correspond with the **two ideological themes** stressed by supporters of the market ever since the seventeenth century: (1) that government **respect the autonomy of the market,** and (2) that government **provide market interests with the structure of law, services, and incentives** deemed optimal for market activity.

Market autonomy is the demand that the primary (if not only) allocation of resources be done through the market (private voluntary transactions between individuals), and that the laws and regulations made by the state interfere as little as possible with the operation of market forces (such as the determination of price through "supply" and "demand"). The second theme, market support, is the demand that the state provide the conditions or infrastructure necessary for individuals to be able to produce, buy, and sell in the market, conditions such as a stable currency, enforcement of contracts, freedom from theft or extortion, etc. While the exchanges which characterize market economies are private voluntary transactions, these rely in turn on a public system of involuntary laws which enforce contracts, protect property from theft, and settle disputes over title. The state has a very important role in establishing the framework of law in which market activity can occur, and in establishing thereby how this market activity will occur. It would certainly be possible to have a market without a supportive state, but not the extensive economic activity we recognize as a market society. The question put properly is not *whether* the state should make policies that affect the market, but rather *how* the state's policies should affect the market. This is where matters become controversial, not least because of differing evaluations of the market, and of who benefits most from its operation.

LIBERALISM AND LAISSEZ-FAIRE

Liberalism was the original ideology of market society, embracing new economic developments and arguing for the conditions of rational government

The Invisible Hand
Adam Smith:

L44 "But the annual revenue of every society is always precisely equal to the exchangeable value of the whole annual produce of its industry, or rather is precisely the same thing with that exchangeable value. As every individual, therefore, endeavours as much as he can both to employ his capital in the support of domestic industry, and so to direct that industry that its produce may be of the greatest value; every individual necessarily labours to render the annual revenue of the society as great as he can. He generally, indeed, neither intends to promote the public interest, nor knows how much he is promoting it. By preferring the support of domestic to that of foreign industry, he intends only his own security; and by directing that industry in such a manner as its produce may be of the greatest value, he intends only his own gain, and he is in this, as in many other cases, led by an invisible hand to promote an end which was no part of his intention. Nor is it always the worse for the society that it was no part of it. By pursuing his own interest he frequently promotes that of the society more effectually than when he really intends to promote it. I have never known much good done by those who affected to trade for the public good. It is an affectation, indeed, not very common among merchants, and very few words need be employed in dissuading them from it."
(*The Wealth of Nations*, 1776)

and economic (social) liberty conducive to the progressive development of market forces. Liberalism was also flexible enough to demand of the state policies corresponding to the nature of the market and the needs of its dominant producers. In the works of some of the early liberals, it is possible to see demands for market support and for the creation of a rational government under the rule of law which would provide the framework of order and appropriate policies for an emerging market economy. As the liberal state replaced the absolutist monarchy of feudalism and as the market became more securely established, liberal thinkers turned their emphasis to policies stressing the need for market autonomy.

By the end of the eighteenth century these policies were most eloquently summed up in Adam Smith's landmark treatise *The Wealth of Nations*; the doctrine of economic liberalism represented by this work came to be known as *laissez-faire*. As this term suggests, the emphasis was on leaving the market as unfettered by regulation and state interference as possible, and the reason for this was to maximize competition among producers, consumers, and labourers. This competition, it was argued, would result in the most efficient and, at the same time, productive use of resources, an economy by which the interests of all would best be served.

According to the model, markets are not only efficient, but progressive: competition improves the standard of living of all by lowering prices that consumers pay for goods, improving the quality of products, encouraging research that produces beneficial goods and byproducts, productively employing the resources of society, and increasing the level of wages paid workers. All this is the unintended consequence of rational self-interested activity in the marketplace; such results were said by Smith to the product of "an invisible hand." According to Smith the beneficial social effects of individual actions will not be produced if governments interfere in the market or artificially determine its outcomes. Therefore this ideal model seeks what has been called a **minimal state**, one that interferes least with the supposed "free" nature of markets. This model works because of the assumptions made about competition and the incentives or penalties imposed by competition between producers and buyers and sellers. Therefore anything that inhibits this competition is deemed harmful and likely to reduce efficiency. The policy that would remove or resist restrictions on trade and thereby completely open markets to competition was known as **laissez faire**, a term which is often employed, and which we shall employ, to refer to the political economic doctrine of a maximum amount of market autonomy and, correspondingly, of a minimal state.

While the *laissez–faire* doctrine calls for a minimal state, it nonetheless relies upon this state to perform some important roles, and to perform them in ways that benefit entrepreneurs or producers. For Adam Smith, these functions were as follows: the administration of justice, provision of defence, provision of public works (necessary to facilitate economic activity), and reform of "various institutional and legal impediments to the system of natural liberty" (Skinner, 1970: 79).

By the nineteenth century, *laissez-faire* had become the dominant economic theory of liberalism and was to become the effective economic policy of the British government, managing what was then the world's most advanced market economy. This last point is important: *laissez-faire* was adopted in Britain when this nation had the most efficient and developed industrial economy in the world and therefore could compete with any state on favourable terms. Where industry is less efficient, or must cope with higher production costs, the commitment to *laissez-faire* will be less strong, and tariffs or other forms of protectionism more popular. *Laissez-faire* was originally the doctrine of successful industrial capitalism — it is therefore not necessarily the optimal policy for less competitive industrial economies, or for other segments of the economy; i.e. merchant capital, finance capital, farmers, or (especially) workers. Thus while *laissez-faire* became the economic theory of classical liberalism, we should not be surprised that other ideologies were critical of this policy and its effects.

EXTERNAL CRITIQUES

Market society has been criticized from any number of directions for its effects on collective and individual human existence. At the risk of caricature, we might summarize some of these critiques as follows:

- the conservative (tory variety) identifies market society with progress (or vice-versa) and progress as corrosive of what is eternal, valuable, and worthy of respect.

- the socialist by contrast believes in progress, and that progress demands proceeding beyond market society in our social and political-economic development.

- the feminist (see Chapter Six) identifies the market with the perpetuation of patriarchal structures and attitudes, and argues for a radically different organization of production and a correspondingly revised set of attitudes about production.

- the environmentalist (see Chapter Six) identifies market society with the destruction of the planetary biosphere.

(There are other objections that are raised against market society, often with compelling force, although they may not be clear about a possible alternative. For example, modern market societies are sometimes criticized for their narrow view of "the good life," with their stress on consumption and pleasure rather than on the development of abilities or on creative human activity. In other words, market society is not just a means of organizing economic life, but organizes our entire life, determines our priorities and values in a narrow fashion. These are important issues, and difficult questions, but in our view they are primarily questions of a different order than political economy issues.)

Tories, as indicated previously, supported the agrarian feudal economy of the medieval period, and tended to view the new market economy as disruptive of established relations and practices. This was not simply a matter of disrupting feudal relations, but also of displacing the landed aristocracy with a new class of capitalists. In some nations the opposition between tory and liberal reflected a distinction between country and city. Market society was associated with urbanization, secularization, commercialism, materialism, and anything else which challenged traditional ways and institutions. Having said that, it is also true that eventually most tories came to accept (and often become very successful in) the market economy.

The rise of industrial capitalism in the nineteenth century and its operation within the bounds of the minimal state had a dramatic effect on the class of industrial workers that it brought into being. It is no accident that the nineteenth century saw the rise of the rival political economic doctrine of socialism. The most formidable socialist critic of the market system or capitalism was Karl Marx.

Marx regarded his work as consistent with the tradition of political economy that included such orthodox market advocates as Adam Smith, David Ricardo, and John Stuart Mill. More than any socialist before him, Marx's critique was based on a close acquaintance with the workings of capitalism and an appreciation of the productive powers it had developed. His critique consisted of roughly five main points.

Instead of the liberal approach of treating market society as simply an association of individuals entering into private economic transactions, Marx analyzed it in terms of classes, where class was determined by the position occupied by individuals within the productive process. Marx argued that industrial capitalism created a two class society, divided between the proletariat (workers) and the bourgeoisie (owners). The latter own or control the means of production and hire labour power for a wage payment; the proletariat is those who sell their labour to the owners (who are owners of capital, hence capitalists). The capitalist and the wage labourer stand at opposite ends of the capitalist mode of production. In time, Marx believed, all other classes in society would disappear, and social life would be dominated by the **class conflict** between these two remaining classes.

Marx argued that the relationship between bourgeoisie and proletariat is exploitive: that is, the worker is paid less than full value for his/her labour by the capitalist, and this surplus extracted from the worker is the source of profits and capital. At various points, Marx also suggested that the capitalist treatment of labour in the effort to maximize profits is dehumanizing, alienating individuals from the full expression of their humanity in creative, self-directed activity.

Marx believed that as capitalism progressed, the proletariat would become **conscious** of itself as an oppressed class, that is, become aware of its collective exploitation by the capitalist class. This would lead to a revolution — which

The End of Capitalism
Karl Marx and Friedrich Engels:

S20 "The productive forces at the disposal of society no longer tend to further the development of the conditions of bourgeois property; on the contrary, they have become too powerful for these conditions, by which they are fettered, and so soon as they overcome these fetters, they bring disorder into the whole of bourgeois society, endanger the existence of bourgeois property. The conditions of bourgeois society are too narrow to comprise the wealth created by them....

But not only has the bourgeoisie forged the weapons that bring death to itself; it has also called into existence the men who are to wield those weapons—the modern working class—the proletarians.

In proportion as the bourgeoisie, i.e. capital, is developed, in the same proportion is the proletariat, the modern working class, developed—a class of labourers, who live only so long as they find work, and who find work only so long as their labour increases capital....

But with the development of industry the proletariat not only increases in number; it becomes concentrated in greater masses, its strength grows, and it feels that strength more....

This organization of the proletarians into a class, and consequently into a political party, is continually being upset again by the competition between the workers themselves. But it ever rises up again, stronger, firmer, mightier. It compels legislative recognition of particular interests of the workers, by taking advantage of the divisions among the bourgeoisie itself. Thus the Ten-Hours Bill in England was carried....

Finally, in times when the class struggle nears the decisive hour ... a portion of the bourgeoisie goes over to the proletariat, and in particular, a portion of the bourgeois ideologists, who have raised themselves to the level of comprehending theoretically the historical movement as a whole....

... The advance of industry, whose involuntary promoter is the bourgeoisie, replaces the isolation of the labourers, due to competition, by their revolutionary combination, due to association. The development of modern industry, therefore, cuts from under its feet the very foundation on which the bourgeoisie produces and appropriates products. What the bourgeoisie therefore produces, above all, are its own grave-diggers. Its fall and the victory of the proletariat are equally inevitable."
(from *The Manifesto of the Communist Party*, 1888)

After Capitalism
(*Marx and Engels recommended the following measures as applicable in "the most advanced countries" for the transition from capitalism to socialism*):

S21 "1. Abolition of property in land and application of all rents of land to public purposes.
2. A heavy progressive or graduated income tax.
3. Abolition of all right of inheritance.
4. Confiscation of the property of all emigrants and rebels.
5. Centralization of credit in the hands of the State, by means of a national bank with State capital and an exclusive monopoly.
6. Centralization of the means of communication and transport in the hands of the State.
7. Extension of factories and instruments of production owned by the State; the bringing into cultivation of waste-lands, and the improvement of the soil generally in accordance with a common plan.
8. Equal liability of all to labour. Establishment of industrial armies, especially for agriculture.
9. Combination of agriculture with manufacturing industries; gradual abolition of the distinction between town and country, by a more equable distribution of the population over the country.
10. Free education for all children in public schools. Abolition of children's factory labour in its present form. Combination of education with industrial production, etc., etc."
(from *The Manifesto of the Communist Party*, 1888)

Marx thought might even occur by democratic means (the election of a proletarian party) — which would replace **class-divided** society with a **classless** community that would organize the economic machinery created by capitalism on socialist principles.

Politically, Marx believed that the chief impediment to socialism was the existence of the state as an instrument employed on behalf of the bourgeoisie. That is to say, the government in capitalist societies not only creates the conditions necessary for capitalism to flourish, but supports and promotes the ideas and ideology that support that economic system. This helps prevent workers from gaining revolutionary class consciousness; instead they accept the legitimacy of the very system that exploits them.

From his analysis of capitalism, Marx concluded that capitalism would self-destruct because of its own internal contradictions; the product of this would be a socialist revolution led by a class–conscious proletariat. These contradictions within capitalism have to do largely with the business cycle (a somewhat cyclical pattern of growth and decline) which in Marx's lifetime had regularly brought market economies into periods of economic depression which seemed increasingly acute and protracted. Marx believed the revolution could very well occur in the most developed industrial societies, like England or Germany.

Marx's critique (which is much more complicated than what I have just presented), like the models of orthodox economists, was based on a variety of assumptions. It was also based on the social and economic realities of the time when Marx was writing, in the middle of the nineteenth century. Industrial capitalism had created an urban working class of factory labourers dependent upon market activity for their existence. Nineteenth–century capitalism *was* exploitive: real wages were lower after the Industrial Revolution than before, urban labourers had much less security than peasants had enjoyed, and the working conditions imposed by industrial capitalism were generally abominable. The state could very well be seen as an instrument for the preservation and support of the interests of the economic elite, especially as long as the government continued to rest on a property franchise. The nineteenth–century did witness increasing class-consciousness on the part of labourers, who attempted to organize to protect their interests, forming Working Men's Associations, unions, working class political parties, etc. Capitalism also regularly exhibited the swings of the business cycle, in which periods of expansion and prosperity were regularly followed by periods of contraction and poverty.

There is little of substance in Marx's critique of British industrial society to illuminate what alternative economic system he thought could take its place. Clearly the private ownership of the productive processes would be replaced with collective ownership by (or in the name of) the people (workers). Marx also seemed to believe that the state should play a transitional role in managing the change from a market economy to a socialist system, and that when this transition was complete, the state would "wither away," having become redundant. The basic point for Marx was that socialism would inherit the tremendous productive forces created by the market system, but organize productive labour in a way so as to eliminate class division and the effects of class exploitation.

The economic systems established in the former Soviet Union and East European countries in the guise of Marxist-Leninism replaced private ownership of production with centralized state ownership, where the state was monopolized by the Communist Party (ostensibly on behalf of the proletariat). It is these command economies which have collapsed in the last decade, and which are being reformed in the direction of market systems at present. The failure of these Marxist-Leninist regimes owes little if anything to Marx, and does nothing to invalidate his analysis of nineteenth–century capitalism, or discredit his reflections on the nature of human creative activity. As with Adam Smith, the limits of Marx's insights into market society are found in his theory, not in the deeds of his disciples.

Whatever the strengths of Marx's analysis of the mature developed industrial capitalism, his prognosis regarding its future health and development was flawed in two principal respects: (1) Marx overestimated the revolutionary potential of the working class, the members of which seem mostly concerned with improving their own living conditions *within* the existing social framework rather than embarking upon a grand social experiment; and (2) Marx underestimated the ability of capitalism to reform itself without abandoning its basic commitment to private property, or to the market as the principle means of allocating resources and values.

The reform of capitalism, which Marx could not have foreseen, entailed moving away from the ideal of *laissez-faire* and, from the middle of the nineteenth century, increasingly involved the state in economic affairs, something that accelerated dramatically after the Depression of the 1930s. While the existence in socialism of a rival economic ideology no doubt influenced liberal theory, the reform of *laissez-faire* was largely the result of pressures internal to developed market economies.

INTERNAL CRITIQUES

One consequence of economic liberalism and its emphasis on market autonomy is to suggest that politics must take second place to economics. Some conservatives, by contrast, will argue that economics should take second place to politics. Thus even while embracing a private property market economy, it is possible for conservatives to argue that the state has a role in directing and shaping the activities of the market for the larger good of the community. One economist who argued this point, and who has largely been ignored in the English-speaking world, was Friedrich List.

List's fundamental point was to argue that the unorganized individual pursuit of self-interest will not necessarily lead to the greater good of all (see C27). Rather, it is requisite for the state to encourage, regulate, erect tariffs if necessary — in short, the state should play an active role in shaping the economy. As List wrote in *The National System of Political Economy*:

Economic Nationalism
Friedrich List:

C27 "The cosmopolitan theorists [e.g. Smith, Ricardo] do not question the importance of industrial expansion. They assume, however, that this can be achieved by adopting the policy of free trade and by leaving individuals to pursue their own private interests. They believe that in such circumstances a country will automatically secure the development of those branches of manufacture which are best suited to its own particular situation. They consider that government action to stimulate the establishment of industries does more harm than good ...

The lessons of history justify our opposition to the assertion that states reach economic maturity most rapidly if left to their own devices. A study of the origin of various branches of manufacture reveals that industrial growth may often have been due to chance. It may be chance that leads certain individuals to a particular place to foster the expansion of an industry that was once small and insignificant—just as seeds blown by chance by the wind may sometimes grow into big trees. But the growth of industries is a process that may take hundreds of years to complete and one should not ascribe to sheer chance what a nation has achieved through its laws and institutions. In England Edward III created the manufacture of woolen cloth and Elizabeth founded the mercantile marine and foreign trade. In France Colbert was responsible for all that a great power needs to develop its economy. Following these examples every responsible government should strive to remove those obstacles that hinder the progress of civilisation and should stimulate the growth of those economic forces that a nation carries in its bosom."
(The National System of Political Economy, 1837)

The forces of production are the tree on which wealth grows. The tree which bears the fruit is of greater value than the fruit itself. ... The prosperity of a nation is not ... greater in the proportion in which it has amassed more wealth (i.e. values of exchange), but in the proportion in which it has more *developed its powers of production*.

As this passage indicates, List was an economic **nationalist**, in contrast to the internationalist (free trade) policies of economic liberalism (*laissez-faire*). James Fallows has pointed out that in Japan the economic ideology of List has been much more influential than the work of Adam Smith ("How the World Works" in *Atlantic Monthly*, December 1993). Written in 1837, List's *The National System of Political Economy* is a non-socialist counterpoint to Adam Smith's *The Wealth of Nations*. In Canada, to cite another example, Conservative governments in the late nineteenth century rejected free trade with the United States and pursued a strategy of economic nationalism (called the National Policy) involving manufacturing tariffs, state-sponsored railway building, and open immigration and settlement policies. Economic nationalism is a policy that can appeal to the kind of conservative we labelled the market tory.

In most Western nations, and certainly in the English-speaking democracies, conservatives have remained economic liberals, that is to say, have continued to support the minimal state of *laissez-faire*. By contrast liberalism, in reforming itself, abandoned *laissez-faire* economics. It did so in part because *laissez-faire* turned out in practice to work less well than in theory, and in part because the coming of political democracy forced liberalism to accommodate the interests of those least well served by *laissez-faire*.

The political economic position of *laissez-faire* rests on an economic model, and as a model it necessarily abstracts from real life to postulate ideal conditions which may never actually be found, and which may in many cases or respects be impossible to obtain. Few (if any) participants in the market ever have perfect information, nor is perfect competition realized, nor are completely rational decisions always made, nor do participants come to the market equal in resources or having benefitted from equal opportunities. This divergence should not surprise us: the point of models is to make abstractions from real conditions for the purpose of comparison, manipulation, or other study. What became problematic for liberals was that the divergences between the real experience of *laissez-faire* and its ideal operation made it difficult to justify the minimal state, particularly from a liberal perspective. Most importantly, the divergence between how markets operate ideally and how they work in practice is a cost that is usually borne by the least advantaged members of market society. Not surprisingly, this is why advocates of *laissez faire* economics in the nineteenth century were often very suspicious of democracy, fearing it would deliver political power to those least advantaged, if not actually disadvantaged, by market society, who might use the state to replace or regulate market mechanisms.

For example, the economic *model* accepts that inequality accompanies a capitalist market economy, and it rationalizes this inequality on two grounds. One is the claim that a market economy will generate prosperity for all and that it is better to be unequal and secure than equal and poor. The second is that "the invisible hand" of the unregulated market will improve the position of the least advantaged by providing for full employment and by constantly increasing the cost of labour while decreasing the margins of profit. In this way inequality is diminished over time. Both these arguments, which rest on certain theoretical assumptions, were not confirmed by experience. Full employment and an increasing price for labour are conditions which *laissez-faire* meets only occasionally, if at all. Very often, there is considerable unemployment and periods of low or diminishing wages. The claim that policies increasing or sustaining market autonomy will benefit everyone needs always to be examined critically in light of the possibility that only some interests will benefit or will benefit disproportionately (*and* that these interests will not be those most in need of benefit). These are considerations to which liberalism is particularly vulnerable, since it claims not to discriminate between individuals, but to give all equal regard. If liberalism is indifferent to the treatment by the market of the poor and working classes, then it risks justifying Marx's claim that it is simply the ideology of the owning classes passing itself off as something more universal.

Market society is the best alternative for the poor and the lesser advantaged only under certain conditions, and it appears that unregulated markets cannot sustain these conditions indefinitely. The supposed benefits that accrue from the efficiency which a market system promotes are accompanied by the costs of weeding out inefficient or outmoded production: competition produces losers as well as winners. It may be true that "in the long run" everyone is better off, and that conditions are improved for all. But who pays the short-term costs? How short is that short-term? How temporary are the human costs of paying that short-term economic cost? Consider for example an economic downturn — what is today called a "recession" and what used to be experienced as a "depression." Someone must pay the costs of this economic contraction as firms declare bankruptcy and close their doors, and as unemployment grows and welfare rolls swell. It may be, as the economist observes, that inefficient producers are being eliminated, that surviving producers and new firms will be forced to be more efficient and that, in this way, eventually all will benefit, but who pays this cost of restructuring? Clearly the owners of the firms which close or are put into receivership lose their investment, but that is generally all they lose. They will not likely need to line up at the soup kitchen or at the unemployment office. The investments of these individuals are in all likelihood a surplus, in which they have a great interest, but upon which they do not depend for their survival. At the very least they will retreat from their investments before their own survival is threatened. The employee, however, is likely to have no surplus: the wage is all that stands between her and the soup kitchen or the unemployment line. The greater economic cost may well be borne by the employer or owner, but the more immediate and human cost is often borne by the worker. Increasing efficiency (the epitome of market rationality) may well, if it involves improving technology or automation, mean less jobs, and there is no reason that this improved efficiency will somehow necessarily result in job creation that sustains those displaced by this rationalization.

The nineteenth century offered considerable real world experience of *laissez-faire*, and it was obvious that often the condition of the working classes was not progressively improving, that often it was the poor and working classes which were most devastated by the periodic economic contractions and restructurings of the market economy. During the latter half of this same century, trade unions, working men's (and women's) associations, and socialist parties began to form and grow. In the late nineteenth century and first decades of the twentieth century, the franchise was extended to all (or almost all) adults. In 1917, the Bolshevik Revolution put a government in power in Russia dedicated to creating a communist utopia, a classless society. It would not be clear for some time that this effort would eventually fail. It is not surprising, then, that reform liberalism abandoned *laissez-faire* economics in search of a political economic policy that might plausibly benefit all members of society. The pragmatic argument that moved them was something like the following.

The kind of market society that can be justified as the best available system for all will be one that can minimize the imposition of the costs of its restructurings, downturns, or modernizations on those who are least advantaged within that system under the best of conditions. This will involve action by the state and will therefore not be true to *laissez-faire* policy with maximal market autonomy and a minimal state. Something more than the minimal state may not be in the interest of producers, entrepreneurs, or investors (although it can be argued that it is), but that is a question of their economic interest, and politically these individuals are only one set of voices seeking policies conducive to their interest. From a political rather than economic standpoint and from the perspective of democracy, it is only reasonable to demand that if those least advantaged in a market society are to be expected to pay the short-term economic costs (which may entail long-term human costs) for the purported long-term benefits of improved efficiency, their consent to this payment should first be obtained. If they should have the opportunity for input on political economic questions, we would expect them to support a state which manages changes in the market economy for the benefit of all, if not primarily for the least advantaged groups. In fact, in the twentieth century, in almost every advanced market economy, *laissez-faire* economic policy was exchanged for something called the *welfare state*.

The distance travelled in the transition from *laissez-faire* capitalism to the contemporary welfare state is enormous (although not all countries have taken the same path or taken it so far), but it has not challenged *primary* reliance on the market as the allocator of resources. Nor has it challenged the private ownership of productive property, or the dependence of the majority of individuals on the wage they receive for their labour. A strong argument can be made, and has been made by supporters and critics of the welfare state alike, that the welfare state has done much to preserve and strengthen the market economy in this century. The reform of capitalism entailed by the welfare state has undermined the appeal of those who would replace private property capitalism with some alternative economy.

Most generally, the welfare state is an *activist* state, a state intentionally involved in the economic life of the nation, a state that performs economic management functions with specific social and political goals in mind. Ringen (1987) emphasizes the redistributive character of the welfare state: its attempt to eliminate poverty and create equality through a system of taxes and transfers. (A transfer is a payment from government to individuals or corporations, and as such has the potential to be strongly redistributive if the class of individuals receiving transfers is largely distinct from the class of individuals paying for them through taxes and other levies. In practice, though, many transfers are universal, eliminating much of their redistributive impact.) By contrast, Mishra talks about the welfare state as a "three-pronged attack on want and dependency," [1990:18] involving (a) a government commitment to **full employment**, (b) the delivery of **universal social programs** – like health care and education – and (c) the provision of a **"safety net"** of assistance for those in need, or what others have referred to as **income maintenance** schemes.

Mishra sees the welfare state as the result of a post-war consensus between the interests of business, labour, and government; others – like Ringen – claim that such a consensus never existed, that business interests always resisted the elements of the welfare state. The truth may well be somewhere in between; a balance of political forces in the post-war period, coupled with a prolonged period of sustained economic growth made the welfare state "affordable." Part of the difficulty here may be that the welfare state was not so much one conscious aim of policy, but rather the result of countless different policy decisions, sometimes only loosely connected or coordinated with each other. Finally, we should note that the welfare state comes in many varieties, ranging from small welfare states in countries like the United States and Switzerland to large welfare states in countries like the Netherlands and Sweden. The "size" of welfare states is simply the share of a nation's economy that can be accounted for by government activity (spending or revenue). Regardless of size though, in all advanced industrial democracies in the last century the role played by the state with respect to the private property market economy has changed significantly. The "welfare state" is a product of these various departures from *laissez-faire* capitalism.

One of the earliest liberal strategies was to reform the market economy through regulations. Such regulation is designed to correct the worst abuses of the capital-labour relationship or to compensate for other consequences of market activity; it does not replace that relationship or alter the fundamental nature of that activity. Many regulations would be taken for granted today: the banning of child labour, minimum wage laws, health and safety regulations, limits on the length of the working day. More recent (and often controversial) regulations concern subjects such as pay equity or smoke-free work environments.

A second significant reform was recognition of the legitimacy of trade unions, formed by workers beginning in the nineteenth century in the effort to improve their conditions within *laissez-faire* capitalism. The union of workers combines the minimal power of individual labourers so that they can bargain collectively on more equitable terms with the producers. The trade union does not threaten or change the capitalist wage-labour relationship, but accepts it as legitimate and, in fact, strengthens it insofar as organization provides a route for grievance within the structure of market society. Unions do not "just happen," but require legislation and enforcement by the state of rights of organization, the legitimization and regulation of the collective bargaining process, and a variety of other possible supports from the state. Labour law varies greatly from country to country, reflecting in part differences in the strength of the working classes, and in part differences in political culture. In many countries, the rise of trade unions and their eventual legal recognition occurred only after considerable struggle, sometimes violent.

The welfare state is also a child of democracy. In the last quarter of the nineteenth century and the first quarter of the twentieth century, most societies with a developed market economy became representative democracies with full adult suffrage. A political party that advocates *laissez-faire* in a representative democracy with full adult suffrage must convince a sufficient portion of the working class that the minimal state is in their best interest. In the latter half of the nineteenth century or early in the present, many members of the working and middle classes did not have fond experiences of the minimal state. Again, not surprisingly, extending the vote to members of the working and middle classes not only made it possible for there to be middle or working class parties,

Contra *Laissez-faire*
John Maynard Keynes:

L45 "Let us clear from the ground the metaphysical or general principles upon which, from time to time, *laissez-faire* has been founded. It is *not* true that individuals possess a prescriptive 'natural liberty' in their economic activities. There is *no* 'compact' conferring perpetual rights on those who Have or on those who Acquire. The world is *not* so governed from above that private and social interest always coincide. It is *not* so managed here below that in practice they coincide. It is *not* a correct deduction from the Principles of Economics that enlightened self-interest always operates in the public interest. Nor is it true that self-interest generally *is* enlightened; more often individuals acting separately to promote their own ends are too ignorant or too weak to attain even these. Experience does *not* show that individuals, when they make up a social unit, are always less clear-sighted than when they act separately.

We cannot therefore settle on abstract grounds, but must handle on its merits in detail what Burke termed 'one of the finest problems in legislation, namely, to determine what the State ought to take upon itself to direct by the public wisdom, and what it ought to leave, with as little interference as possible to individual exertion.'"
("Laissez-Faire and Communism," in *The New Republic*, New York, 1926)

but made it more likely that all parties would begin to support regulation of the market economy.

At least in part, if not in large part, in response to pressures generated by representative democracy, the state has grown enormously in market societies in the twentieth century. There are many circumstances and factors involved here: the role of the state in fighting and then rebuilding after two world wars, the response of the state to the Depression of the 1930s, the demand for services and the need for infrastructure created by social and technological change — which seems to have proceeded at an accelerating pace — and, as important as any of these, the adoption of Keynesian fiscal policy.

Keynes was an economist whose major work — *General Theory of Employment, Interest and Money* — was published in 1936. Following the war and in the attempt to avoid more periods of pronounced stagnation like the Depression of the 1930s, governments in market societies adopted the fiscal policy Keynes recommended. Keynes argued that the periodic slumps experienced by capitalism arise from a combination of overproduction and insufficient demand —that there is not enough money to keep the exchange of goods and labour in equilibrium. What Keynes proposed was the concept of **demand management**, whereby governments would stimulate consumer demand in slow times and put a brake on it in good times, thereby evening out the cycle. The means of accomplishing this was for governments to unbalance their books. Until this time, governments had believed that their accounts should "balance" —government expenditures should always equal government revenues. Keynes had proposed that when the economy slows down, the government should spend more money than it collects and accumulate a deficit on its books — go into debt. By putting more money into the economy than was taken out, the government would stimulate flagging demand and production. Conversely, when the economy is booming, the government should collect more money than it spends, thus removing demand from the system and slowing down economic expansion. The surplus accumulated in good years should erase the deficits accumulated in lean times. Western industrial nations adopted Keynes's strategy of demand management, although they found that it was always easier to accumulate deficits than surpluses.

The growth of the state with regard to the economy takes many forms. Public works programs are one way; assuming ownership of companies, for strategic or political reasons, is another. The increase in the size of the state has its own impact in terms of the number of employees, government purchases in the economy, and so on. A fourth area of economic influence by the state is the transfers it makes to citizens: payments or entitlement to goods like health care or education for which the state must pay. These payments are central to the welfare state, and they are made for several reasons. One is to provide relief to those disadvantaged, often through no fault of their own, because of the inability of the market economy to sustain them. Another is to alleviate some of the inequality which the market system tends to reproduce. These payments are also a means by which governments can inject money into the economy when it stagnates. They take many forms and have come about over many decades. Like other phenomena, the welfare state is not uniform, but varies from one advanced industrial country to another under the influence of history, political culture, and economic circumstance. The net effect of all of these was the creation of a significant **public sector**, which characterizes all modern welfare states.

Now whether or not Mishra is accurate in describing the welfare state as a compromise between the interests of business, labour, and the state, it is clear that in many ways the welfare state represented a compromise or even consensus among ideologies. Reform liberals, social democrats, and even market tories (or European Christian Democrats) could find reason to agree on the continued justification of the welfare state, even though they might disagree on its optimal size or on the particular programs it should encompass. Standing outside this consensus would be those economic liberals (i.e. conservatives) who advocate a return to the minimal state, and on the other hand those radical socialists (i.e. communists) who still believe that a private property market economy can and should be overthrown. Such socialists are difficult to find today in any great number, but economic liberalism has made a significant comeback, so much so that many see the contemporary welfare state as a state in crisis. As is so often the case in ideology, what has shifted is the context, and the result is that a question that seemed more or less settled a few decades ago, the proper role of the state in the economy, has once again become central to ideological debate.

BEYOND THE WELFARE STATE?

For a considerable period after the Second World War, the Keynesian welfare state worked; market economies were able to achieve relatively stable economic growth in conditions of relatively full employment and low inflation. At the same time government services and transfers continued to be introduced and enriched. After 1970, for a variety of reasons, the Keynesian strategy seemed to fail. While previously there had been a trade-off between unemployment and inflation, so that governments could tackle at least one of these conditions at the expense of the other, after 1970 both inflation and unemployment persisted (what was called "stagflation"). This and other factors led to a prolonged period of government deficits, which led to ever-larger levels of accumulated indebtedness. Keynesian economics fell out of favour with economists, replaced by monetarism: instead of practicing demand management, governments should attempt to influence the rate of economic growth through their control of the money supply (hence "supply-side economics") and the use of instruments such as interest rate policy.

While governments were no longer committed to Keynesian policies, they continued to spend more than they were raising in revenue. There is considerable debate about why deficits have seemed so irreversible. Certainly governments have found it difficult to cut expenditures, and the difficult economic times that have often arisen since the mid-1970s have made it even less easy to cut social welfare expenditures. At the same time, it is difficult to raise more revenue to match continued spending commitments. In an age of multi-national corporations and increasing free trade, it is relatively easy for wealthy individuals and corporations to move investments away from regimes which impose higher taxes. The middle class has borne an increasingly higher proportion

The Limits of Markets
John Kenneth Galbraith:

L46 "There are certain things the market does not do, products and services it does not provide. And from the free operation of the market there is injustice, pain and hardship, which no society, either from compassion or wisdom, can tolerate. This we accept; from this acceptance comes the complementary role of the state. This role we support not with reluctance or apology but with fully avowed belief in its necessity and advantage.

There are some matters on which the market is in inescapable default. In no industrial country does it supply good housing to people of moderate income or below. Nor does it supply medical and health services to the least advantaged people. Or good mass transportation in the cities. Or, needless to say, education of the required universality and quality....

In the market economy of the last century, which numerous conservatives now seek romantically to recover, the old were discarded without income. So also were workers when no longer needed. Children were ruthlessly exploited, as also their mothers.

It was one of the great civilizing steps of modern society when these (and other) oppressions were corrected. Without this action—old-age pensions, unemployment compensation, aid to the otherwise financially distressed, public housing, medical care—capitalism would not have survived....

There is a further matter on which liberals take an adverse view of current ideological fashion. As always, we seek an economic world in which all can participate and from which all have a decent return. We want progress toward greater equality of return; we see this as a broadly civilizing tendency in modern society. In support of this goal we stand firmly for the principle of effectively progressive taxation and for income and other welfare support to the disadvantaged and the poor." ("What It Means to be a Liberal Today,"
The Financial Post, September 21, 1987:10.)

of the tax burden, but has also shown its willingness to punish governments that tax too highly. While the debate about the causes and the cures of government deficits continues, the seriousness of the mounting debt-load is increasingly recognized by left and right alike. Not so long ago, one could distinguish adherents of ideologies by their attitude towards deficits, fiscal conservatives (economic liberals) abhorring them, and reform liberals and social democrats dismissing them as a short-term expedient that could be paid down at some point in the future (presumably once the economy turned around). The practical problem is that governments must at least meet interest payments on the debt they have accumulated over the years. As the level of this debt has risen, the interest payments have consumed an ever larger portion of government expenditure, inhibiting the ability of governments to implement the policies to which they are committed. More and more government revenue goes to pay bondholders and other investors from whom governments have borrowed, and proportionately less is spent on services or transfers to the public. This is a situation which compels even reform liberals and democratic socialists who still might be committed to Keynesianism in principle to question the ability of governments to continue to finance deficits.

Given the difficulty governments experience in trying to increase revenues, deficit reduction or elimination appears to require reductions in government spending. This means reducing the size of the public sector, cutting back or eliminating government programs, or reducing government transfers. Clearly then, the fiscal crisis that many states have experienced has placed the continued shape (if not existence) of the welfare state in question. In the debate about how to downsize government and about the impact of this exercise on the welfare state, competing ideologies are at work.

Fiscal conservatives (who are economic liberals) have found in the mounting debt of market economy governments confirmation of their argument that the welfare state ought to be dismantled. The so-called neo-conservative revolution of the Thatcher and Reagan decade (the 1980s) was premised on this basis (although government deficits rose under the Reagan administration, largely because of military outlays). Many elements of the Gingrich Republicans' "Contract With America" have in mind a rolling back of the public sector. Liberals who once participated in the design and expansion of the welfare state now discuss the need to reform the welfare state, to redesign programs, to "do more with less." Driven by the context of government debt, reform liberals have started to resemble neo-liberals (see above). Ultimately, the only defense of the welfare state as we have known it, comes today from the left, from democratic socialists or social democrats, who a generation ago would have argued that the welfare state does not go far enough in redressing inequalities created by a market economy. It is also the case today that even socialists, when in power, have found themselves holding the line on, or even limiting, government expenditures.

At the end of the twentieth century, in light of the collapse of East European and Soviet non-market command economies, the political economic question appears to be not "whether markets?" but "whither markets?" In which directions is market society heading, and in particular, how will the relationship of the state to the economy be defined? Conservatives and conservative liberals will argue for more market autonomy. This is not necessarily the demand for a classic *laissez-faire* economy with a minimal state; in the present realities this may not even be feasible, let alone desirable, and many supporters of market autonomy recognize this. Their concern is rather to generate more autonomy, less government activity, less regulation, less extensive or expensive social programs, and as a result of all these reductions in the role of the state, to create greater investment and greater opportunities for investors. The justification for this increase in market autonomy continues to hinge upon the claim that all will benefit from this autonomy, if not equally, then at least in ways substantial enough in the long term to justify hardship in the short term. The evidence to support this claim is, at the least, mixed. Moreover, while the current economic orthodoxy appears to be for a less rather than more active state, signalled particularly by the commitment to "free" or "unmanaged" trade and the creation of larger common markets, there does remain (particularly outside the English-speaking world) a belief among some supporters of market capitalism in the continued viability (if not necessity) of promoting a national economy through an active sympathetic state. Here the emphasis is not on market autonomy, but on market support.

For another group too the solution is not less government activity, but an activist focus by the state in economic management. This may mean a greater role in job creation through public works, or increased regulation of the economy, or expanding the network of social services, or even government ownership of key sectors of the economy. Here too the justification is the belief that in this way the power of the state can provide economic opportunity, if not equality, for everyone, and only in this expanded role counter the tendencies of the market to generate inequality and frustrate opportunities.

Finally, there are those who do not call for an expansion of the state's activity, but a refinement or redefinition of that role with respect to the market. This may mean neither abandoning nor expanding social programs, but redesigning them to meet the double end of serving those in need without needlessly expending resources. For a country like Canada, the future may involve drawing on the experience of countries like Germany or Japan, where the role of the state is much more closely linked to participation by both business and labour interests in shaping policy goals and in implementing programs to meet the challenges of a changing world. The ultimate question will be: who benefits from the shape of the state after the welfare state? In a democratic age, those who benefit and those who are disadvantaged by changing policies at least have the opportunity to express their consent or dissent through the political process.

SUGGESTED READING:

[Publishing information is not provided for texts in political thought which are either out of print, or widely available in contemporary editions.]

Friedman, Milton. (1963). *Capitalism and Freedom*. Chicago: University of Chicago Press.

Galbraith, John Kenneth. (1973). *Economics and the Public Purpose*. Boston: Houghton Mifflin.

Heilbroner, Robert L. (1970). *Between Capitalism and Socialism*. New York: Random House.

Howe, Irving, ed. (1982). *Beyond the Welfare State*. New York: Schocken Books.

Lindblom, Charles. (1979). *Politics and Markets*. New York: Basic Books.

List, Friedrich. (1837). *The National System of Political Economy*.

Marx, Karl. (1849). *Wage Labour and Capital*.

Mishra, Ramesh. (1990). *The Welfare State in Capitalist Society*. Toronto: University of Toronto Press.

Novack, Michael. (1982). *The Spirit of Democratic Capitalism*. New York: Simon & Shuster.

Ringen, Stein. (1987). *The Possibility of Politics*. Oxford: Clarendon Press.

Schumpeter, Joseph A. (1962). *Capitalism, Socialism, and Democracy*. New York: Harper & Row.

Smith, Adam. (1776). *The Wealth of Nations*.

Chapter Six

Third Generation: Challenging the Consensus

SO FAR OUR FOCUS HAS BEEN ON THE mainstream ideologies (or families of ideologies) that have managed by the end of the twentieth century to fashion a rough consensus about the central institutions of contemporary liberal democracy. Conservatism, liberalism, and socialism do not manage, though, to cover all the ideological bases. In this chapter and the next, we will consider some different "isms," first those which challenge from within the consensus of the second generation ideologies, and then those systems or types of thought which stand outside (if not in direct opposition to) that same consensus. (The essential nature of nationalism, as we will note, is not captured by either characterization.) Some of these "isms" can be seen as satisfying our definition of an ideology; that is, they have a vision, a perspective, and a program. Others satisfy this only in part, and others still are best described as "dispositions" which are compatible with more than one ideological position.

Some of the ideologies we consider here (specifically feminism and environmentalism) have been described as "post-materialist" ideologies, identified with a post-materialist politics said to have developed since the 1960s. Confusion about what "post-materialist" signifies is such that we will simply suggest two ways in which the term indicates something significant about these (and possibly other) ideologies. One is that, unlike the mainstream ideologies discussed earlier, these newer ideologies are not (or not primarily) concerned with the problems of political economy, with conquering scarcity, nor with the economic management function of the state in market economies. These ideologies have other primary concerns, and their focus on these other concerns may rest on assumptions about political economy, as we shall see. A second, more technical sense of "post-materialist" has to do with Marx's view of ideologies as systems of thought reflective of particular ways in which societies organize production. Thus, for Marx, classic liberalism is the ideology of a capitalist (private property, market society) mode of production, toryism is the ideology of feudal

Libertarian Anarchism
Sebastien Faure:

An1 "There is not, and there cannot be, a libertarian *Creed or Catechism*.

That which exists and constitutes what one might call the anarchist doctrine is a cluster of general principles, fundamental conceptions and practical applications regarding which a consensus has been established among individuals whose thought is inimical to Authority and who struggle, collectively or in isolation, against all disciplines and constraints, whether political, economic, intellectual or moral.

At the same time, there may be—and indeed there are—many varieties of anarchist, yet all have a common characteristic that separates them from the rest of humankind. This uniting point is *the negation of the principle of Authority in social organizations and the hatred of all constraints that originate in institutions founded on this principle.*

Thus, whoever denies Authority and fights against it is an Anarchist."
(*Encyclopédie anarchiste*, no date)

Leo Tolstoy:

An2 "Many constitutions have been devised, beginning with the English and American and ending with the Japanese and the Turkish, according to which people are to believe that all laws established in their country are established at their desire. But everyone knows that not only in despotic countries, but in the countries nominally most free—England, America, France, and others—laws are made not by the will of all, but by the will of those who have power, and therefore always and everywhere are such as are profitable to those who have power: be they many, or few, or only one man. Everywhere and always the laws are enforced by the only means that has compelled, and still compels, some people to obey the will of others, i.e., by blows, by deprivation of liberty, and by murder. There can be no other way."
(*The Slavery of Our Times*, 1900)

society, and socialism is the ideology of the post-capitalist mode of production to be realized in communist society. This view of ideology is rooted in Marx's "historical materialism," which explains all phenomena associated with consciousness (as is ideology) as ultimately grounded in our material (i.e. economic) relations. In this sense then, I believe, individuals have used post-materialist to indicate ideologies which are not so simply associated with a particular mode of production, but are founded on another basis altogether.

A: ANARCHISM

It may seem curious to include anarchism (from the Greek *an*: "without" and *archon*: "a ruler") as an internal challenge to the ideological consensus of the West, insofar as it is a system of thought organized around the idea that humankind can (and ought to) live without a government, or at least without government organized through the complex of institutions we recognize as the state. Nonetheless, there are certain reasons why it is hard to imagine anarchism arising anywhere but in the context of liberal society and its institutions. (Anarchists trace their roots to strains in medieval and classical thought, but as George Woodcock notes: "as an activist movement, seeking to change society by collective methods, anarchism belongs only to the nineteenth and twentieth centuries." (1977:12))

We have observed that modern states seek legitimacy, and do so because this means being able to rule through the exercise of authority (which implies consent) rather than resorting to power (which involves coercion, force). It remains true, though, that even those states which have secured considerable legitimacy continue to be recognized as the sole institutions which, in their societies, can legitimately employ force. (Even in regimes which are considered legitimate, it is often necessary to use force to protect the majority who concede that legitimacy, from the minority who don't.) What the anarchist seeks is not necessarily the absence of authority, but the elimination of force or coercion from public life. There are three particularly modern sources of the thinking that this might be possible. The first is simply liberal individualism taken to its extreme conclusion. We observed that many liberals began with a conception of a "state of nature," a condition of human life without government. On the basis of some supposed feature of this state of nature (Hobbes: perpetual war; Locke: the insecurity of property; Rousseau: the threat to individual liberty and equality) liberals then concluded that the state was necessary and legitimate insofar as it exercised a rule of law permitting as much individual liberty as is compatible with social peace. Suppose instead that it were possible to remain in the state of nature, to have a peaceable social existence without the creation

Communitarian Anarchism
William Godwin:

An3 "Every man should be urged to the performance of his duty, as much as possible, by the instigations of reason alone. Compulsion to be exercised by one human being over another, whether individually, or in the name of the community, if in any case to be resorted to, is at least to be resorted to only in cases of indispensable urgency....

For, let it be observed that, not only no well-informed community will interfere with the quantity of any man's industry, or the disposal of its produce, but the members of every such well-informed community will exert themselves, to turn aside the purpose of any man who shall be inclined, to dictate to, or restrain, his neighbour in this respect.

The most destructive of all excesses, is that, where one man shall dictate to another, or undertake to compel him to do, or refrain from doing, anything (except, as was before stated, in cases of the most indispensable urgency), otherwise than with his own consent."
(*Of Property*, 1793)

Anarchism and Liberalism
Peter Kropotkin:

An4 "It will perhaps be objected that during the last fifty years, a good many liberal laws have been enacted. But, if these laws are analyzed, it will be discovered that this liberal legislation consists in the repeal of the laws bequeathed to us by the barbarism of the preceding centuries. Every liberal law, every radical program, may be summed up in these words,—abolition of laws grown irksome to the middle-class itself, and return and extension to all citizens of liberties enjoyed by the townships of the twelfth century. The abolition of capital punishment, trial by jury of all 'crimes' (there was a more liberal jury in the twelfth century), the election of majistrates, the right of bringing public officials to trial, the abolition of standing armies, free instruction, etc., everything that is pointed out as an invention of modern liberalism, is but a return to the freedom which existed before church and king had laid hands upon every manifestation of human life."
(*Law and Authority*, 1886)

or maintenance of the state. Such a notion is at the heart of anarchism. Anarchists such as William Godwin (1756-1836) and Peter Kropotkin (1842-1912) seem to have been inspired by such notions of natural liberty.

Another source of inspiration for anarchism was the discovery by Europeans of societies elsewhere (e.g. in the New World) that flourished without evident political institutions or government (or, in some cases, without institutions recognizable as such to Europeans). Such anthropological evidence seemed to provide confirmation of the human ability to live peaceably without a coercive state. Moreover, the nineteenth century, the century of Romanticism, witnessed several "back to Nature" movements in which individuals sought refuge from the increasing complexity of modern life through a more simple existence in harmony with "nature." This is certainly one element in the thought of the celebrated American writer, Henry Thoreau (1817-1862).

Ironically, the last modern current which feeds anarchist thought is the modern notion of progress. Once humans have developed and organized their material and social lives and learned to balance the conquest of scarcity with proper respect for the imperatives of nature, the state may be seen to be superfluous. Modern technology and science become instruments which offer the possibility of realizing the anarchist vision. One line of thought in this direction is supplied by those communists who have taken literally Marx's notion that eventually in a socialist future, the state might indeed "wither away," its tasks accomplished, and future social management entrusted to voluntary cooperation.

For all these reasons, then, anarchism is a product of the forces and contexts we have identified with our ideological mainstream. While the latter has been refining a consensus about the modern state, anarchism rejects that consensus in two very different versions, one intensely individualist, and one very collectivist.

In common usage, the word anarchy is often used as a synonym for "chaos," a condition of disorder, confusion, and even destruction. This set of images is wholly inappropriate to the anarchist vision. The anarchist seeks to remove coercion, not order. The power of the state is to be replaced by the authority of the community, and that authority is to be largely, if not entirely, the kind of unforced, shared decision-making that we identified as voluntary cooperation. This presupposes some sense of common identity and some common sense of good, a mutual respect and courtesy, and either a common set of purposes, or a willingness to tolerate diverse ends. In other words, it is a vision of a moral community which, because it functions as a moral community, does not need to establish a formal political community. Most of those who see themselves as anarchists subscribe to some form of communitarian or collectivist thinking. What separates these anarchists from other collectivists, such as socialists, is their insistence that the community must always rest on the voluntary consent of all its members. There is no instance, and indeed no means, where some portion of the community can force some other portion to follow their decision.

An almost diametrically opposed strain of anarchist thought is intensely individualist. Thinkers like the German Max Stirner (1806-1856), and the American Benjamin Tucker (1854-1939) remain influential among anarchists for their denunciations of the state and its structures of power and authority, but their purpose was solely to expand the freedom of the individual, to remove obstacles to *whatever* conduct individuals might choose to engage in. In the case of Stirner, at least, it was clear that others serve simply as means for the purposes of the individual (or "ego"). Such thinkers provide the most extreme examples of *libertarianism*, a brand of political thought that seeks simply to remove as many obstacles to individual liberty as can possibly be dismantled. This means opposing almost any activity or regulation by the state; the libertarian supports the minimalist of minimal states. By the same token, the libertarian finds the moral authority which organizes collectivist anarchism no better than the coercion of the state. For individualist anarchists the fundamental human relation is a contract, a voluntary agreement between two parties. One way to see libertarians is as simply the most radical of liberals, a point which brings us back to where we began our discussion of anarchism.

Anarchism has not been a dominant ideology, and it is difficult to see in the near future how it might be. Given the tremendous expansion of the state in the twentieth century, it becomes increasingly difficult to imagine a stateless society, particularly given the complexity and size of contemporary societies. If collectivist anarchism is to be a possibility, then communities need to be small and homogenous; presently societies are becoming larger and more pluralist. The prospects seem better in this respect for individualist anarchism, but their challenge is not only to convince the majority of people that they would be better off without a state, but also to demonstrate over the long term that this is actually the case. Short of the elimination of the state, libertarians lobby for the rollback of legislation and regulations which confine individual liberty, a liberty defined in classically liberal terms as the absence of legal restraint. A liberal individualist whose thought has enjoyed something of a revival in recent years is the American Ayn Rand (1905-1982). Reactions against the modern welfare state often draw upon, or are enthusiastically supported by, libertarian thought. In the economic realm, libertarians and liberal conservatives can often make common cause, but true libertarians reject the moral authority that most modern conservatives would preserve or enhance.

B: POPULISM

Unlike anarchism, but like nationalism (see next chapter), populism is more of a disposition than a full-fledged ideology. It is a current within political movements and generally complements another ideological agenda. As the name suggests, populism is an anti-elitist celebration of the wisdom of the ordinary citizen. Peter Wiles has suggested that populism is "any creed or movement based on the following major premise: *virtue resides in the simple people, who are the overwhelming majority, and in their collective traditions*" (1969:166 Further see P1). In the United States, populism was a movement of disaffected farmers who formed the Populist or People's Party of the 1890s. This agrarian basis has been a common theme of populist movements, which have championed the virtue of the independent farmer and fought against opposing interests represented by banks, railroads, and urban capitalists. This context explains the demand of American Populists in the 1890s for a progressive income tax, government ownership of the railroads and telegraph companies, and low-interest loans to farmers. Similar movements based on the interests of agricultural producers have been found around the world.

More generally, populism survives — and is capable of being tapped — as a resentment of privileged elites, or of their clients, identified as "special interests." In its celebration of "ordinary people" and their values, populism resents change on behalf of new groups or newly empowered interests in society. In part, populism often reflects an alienation produced by social transformation and modernization. Parties of protest not only draw upon, but often fuel popular resentments as a source of their strength. Political power should remain with the ordinary people, and not be monopolized by politicians unaccountable to the public they are supposed to represent. "Special interests" is a handy term for those who have (or it is imagined have) captured the attention and concern of politicians, thereby excluding the voice or interests of the "silent majority." In extreme forms, populism draws on conspiracy theories of how public policy is made by or in the service of a small elite.

To a considerable degree, populism seems very much in the democratic mould, and modern populists in North America at least have been strong advocates of using or introducing instruments of direct democracy like referendums, initiatives, and the process of recall for elected representatives. Nonetheless, there are three qualifications to keep in mind. First, populism is often employed by one set of elites against another; individuals who have much to gain by exploiting public discontent are often the loudest supporters of "the people," without intending actually to have the people take unreserved control of affairs. Secondly, the voice of the people is raised against political elites, but rarely

Populism
Peter Wiles:

Pop1 "To me, populism is any creed or movement based on the follow-ing major premise: *virtue resides in the simple people, who are the over-whelming majority, and in their collective traditions*....

The following things, then, tend to follow from the major premise.
1 Populism is moralistic rather than programmatic....
2 This means that unusually much is demanded of leaders in respect of their dress, manner and way of life....
4 Populism is in each case loosely organized and ill-disciplined: a move-ment rather than a party.
5 Its ideology is loose, and attempts to define it exactly arouse derision and hostility.
6 Populism is anti-intellectual. Even its intellectuals try to be anti-intellec-tual.
7 Populism is strongly opposed to the Establishment ... It arises precisely when a large group, becoming self-conscious, feels alienated from the cen-tres of power...."
(*A Syndrome, Not a Doctrine*, 1969)

against other elites like business interests or pressure group leaders. Lastly, popu-lism often champions an uninformed public opinion (what academics call the anti–intellectual strain in populism), and to the degree that this is so, risks ele-vating ignorance at the expense of informed, rational debate and decision.

In theory, in an age of democracy, one would expect that any ideology might be susceptible to populism; in practice, populism is most likely to be em-ployed by ideologies that wish to limit or restrict the role of the state. (Al-though in Canada the social democratic CCF and NDP have periodically been beneficiaries of Western populist sentiment, that sentiment has found stronger expression in the Social Credit Party and more recently in the Reform Party, which has drawn heavily on the ideas of American conservative liberalism.) For this reason, populism today is often a disguised (or even not disguised) form of conservatism: because its apparently progressive or reforming stance is directed against the state, it remains (even if by default) largely complacent about the so-cio-economic status quo.

If many populist movements of the past were based on alienated rural inter-ests in increasingly urbanized societies, populism remains a potential political force today because of the ability of modern society to alienate so many different interests. The middle class has become a fertile ground for populist appeals as modern states have shifted much of the tax burden of the welfare state onto the backs of middle class constituents. Blue collar skilled labour and white collar managers displaced by "restructuring" or the export of production to the developing world represent another possible constituency for populism. Those traditionally privileged groups in society that feel threatened by progressive social programs and hiring practices designed to empower historically disadvantaged groups constitute yet another base for populism (e.g. the backlash against "political correctness"). The success of Ross Perot in the 1992 Presidential campaign in the United States, the rise of the Reform Party in Canada in the 1990s, and the surge of support for far-right (anti-immigrant) parties in Europe in the past decade are all examples of the continuing capacity of political actors to capitalize on populist appeals. This is not to suggest that Ross Perot, the Reform Party, and European far-right politicians are interchangeable, but rather that populism takes many forms and succeeds in many different contexts.

C: FEMINISM

Unlike populism, feminism has a strong claim to be considered a full-fledged ideology for it has a vision, a perspective, and a program. On the other hand, it can be argued that it is misleading to speak of "feminism" when there are so many competing feminisms. No more than we would be willing to equate social democracy and communism, should we be willing to treat the various schools of feminist thought as one and the same ideology. In some cases, these varieties of feminism are the feminization of the ideologies with which we are already familiar: hence liberal feminism, Marxist feminism, social democratic feminism, anarcha-feminism, etc. Other currents, particularly radical and postmodern feminism, appear to reject any accommodation with ideologies from the past. My approach here will be to outline what all these feminisms share to the degree they have a common vision and perspective, and, then, to indicate however briefly the grounds of division within feminism.

Like socialism, feminism is in some senses easiest to approach through its perspective, its particular diagnosis of the *status quo*. Feminists see contemporary social relations as expressions of patriarchy, a structure of domination of women by men. The primary goal of feminism is to create gender equality, and thus to dismantle patriarchy. Susan Moller Okin defines gender as "social institutionalizations of sexual difference," and notes that much of this sexual difference is not immutably biological, but is "socially constructed" (Held, 1991: 67). Melissa Butler defines patriarchy as "the rule of women by men, and of young

Sexism
Juliet Mitchell:

F1 "What does our oppression within the family *do* to us women? It produces a tendency to small-mindedness, petty jealousy, irrational emotionality and random violence, dependency, competitive selfishness and possessiveness, passivity, a lack of vision and conservatism. These qualities are *not* the simple produce of male chauvinism, nor are they falsely ascribed to women by a sexist society that uses 'old women' as a dirty term. *They are the result of the woman's objective condition within the family*—itself embedded in a sexist society. You cannot inhabit a small and backward world without it doing something to you."
(*Woman's Estate*, 1971)

Patriarchy
Kate Millet:

F2 "... our society, like all other historical civilizations, is a patriarchy. The fact is evident at once if one recalls that the military, industry, technology, universities, science, political office, and finance—in short, every avenue of power within the society, including the coercive force of the police is entirely in male hands. As the essence of politics is power, such realization cannot fail to carry impact. What lingers of supernatural authority, the Deity, "His" ministry, together with the ethics and values, the philosophy and art of our culture—its very civilization—as T.S. Eliot once observed, is of male manufacture.

If one takes patriarchal government to be the institution whereby that half of the populace which is female is controlled by that half which is male, the principles of patriarchy appear to be two fold: male shall dominate female, elder male shall dominate younger. "
(*Sexual Politics*, 1970)

men by older men" (1978:135). Feminists work to overturn these social institutionalizations of sexual difference and to deconstruct those social constructions of sexual difference which have come at women's expense. In general, feminism seeks to create a world of structural equality and one in which women, as women, have full autonomy. More specifically, achieving these goals requires action on a variety of policy issues such as pay equity, reproductive choice, and day care. One of the distinguishing marks of feminism has been its insistence on examining the dynamics of power within what is often regarded by "mainstream" political science as the private sphere — that is to say, the relations within families, within marriage, or the sexual relations of individuals. This focus is captured in the phrase "the personal is the political," which rejects the more orthodox dichotomy of private/public on the basis that what occurs within either of these spheres cannot be understood in isolation from the other.

As with other ideologies, feminism attracts various levels of commitment; its adherents differ in the intensity of their involvement or in the thoroughness of their conviction (that is, the degree to which their perspective is wholly feminist). Just as there are radical and not-so-radical socialists or conservatives, there are radical feminists and not-so-radical feminists. "First wave" feminism sought to increase opportunities for women within the existing structures and processes of capitalist, liberal (patriarchal) society, without challenging their legitimacy. Important strides were made in terms of gaining rights for women that were previously lacking or inadequately enforced, but many felt this was insufficient. Second wave feminists go further and challenge the very structures by which gender inequality has been reinforced and perpetuated. Second wave feminism, then, in many ways, and certainly for its more "radical" adherents, is a revolutionary perspective that calls for a fundamentally different kind of society and of social relations.

One effect of feminism upon the narrowly-defined political realm has been a marked increase in the number of women in politics over the past generation. In some respects this has been even more noticeable in the number holding high political office. Recent women leaders have included Margaret Thatcher (British Prime Minister, 1979-1990), Gro Harlem Brundtland (twice Prime Minister of Norway), Benazir Bhutto (Prime Minister of Pakistan), and Kim Campbell (briefly Prime Minister of Canada). Nonetheless, women remain badly underrepresented in politics, even in the most "advanced" democracies. In addition, there have been few signs of a "feminization" of the political process. It was predicted that the rise of women to positions of power would be accompanied by a shift to a politics less confrontational, adversarial, and partisan; that there would be a more constructive opposition of viewpoints. As yet such a change has not been evident. Perhaps those women who have succeeded in

Liberal Feminism
Zillah R. Eisenstein:

F3 "The United States is as patriarchal as it is capitalist. This means that the politics of society is as self-consciously directed to maintaining the hierarchical male-dominated sexual system as to upholding the economic class structure. The forms of order and control in both systems remain mutually supportive until changes in one system begin to erode the hierarchical basis of the other. For example, such erosion in the patriarchal system began to occur when structural changes in the marketplace, changes in the wage structure, and inflation required white married women to enter the labour force.

... The problem is rather the kind of society we live in, which is both patriarchal and capitalist, which would return individuals to self-reliance while maintaining structural barriers related to economic, racial, and sexual class that limit and curtail the individual. It is up to feminists of all political persuasions, left-liberals, and leftists to shift the critique from the welfare state to the patriarchal society that creates it. As feminists we need to marshal the liberal demands for individual self-determination, freedom of choice, individual autonomy, and equality before the law to indict capitalist patriarchal society. This use of liberal ideology by feminists will permit us to direct the public's consciousness to a critique of capitalist patriarchy, not merely of the welfare state." ("The Sexual Politics of the New Right", in *Signs: Journal of Women in Culture and Society* 7, no.2, 1982)

politics have been forced to play by the "old rules"; perhaps partisan confrontation is a feature of the political system and not of its male actors; perhaps it is just too soon to judge.

Increasing numbers of women (and men) have embraced principles and goals of feminism, although it is fair to speculate about how many, outside the academic and intellectual communities, have progressed from "first wave" to "second wave" feminism. For those who have not, feminism may be a less than complete ideology, one which supplements (or is supplemented by) another perspective or program. While feminism is committed to ridding society of sexism and its consequences, not all feminists may see all political issues as "feminist issues," nor contend that there is a uniquely feminist position on all issues. Moreover, feminism has, like nationalism or populism, found its home within many ideologies; only those which remain unabashedly traditionalist on moral and social questions are impervious to feminism. It is possible to speak with sense then of liberal feminism, socialist feminism, Marxist feminism, radical feminism, and anarcha-feminism; varieties which are distinguished by their respective focus, and by the kinds and degrees of change which they advocate as necessary and desirable.

Among the earliest feminists – e.g. Mary Wollstonecraft (1759-1797), Harriet Taylor (1807-1858), and John Stuart Mill (1806-1873) – were liberals driven by the abstract egalitarianism that we have identified with the liberal concept of "the individual." The liberal feminist program was (and is) to rid society of male privilege through the realization of equality, autonomy, and freedom of choice. The institutions of society must be reformed or replaced with gender-neutral substitutes. In Mill's day, the issues were the inability of women to own property, the difficulties of obtaining divorce, and the lack of a female suffrage. A favourite instrument for early liberal feminists was individual rights, the challenge being to extend to women the same rights, in theory and in practice, as were enjoyed by men. Speaking of his own essay *The Subjection of Women* (1869), Mill wrote "The purpose of that book was to maintain the claim of women, whether in marriage or out of it, to perfect equality in all rights with the male sex" (CW, XVII, 1751). As liberals found in other spheres, obtaining equality of rights was not sufficient to eliminate patriarchy. Liberal feminism, like other aspects of liberalism, moved to programs that would provide positive enhancement of opportunity.

Like all Marxism, Marxist feminism proceeds from a class analysis, with the added insight here of the ways that patriarchy is rooted in or sustained by the structures of capitalism. Early Marxist feminists took the position that the emancipation of women would follow from the emancipation of the proletariat and the creation of a classless society. Modern Marxist feminists rarely take such a simple view of the challenges which confront women. They observe that classical Marxism, much like classical liberalism, could simultaneously support formal equality for women while supporting the traditional division of roles within the family. Some feminists are Marxists, not so much because they subscribe to Marx's vision of a socialized mode of economic production, but because they have been inspired by Marx's methodology, his analysis of social relations. They seek, in other words, to apply a transformed historical materialism to explain women's condition in patriarchal societies. As Hartstock (1983) argues, just as the standpoint of the oppressed class (the proletariat) is privileged for Marx as the foundation from which a revolutionary consciousness can emerge to transform society, so too within patriarchal society the standpoint of the oppressed sex can provide the consciousness that perceives most clearly the exploitative relations within society.

Marxist Feminism
Heidi I. Hartman:

F4 "In a Marxist-feminist view, the organization of production both within and outside the family is shaped by patriarchy and capitalism. Our present social structure rests upon an unequal division of labour by class and by gender which generates tension, conflict and change. These underlying patriarchal and capitalist relations among people, rather than familial relations themselves, are the sources of dynamism in our society. For example, the redistribution that occurs within the family between wage earners and non-wage earners is necessitated by the division of labour inherent in the patriarchal and capitalistic organization of production. In order to provide a schema for understanding the underlying economic structure of the family form prevalent in modern Western society—the heterosexual nuclear family living together in one household—I do not address in this essay the many real differences in the ways people of different periods, regions, races, or ethnic groups structure and experience family life. I limit my focus in order to emphasize the potential for differing rather than harmonious interests among family members, especially between women and men."
("The Family as the Locus of Gender, Class, and Political Struggle," in *Signs: Journal of Women in Culture and Society* 6, no.3, 1981)

The difference between Marxist feminism and socialist feminism is something like the difference between Marxism and social democracy. Socialist feminism seeks to move beyond the narrow, class-based focus of Marxism, appealing to the common experience of women in all classes, and looking at the interplay not only of class and patriarchy, but also of racism and ageism, etc. In contrast to the Marxist focus on the "public" relations of production, socialist feminism examines the oppression of women in the private realm (in fairness, Marxist feminists have also considered the labour women perform within the family and home as part of the larger picture). As Jagger argues (see F7), socialist feminism seeks economic reform that will allow access to birth control, abortion, and child care, and provide adequate income maintenance for mothers.

Radical feminism is concerned with a dimension that traditional ideological approaches to feminism seem to have more difficulty coming to terms with: namely the social construction of gender. In particular, radical feminism is concerned with the social constructions of female sexuality that sustain male domi-

Radical Feminism
Catherine MacKinnon:

F5 "A feminist theory of sexuality would locate sexuality within a theory of gender inequality, meaning the social hierarchy of men over women. To make a theory feminist, it is not enough that it be authored by a biological female. Nor that it describe female sexuality as different from (if equal to) male sexuality, or as if sexuality in women ineluctably exists in some realm beyond, beneath, above, behind—in any event, fundamentally untouched and unmoved by—an unequal social order. A theory of sexuality becomes feminist to the extent it treats sexuality as a social construct of male power: defined by men, forced on women, and constitutive in the meaning of gender. Such an approach centers feminism on the perspective of the subordination of women to men as it identifies sex—that is, the sexuality of dominance and submission—as crucial, as a fundamental, as on some level definitive, in that process. Feminist theory becomes a project of analyzing that situation in order to face it for what it is, in order to change it.

... Dominance eroticized defines the imperatives of its masculinity, submission eroticized defines its femininity. So many distinctive features of women's status as second class—the restriction and constraint and contortion, the servility and the display, the self-mutilation and requisite presentation of self as a beautiful thing, the enforced passivity, the humiliation—are made into the content of sex for women. Being a thing for sexual use is fundamental to it. This identifies not just a sexuality that is shaped under conditions of gender inequality but this sexuality itself as the dynamic of the inequality of the sexes."
("Sexuality, Pornography, and Method," in Sunstein, 1990)

nance. This involves asking what it means to be a woman, to be "feminine," and means unmasking and rejecting the ways in which being woman has been defined by males or by the patriarchal structures of society which reinforce female submission to men. One strain of this feminism is suspicion or critique of that heterosexual practice which expresses male dominance, often through violence (see F5). In policy terms this means, among other things, struggling against pornography, prostitution, sexual harassment, rape, and wife battering.

Finally, and not surprisingly, anarcha–feminism opposes all hierarchy and domination, especially opposing the institutions and structures which sustain

Socialist Feminism
Barbara Ehrenreich:

F6 "The discovery of the importance of women's domestic work put some flesh on the abstract union of capitalism and patriarchy. First, it gave patriarchy, which had otherwise had a somewhat ghostly quality (stretched as it was to include everything from rape to domestic slovenliness), a 'material base' in 'men's control over women's labor power.' Second, it revealed a vivid parallel between 'the private sphere' where patriarchy was still ensconced, and the 'public sphere,' where capital called the shots. In the public sphere, men labored at production, and in the private sphere women labored at 'reproduction' (not only physical reproduction, but the reproduction of attitudes and capabilities required for all types of work). Finally it showed how essential patriarchy was to capitalism: most capitalist institutions produced only things, but the quintessential patriarchal institution, the family, produced the men who produced things—thanks to the labor of women."
("Life Without Father: Reconsidering Socialist-Feminist Theory", in *Socialist Review* 14, no.1, 1984)

Alison Jaggar:

F7 "This is not to say, of course, that women's oppression stems from capitalism alone, nor that the abolition of capitalism would eliminate that oppression. The abolition of capitalism would end the specifically capitalist form of women's oppression, but there is no reason to suppose that it could not be succeeded by a new form of 'patriarchy' or male dominance and perhaps by new modes of alienation. The socialist feminist analysis of women's oppression shows that women's liberation requires totally new modes of organizing all forms of production and the final absolution of 'femininity.' Traditional Marxism has taken the absolution of class as its explicit goal, but it has not committed itself to the abolition of gender. Socialist feminism makes an explicit commitment to the absolution of both class and gender."
("The Politics of Socialist Feminism," in *Feminist Politics and Human Nature*, 1989)

Early Liberal Feminism
J. S. Mill:

F8 "[T]he principle which regulates the existing social relations between the two sexes—the legal subordination of one sex to the other—is wrong in itself, and now one of the chief hindrances to human improvement; and that it ought to be replaced by a principle of perfect equality, admitting no power or privilege on the one side, nor disability on the other....

[T]he adoption of this system of inequality never was the result of deliberation, or forethought, or any social ideas, or any notion whatever of what conduced to the benefit of humanity or the good order of society. It arose simply from the fact that from the very earliest twilight of human society, every woman (owing to the value attached to her by men, combined with her inferiority in muscular strength) was found in a state of bondage to some man. Laws and systems of polity always begin by recognising the relations they find already existing between individuals. They convert what was a mere physical fact into a legal right, give it the sanction of society, and principally aim at the substitution of public and organized means of asserting and protecting these rights, instead of the irregular and lawless conflict of physical strength.... But this dependence, as it exists at present ... is the primitive state of slavery lasting on, through successive mitigations and modifications occasioned by the same causes which have softened the general manners, and brought all human relations more under the control of justice and the influence of humanity."
(*The Subjection of Women*, 1869)

---

this inequality. As Tuana and Tong (1995) point out, the anarcha–feminist criticizes liberal feminism for seeking to replace patriarchal privilege with gender blind privilege and Marxist feminism for its accommodation with hierarchical revolutionary structures.

What these different currents within feminism speak to is its growing maturity and self-confidence. Whereas mainstream ideology in the West has been converging on the centre and with this convergence has been fashioning a consensus about central institutions, feminism has become more rich and textured as it has become established, gained legitimacy, and found its voices.

D: ENVIRONMENTALISM

In 1962 Rachel Carson published *Silent Spring*, which documented in a powerful way the effect of pesticides, herbicides, and other man-made chemicals upon the environment; many date the beginning of the environmental movement to the public awareness created by this book. Terminology is very much contested in this field, but I will follow others in regarding *ecology* (from the Greek *oikos*, or "home" — as is the word economy) as a word indicating a science concerned with the relationship of living things to their environment, and *environmentalism* (or "Green politics") the political movement(s) inspired by ecology. Ecology supplies the perspective, the way of seeing the world, that informs environmentalism.

The ecological perspective is one of interdependence, looking at humanity and Nature through a systems approach that seeks to understand how species and their environment move in and out of balance with each other. The "good" to which Nature seems to tend is exactly this notion of a balance or equilibrium between creatures and the world they depend on. Ecologists point out the ways that human activity in the world upsets the balance between creatures and their environment by destroying habitats, polluting the environment, using up non-renewable resources, transforming the climate, crowding out other species by over-populating the planet, etc. As humanity progressively makes the world a less hospitable place for life, which in its diversity is steadily diminishing, the quality of life lived by humans is also diminished, or so those concerned with environmental issues argue. Ultimately, as the ecological perspective reminds us, there is a finite limit on the ability of the planet to sustain life. The human population and the resources it expends cannot continue to grow *ad infinitum*. The ultimate danger is that by the time humanity becomes aware that it has overtaxed the planet's capacity to sustain life, it will be too late.

The concern of environmentalism, informed by this ecological perspective, is to slow down and ultimately reverse the trend of an ever-increasing human consumption of resources and human domination and despoliation of "the environment." The vision of environmentalists, then, is a world of nature in balance, although there are competing visions of what this balance entails and what it would permit of humanity. Certainly one obvious issue is the question of uneven economic development and the desire of much of the world's nations to "catch up" to the standard of living of advanced industrial societies, a process which would involve a tremendous acceleration in the consumption of resources and the production of associated wastes. Interestingly, though, its long-term effect might be to stabilize population, since there seems to be a strong inverse relationship between birth rate and standard of living. (For an

Connectedness
David Suzuki:

E1 "Johnny Biosphere [ecologist Jack Valentyne] tells of an Indian who, on a hot day hundreds of years ago, swam in Lake Superior. Sodium ions from the sweat of his body are still contained in each drink of water that we take from Lake Ontario. And when one realizes that everything we eat for nutrition was itself once living, we realize that we remain inextricably linked to the rest of life on this planet. Seen in this perspective of sharing and connectedness, we have to behave in a radically different way when we dispose of our wastes or apply new technologies that affect other parts of the ecosystem.

Throughout human history, the boast of our species has been that we love our children and hope that they will have a richer, fuller life than we did. Yet now, for the first time, we know with absolute certainty that our children's lives will be immeasurably poorer in bio-diversity and filled with massive problems that we have foisted on them in our shortsighted pursuit of immediate profit and power."
(in *The Globe and Mail*, April 23, 1988)

---

environmentalist, the measure of "standard of living" in terms of output, or consumption, or purchasing power, is a symptom of the skewed perspectives of industrial societies.) Accordingly, much attention in recent years has focused on the notion of "sustainable development," a term implying a modernization and enrichment of life that is neutral in its effects on the environment, or, as defined by the World Commission on Environment and Development (WCED, 1989), "development that meets the needs of the present without compromising the ability of future generations to meet their own needs."

As the issue of sustainable development indicates, environmentalism challenges the very economic and political-economic assumptions that have been central to the ideologies of the modern world, for conservatism, liberalism, and socialism alike have accepted the desirability of economic growth and development without limits. According to the dominant schools of economic thought, and to most economic policy makers, the economy is "working" when it is growing, not when it is shrinking or even in equilibrium. Environmentalism is thus seen to be post-industrialist and post-materialist; a popular slogan among Greens has been "neither right nor left nor in the centre," indicating their distinction from all established parties.

The "Conquest" of Nature
Fritz Schumacher:

E2 "One of the most fateful errors of our age is the belief that 'the problem of production' has been solved. Not only is this belief firmly held by people remote from production and therefore professionally unacquainted with the facts—it is held by virtually all the experts, the captains of industry, the economic managers in the governments of the world, the academic and not-so-academic economists, not to mention the economic journalists. They may disagree on many things but they all agree that the problem of production has been solved: that mankind has at last come of age. For in the rich countries, they say, the most important task now is 'education for leisure' and, for the poor countries, the 'transfer of technology.' ...

The arising of this error, so egregious and so firmly rooted, is closely connected with the philosophical, not to say religious changes during the last three or four centuries in man's attitude to nature.... Modern man does not experience himself as a part of nature but as an outside force destined to dominate and conquer it. He even talks of a battle with nature, forgetting that, if he won the battle, he would find himself on the losing side. Until quite recently, the battle seemed to go well enough to give him the illusion of unlimited powers, but not so well as to bring the possibility of total victory into view. This has now come into view, and many people, albeit only a minority, are beginning to realize what this means for the continued existence of humanity."
(*Small is Beautiful*, 1974)

The program of environmentalism is diverse, comprehensive, and very much contested by different currents within the movement. All agree on the need to reduce, if not somehow eliminate, the production and eventual release by humans into the environment of toxic substances. How this should be done is a question of competing strategies: while some will look for non-toxic alternatives (using organic rather than chemical fertilizer on the lawn), some will stress eliminating the need for such substances at all (eliminate the lawn, let natural grasses and wildflowers grow). Some will be concerned with the regulatory mechanisms in place (or not), while others will urge using market mechanisms to provide incentives for polluters rather than legal sanctions as disincentives. Fritz Schumacher wrote a famous book *Small is Beautiful* (1974) in which he challenged the assumption that bigger is always better, as implied in the notion that larger organizations always employ economies of scale that mean efficiency (Schumacher did *not* think small was necessarily right; the imperative is to use what is the *appropriate* scale of technology or organization). An issue of some debate is whether it is more appropriate to develop new ecologically sound technologies, such as alternative energy sources (wind, solar panels, etc.), or to work to change the structure of societies and accordingly human consumption habits. Murray Bookchin, who advocates "social ecology," and is something of an anarcha-ecologist, sees the whole environmentalist movement as faddish, as more "tinkering with existing institutions, institutions, social relations, technologies and values than [concerned about] changing them" (1980). Again, all environmentalists wish to stop new development that is harmful to the environment, all wish to clean up or eliminate those activities which are currently harming the environment; the question for many is, is this enough? Or does sustaining the planet which sustains us require us to change our lives more drastically? Edward Goldsmith, the founder of *The Ecologist* has distinguished between the real world (the biosphere) and the surrogate world (the technosphere). Humans have been engaged in constructing the latter at the expense of the former. Can this be reversed? Must humans now consider a process of de-industrialization? Finally, many have seen the root of the problem in the Enlightenment elevation of human reason, in the faith that through science we can solve tomorrow any problem we create today. These observers call for a post-humanist philosophy that recognizes our place within Nature as limited, fallible creatures.

A final area of considerable debate and disagreement within environmentalism and among "Greens" concerns the political strategy of the movement/party. Should "Greens" be active as a political party, thus giving legitimacy to the very system that sustains a materialist, unsustainable development? Green parties have become active in almost every European country in the past two decades or so, but have had only limited electoral success to date. The closest they have come to power is in Germany, where the nature of the party system means they have the potential to be a junior coalition partner in the national government (as they have been in a couple of state-level governments). Such a situation presents another dilemma: should the Greens be fundamentalists (sticking to their principles on all issues, without making exceptions), or should they be realists (willing to make compromises, make or accept policy that is not necessarily justifiable on party principles)? Another, somewhat related issue, is whether environmentalists should be trying to gain power, or concentrating on getting their message across to the general public. It can be argued that Green parties and environmental interest groups have had consid-

Real and Surrogate Worlds
Edward Goldsmith:

E3 "If it [development] has occurred at all, it is that over the last few thousand million years the primaeval dust has slowly been organized into an increasingly complex organization of matter—the biosphere, or world of living things—or the 'real world' as we might refer to it—which provides the resources entering into this process. Industrialization is something which is happening to the biosphere. *It is the biosphere, in fact—the real world*—that is being industrialized.

In this way, a new organization of matter is building up: the techno-sphere or world of material goods and technological devices: or the *surrogate world.*

This brings us to the second important feature of industrialization: the surrogate world it gives rise to is in direct competition with the real world, since it can only be built up by making use of resources extracted from the latter, and by consigning to it the waste products this process must inevitably generate....

It must follow that all three steps involved in the process of building up the surrogate world give rise to a corresponding contraction and deterioration of the real one. Economic growth, in terms of which the former process is measured, is thereby biological and social contraction and deterioration. *They are just different sides of the same coin.*

Unfortunately, we are part of the real world not the surrogate one. In fact, we have been designed hylogenetically (and at one time culturally, too) to fulfil within it specific differentiated functions. It would be very naive to suppose that its systematic destruction would not effect us in some way. To understand exactly how, we must consider the basic features of the real world. Unfortunately, these tend to be disregarded by most of today's scientists, who are more concerned with accumulating trivia than in understanding basic principles."
(*The Great U-turn: De-Industrializing Society*, 1988)

erable success on the front of public education. The surest proof of this is the tendency of *all* political parties today to at least make the right noises about their concern for environmental issues, even if their policies don't always demonstrate this. It is also difficult to escape the conclusion, though, that public concern for environmental issues is fickle and, to a certain degree, a luxury. It is those societies and those governments least concerned about job creation, or economic development generally, which have the greatest ability or flexibility to engage in environmental policy-making. By the same token, when economies stagnate or decline, when restructurings result in lay-offs, people are less concerned with environmental impact than with economic opportunity. This is why the often-sought alliance between "Greens" and the democratic left often fails to work; socialism is most concerned with preserving the jobs of workers, while environmentalists may seek to shut the very factories, mines, or logging operations on which those jobs depend.

If the perspective which ecology brings is at all accurate, then we can only put-off addressing the concerns which environmentalists raise. Sooner or later we will surpass what Schumacher calls the "tolerance margins of benign nature," and the results will be impossible to ignore. At that point, perhaps, all ideologies will draw on the environmentalist account.

SUGGESTED READING:

[Publishing information is not provided for texts in political thought which are either out of print or widely available in contemporary editions.]

Bakunin, Mukhail. (1873). *Statehood and Anarchy*.
Bookchin, Murray. (1980). *Toward an Ecological Society*. Montreal: Black Rose Books.
Carson, Rachel. (1965). *Silent Spring*. London: Hamish Hamilton.
Dobson, Andrew, ed. (1991). *The Green Reader*. London: André Deutsch.
Dworkin, Andrea. (1976). *Our Blood: Prophecies and Discourses on Sexual Politics*. New York: Harper & Row.
Eisenstein, Zillah. (1981). *The Radical Future of Liberal Feminism*. New York: Longman.
Friedan, Betty. (1963). *The Feminine Mystique*. New York: W.W. Norton.
Hartsock, Nancy C.M. (1983). *Money, Sex, and Power: Toward a Feminist Historical Materialism*. New York: Longman.
Jagger, Alison M. (1983). *Feminist Politics and Human Nature*. Totawa, N.J.: Rowman & Allanheld.
Kropotkin, Peter. (1886). *Law and Authority*.
Millet, Kate. (1970). *Sexual Politics*. Garden City, N.Y.: Doubleday.
Nozick, Robert. (1974). *Anarchy, State, and Utopia*. New York: Basic Books.

Phillips, Anne. (1991). *Engendering Democracy*. Oxford: Polity Press.

Schumacher, E.F. (1974). *Small is Beautiful*. London: Random Century Limited.

Stirner, Max Stirner. (1845). *The Ego and His Own*.

Sunstein, Cass R., ed. (1982). *Feminism and Political Theory*. Chicago: University of Chicago Press.

Wolff, Robert Paul. (1970). *In Defense of Anarchism*. New York: Harper Torchbooks.

Woodcock, George, ed. (1977). *The Anarchist Reader*. London: Fontana.

Chapter Seven

Outside the Consensus

THE DISCUSSION IN THE PREVIOUS CHAPTERS has been inevitably and necessarily Eurocentric: that is to say, confined (mainly) to the context of European states, or of states that were once European colonies and which remain governed by ideas and institutions originating in that European culture which was a product of the Enlightenment, the Reformation, and the rise of the market economy. Our focus has been inevitably and necessarily thus because the word ideology and the specific systems known as ideologies that we have been examining were mainly products of the context and evolution of European societies. Nonetheless, however broadly European ideas may have been exported, and however often these ideas have been inspiration for, or a model for, or indeed, imposed upon, non-European societies, they are not the whole picture. We need to at least consider the possibilities provided for and by ideology in non-democratic contexts.

A: AUTHORITARIANISM

The observation has been made that democracy accounts for less than one—quarter of the world's nation states (although if we conclude that democracy has been successfully established in Eastern Europe and some of the republics of the former Soviet Union, then this proportion rises to closer to 30 percent). In the rest of the world – and for the most part in what is called the "developing world" – by any objective criteria, democracy is not in place, and instead, the vast majority of these other states can be characterized as **authoritarian**.

One irony here is the use of the word "authoritarian" to indicate regimes where often the maintenance of order and stability depends much more on power than on authority. This is only sometimes true, though, and often only partially true when it is true. We need to recall that there have been other forms of government than democracy which have been regarded as legitimate,

Totalitarianism
Mao Tse-tung:

Au3 "What should our policy be towards non-Marxist ideas? As far as un-mistakable counter-revolutionaries and saboteurs of the socialist cause are concerned, the matter is easy: we simply deprive them of their freedom of speech. But incorrect ideas among the people are quite a different matter. Will it do to ban such ideas and deny them any opportunity for expression? Certainly not. It is not only futile but very harmful to use summary methods in dealing with ideological questions among the people, with questions concerned with man's mental world. You may ban the expression of wrong ideas, but the ideas will still be there. On the other hand, if correct ideas are pampered in hot-houses without being exposed to the elements or immunized from disease, they will not win out against erroneous ones. Therefore, it is only by employing the method of discussion, criticism and reasoning that we can really foster correct ideas and overcome wrong ones, and that we can really settle issues".

"Communism is at once a complete system of proletarian ideology and a new social system. It is different from any other ideology or social system, and is the most complete, progressive, revolutionary and rational system in human history. The ideological and social system of feudalism has a place only in the museum of history. The ideological and social system of capitalism has also become a museum piece in one part of the world (in the Soviet Union), while in other countries it resembles 'a dying person who is sinking fast, like the sun setting beyond the western hills,' and will soon be relegated to the museum. The communist ideological and social system alone is full of youth and vitality, sweeping the world with the momentum of an avalanche and the force of a thunderbolt. The introduction of scientific communism into China has opened new vistas for people and has changed the face of the Chinese revolution. Without communism to guide it, China's democratic revolution cannot possibly succeed, let alone move on to the next stage. This is the reason why the bourgeois die-hards are so loudly demanding that communism be 'folded-up.' But it must not be 'folded-up,' for once communism is "folded-up," China will be doomed. The whole world today depends on communism for its salvation, and China is no exception...."
(Five Articles by Chairman Mao Tse-tung, 1968)

and other justifications for authority than the legal-rational authority of Western liberal democracies. While authoritarian regimes are not legitimate from the standpoint of the citizens who live in Western democracies, they are very often regarded as legitimate by their own citizens on the basis of other (typically non-Western) values. Most certainly, these regimes stand outside the consensus about central institutions and political values that we discussed in Chapter Four. Again, though, it is sometimes important to realize that they may indeed sometimes stand with one foot inside that consensus. While authoritarian regimes are, by definition, not democratic, they sometimes *claim* to be democratic and, even more often, appeal to the principle of *popular sovereignty* by claiming that their policies and actions are consistent with the will of the people or are consistent with what the people need or require. Almost without exception, moreover, these regimes will also claim to provide "justice" for their citizens. Their norms of justice, or the applications that they make of these norms, are what clashes with the sensibilities of non-authoritarian cultures.

As this discussion has made clear, it is often easier to describe authoritarian regimes in terms of *what they are not*, rather than what they are. In this sense, we have no grounds for considering authoritarianism to be *an* ideology; there is no *one* authoritarian vision, nor is there *an* authoritarian perspective, nor *an* authoritarian program. What authoritarian regimes do have in common is a commitment by those in power not to relinquish it. Other general features of authoritarian states can be identified by understanding those elements of the liberal democratic consensus that are missing in such regimes. As indicated, authoritarian regimes are not democratic. Those who occupy top political offices have not been elected to them or, having been elected, have since suspended or abolished democratic political processes. This means that they have become unaccountable to the public. One thing democracy does (some might argue the *only* thing it does) is provide a means by which the public can peacefully replace those who rule them. Such an avenue is missing in an authoritarian regime, and the replacement of rulers requires violence (coups, assassinations, revolutions, etc.).

TOTALITARIANISM

A distinction is often made between authoritarian and *totalitarian* regimes. In this author's view, totalitarian regimes form a special category of authoritarian government. What distinguishes totalitarian regimes is the extent of the power which is exercised by the state: it is total, complete, reaching into virtually every sphere of life. All authoritarian systems have the potential to become totalitarian (because they do not recognize limits on their power), but in practice

Nazi Fascism
Adolph Hitler:

Au1 "The program of the German Workers' Party [name changed in 1920 to the National Socialist German Workers' Party] is limited as to period. The leaders have no intention, once the aims announced in it have been achieved, of setting up fresh ones, merely in order to increase the discontent of the masses artificially, and so ensure the continued existence of the party.

1. We demand the union of all Germans to form a Great Germany on the basis of the right of self-determination enjoyed by nations.
2. We demand equality of rights for the German people in its dealings with other nations, and abolition of the peace treaties of Versailles and Saint-Germain.
3. We demand land and territory (colonies) for the nourishment of our people and for settling our excess population.
4. None but members of the nation may be citizens of the state. None but those of German blood, whatever their creed, may be members of the nation. No Jew, therefore, may be a member of the nation.
5. Anyone who is not a citizen of the state may live in Germany only as a guest and must be regarded as being subject to foreign laws.
6. The right of voting on the leadership and legislation is to be enjoyed by the state alone. We demand therefore that all official appointments, of whatever kind, whether in the Reich, in the country, or in the smaller localities, shall be granted to citizens of the state alone. We oppose the corrupting custom of Parliament of filling posts merely with a view to party considerations, and without reference to character or capacity.
7. We demand that the state shall make it its first duty to promote the industry and livelihood of citizens of the state. If it is not possible to nourish the entire population of the state, foreign nationals (non-citizens of the state) must be excluded from the Reich.
8. All non-German immigration must be prevented...."
("Twenty-five Points of the German Workers' Party," 1920)

only a few actually take this route. It is possible, for example, for authoritarian regimes to grant considerable levels of autonomy to market forces within their jurisdiction; this is not as likely in a totalitarian regime. (The openness of authoritarian regimes to capitalism has often meant that Western nations — particulary the United States — have been willing to support such governments in their suppression of democratic or popular oppositions that might be less welcoming to foreign investment.) The driving imperative for most authoritarian regimes is to maintain a hold on power. In this respect they are profoundly conservative of a *status quo*. Totalitarian states usually arise when the driving imperative of the ruling class is to change the world in ways which require a spectacular mobilization of the public, or a profound transformation of human nature. For examples of both, consider Germany under Hitler (see below on fascism), or China under Mao Tse-tung (Zedong).

AUTHORITARIANISM AND THE LIBERAL CONSENSUS

It should not come as a surprise to learn that in regimes where rulers do not expect to give an accounting of their actions to the public, rulers often act as if they are outside the law or above it. They may profess belief in the principle of the rule of law, but what is missing is the requirement that all citizens, rulers and ruled alike, be subject to the rules and sanctions contained in the law. Not surprisingly, in such societies the application of the rule of law may also be suspect; widespread corruption among the police, the military, and even judicial authorities is not uncommon.

If the liberal understanding of the rule of law is foreign to the practice of authoritarian regimes, the liberal respect for and reliance upon individual rights is almost inconceivable. Legal rights which are genuinely enforceable put limits on the actions of the state or on its members (the government), and limits on the state or on rulers are, by definition, contrary to the nature of authoritarian regimes. Most often, the only limitations on their actions that rulers acknowledge in such regimes are those which they impose on themselves. (It is not unknown for states to possess a very comprehensive constitutional declaration of rights and an enunciation of the principles of the rule of law, which is ignored or violated whenever it suits the rulers' purposes. In these cases the constitution is a façade.) A result of authoritarian disdain for the liberal rule of law and respect for individual rights is a very incomplete comprehension of "the individual" as an abstract unit of legal personality. Consequently, those who fall afoul of the law (or more accurately, and thereby emphasizing our point, fall afoul of "the authorities") in authoritarian regimes are often subjected to treatment regarded as abusive by liberal standards.

Fundamentalism
Ayatollah Khomeini:

Au3 "It is our duty to stand up to the superpowers and we have the ability to stand up against them, provided that our intellectuals give up their fascination with Westernization or Easternization and follow the straight path of Islam and nationalism.

We are fighting against international communism to the same degree that we are fighting against the Western world—devourers led by America, Israel and Zionism. My dear friends, you should know that the danger from the communist powers is not less than America and the danger of America is such that if we show the slightest negligence we shall be destroyed. Both superpowers have risen for the obliteration of the oppressed nations and we should support the oppressed people of the world.

We should try hard to export our revolution to the world, and should set aside the thought that we do not export our revolution, because Islam does not regard various Islamic countries differently and is the supporter of all the oppressed people of the world.... We should clearly settle our accounts with the powers and superpowers and should demonstrate to them that, despite all the grave difficulties that we have, we shall confront the world with our ideology".

("We shall confront the world with our ideology," 1980)

Perhaps not surprisingly, the commitment to equality is even weaker in authoritarian regimes than it is in democracies. Any thorough belief in equality is sure to undermine the justifications which sustain the rulers in their permanent monopoly of power. It might well be objected that in some authoritarian systems, including but not restricted to those that have drawn on Marxist-Leninism, there is a strong commitment to social and economic equality. While this is true, we may make two qualifications. One is that such a commitment has often turned out to be stronger in theory than in practice; the classless society remains a goal to be realized rather than a present reality. The other is that in such societies political inequality is total and will accept no challenge.

Clearly then, the ideologies that support authoritarianism will be characterized by elitism rather than egalitarianism. Strictly speaking, elitism is the belief in the necessity and desirability of the concentration of power and authority, political or economic or social, in the hands of a small ruling group. Natural elitism is the belief that there is a superior group or class of individuals, endowed by Nature (or by God through natural ability) with the talents, abilities, or wisdom which fits them to rule others. Typically, some variety of natural elitism is used to justify the government by some small group who have held or seized power. Natural elitism is of course anti-democratic, but it is not unheard of for elites to govern with the support of non-elites who for some reason have accepted the assertions of natural elitism. Functional elitism, on the other hand, argues that the nature of organizing and carrying out tasks in complex societies requires the exercise of authority and power by a small group rather than by the whole population. Functional elitism is not anti-democratic in principle, but for reasons of efficiency or expedience. Unlike natural elitism, functional elitism advocates that those who exercise power be those most capable of fulfilling the functions in question, so that education, or merit, or demonstrated skill are the means of attaining elite positions. It is the position which in fact is privileged, and not the individual who occupies it (or rather, the individual is only privileged so long as they occupy that position). This distinction between positions and individuals allows the latter to be held accountable by the public for their performance of the role identified by the position. Functional elitism is in fact a part of every liberal democracy today.

A further important distinction concerns the place of religion within the authoritarian state. Very often authoritarian regimes do not acknowledge the separation of church and state which in the West was a product of the Reformation and the Enlightenment. In the liberal consensus, what people believe and are obliged to do because of their beliefs is a completely autonomous realm from what people are obliged to do as citizens. The law of the state is divorced from the commandments of faith. As a result, public policy is not supposed either to reflect or favour the influence of any particular religious creed. This separation of "church" and state was in part simply a practical recognition of growing religious diversity in Western culture, a diversity that began with the Reformation. It is also true that in Western nations where the population is religiously homogeneous the separation of church and state has sometimes been longer in coming and less completely realized. In authoritarian regimes, quite often religion is a source of justification (sometimes *the* source) for the rulers' power. Here there may be a high degree of conformity between the civil and the religious laws, or the authority of the state may be used to enforce religious edicts and to ensure religious conformity. In such systems the degree of religious tolerance will be low, if it exists at all. The case of religion illustrates a more general observation, namely that authoritarian regimes are less likely to celebrate plurality within their society, and more likely to work to maintain, or even forcibly create, an homogeneity within the population in terms of language, culture, religion, and sometimes, even race.

Authoritarianism, then, does not denote an ideology but is a term indicating a broad category of political regimes characterized by a government whose ruling members are not accountable to those they rule. (A typology of authoritarian regimes would include dictatorships, monarchies, juntas, theocracies, and dynasties). This permanence in office may seem to indicate stability, but there are two senses in which this is misleading. Precisely because authoritarian rulers are not regularly replaced by peaceful means, their governments are susceptible to violent challenges such as insurrection or revolution. At the same time, the fear of this happening and the attempt to stifle any competition lead to repressive actions and agencies (secret police, bureaus of censorship, etc.) which impose stability through coercion and intimidation. Most importantly, authoritarian rulers will seek to justify their hold on power in order to stabilize their regimes. Their distaste for public involvement in decision-making or in selecting rulers goes hand in hand with a desire to receive public approval of their actions and policies. One of the instruments employed by authoritarian rulers will be ideology.

The ideologies which justify authoritarian regimes, with one exception, fall outside the liberal democratic consensus that we have identified. This exception is the façade of democratic elections. As noted, almost all regimes claim to embody justice and popular sovereignty and, in making this claim, seek to establish their legitimacy. Regimes which do not have elections claim to represent or embody the public will in some other way. In many authoritarian regimes, elections *do* take place, but they do not meet the standards that most observers regard as satisfying the criteria of democracy. The most obvious example is elections in which there is no choice: the people are allowed to cast a ballot, but there is only one candidate. Or they are allowed to choose among candidates, but all candidates belong to the same (the ruling) party. What amounts to the same thing is elections in which there is a choice among candidates and parties but, nonetheless, the ruling party is guaranteed victory — either through corruption or fraud, through special rules, or through control of other institutions like the mass media, the police, etc. (Mexico is a well-known example of a state with contested elections which always manage to return the ruling party to power.) The ideologies of liberal democracy are, by and large, ideologies *of the people*, accepting and building upon the notion that authority is grounded in the people, is exercised by rulers as a trust from the people, and serves the public welfare. The various ideologies fashioned to justify authoritarian regimes are better understood as ideologies *of the state*.

Our concern in the remainder of this chapter will be to examine the ideologies that have provided support for authoritarian systems. (There is much more that could be said about authoritarian regimes but this is, after all, a book on ideologies, not on types of constitutions or governments.)

B: NATIONALISM

Immediately, we should state that there is nothing necessarily authoritarian about nationalism — as our discussion of nationalism within the context of non-authoritarian systems should have made clear. Nonetheless, nationalism provides a powerful vehicle for authoritarian rulers to employ in justifying their grip on power and in the attempt to secure legitimacy in the eyes of the public. It may be useful to think of nationalism in liberal democracies as a (usually) subordinate element within the broader ideologies of conservatism, liberalism, and socialism. By contrast, in authoritarian regimes, nationalism can become the dominant element in the ideology of the state. To put it another way, in the context of liberal democracies, nationalism is less an ideology than a disposition which may be present or absent within ideologies. In authoritarian systems (and certain other special contexts) nationalism often becomes *the* ideology.

THE NATION

By nationalism we may mean several things, but behind them all stands the idea of "the nation," a rather fuzzy term indicating a common identity and purpose which unites people for political purposes. A nation exists where a people share a common language, culture, religion, customs, and a shared understanding of their collective history as a people. If a clan or tribe is like a family only larger, then a nation is like a tribe but larger, more comprehensive, and corresponding to the larger political units that have emerged in relatively modern times. In the history of humanity, the nation is relatively young. Nation-states as we understand them today only emerged in Western Europe at the end of the feudal period as the patchwork system of feudal kingdoms, duchies, and principalities was forged into larger territorial units under the developing authority of absolute monarchs. The work of creating an identity among citizens corresponding to these larger political units was something accomplished after the demise of feudal society and owes much both to the first and second generation ideologies we have discussed and to the institutions and practices they have established and sustained. The notion of a national identity depends to a large degree on the development of means of communication and travel and on the standardization of laws and institutions. Each of these serves to break down the differences which define local communities and provide them with their own unique identity. Nationalism, then, is the political dispositions which promote and maintain the interests of "the nation," so understood. There are three general forms in which we might encounter nationalism.

SELF-DETERMINATION

The first sense of nationalism is *the goal of achieving political autonomy or independence for a people* (that is, for the "nation"). Typically this nationalism is a movement by a specific people within a larger society for self-determination, which may be seen to require the separation of a territorial unit inhabited by the "nation"; the departure of a ruling colonial power; or, less drastically, the granting of various measures of political autonomy. The nationalism of self-determination seeks greater autonomy (e.g. state-building) for a people whose common identity marks them as a "nation" (which may itself be contested). This is the nationalism that inspired revolutions (or national liberation movements) within territories in the developing world that were ruled as colonies by European powers. It is also the nationalism that motivates action for self-determination by a people not successfully integrated into the larger identity of a nation-state, a people who usually constitute a cohesive minority within that state. This is the way that nationalism most often becomes problematic within liberal democracies. The desire of a significant portion of the Québécois in Canada for political autonomy is perhaps the closest example at hand for students reading this. Finally, the desire for self-determination is the nationalism that feeds the dreams of peoples without a state to establish one; e.g. the creation of Israel, or the desire of Kurds for their own homeland.

NATION-BUILDING

A second sense of nationalism has the goal of creating, fostering, or sustaining a common identity among the citizens of a political state. In many cases this is an attempt to unite those who otherwise do not see themselves as sharing a common identity (an exercise often called nation-building). This is the nationalism that lay behind the creation of modern nation-states out of smaller communities and societies. That nations are often so constructed is more obvious perhaps to citizens of newer nations like the United States, Canada, and Australia, where peoples of various backgrounds and experiences share a nation state. In the case of Canada, at least, the question of national identity (i.e. what it means to be a Canadian) is very much still in debate. On the other hand, the disintegration of what once was Yugoslavia, the divorce of the Czech Republic and

Slovakia, and the falling apart of the former Soviet Union, all indicate how the nationalism of nation-building can sometimes fail to overcome and supplant the more particular identities of ethnic and linguistic communities which maintain their integrity within the larger nation-state. In the absence of integration into a large whole, it is perhaps inevitable that such communities look for a degree of self-determination. The failure to create a common Yugoslavian identity is reflected in the desire of Croats, Serbs, Bosnians, Slovenians, etc. to obtain and preserve their own geo-political autonomy — and in their willingness to engage in brutal warfare and widespread civilian destruction for that purpose.

NATIONAL PREFERENCE

The third sense which we may attach to nationalism is an emphasis on the integrity or priority of the nation-state. This is a rather vague description that covers a variety of stances which oppose something we might with similar vagueness call internationalism. The tendency in foreign policy, for example, to act unilaterally, rather than in concert with other nations or through supranational organizations such as the UN is one such expression; isolationism, in which a country withdraws from activity in the international arena, is another. (The United States has at various times during this century exhibited both of these tendencies.) Free traders are economic internationalists; their counterparts are economic nationalists, who may advocate protectionism or national standards with respect to employment or environmental policies, or restrictions on foreign investment. In Canada the protection of cultural industries and the general concern to prevent cultural assimilation by the United States is a familiar example of nationalism in this last, and perhaps most politically benign, sense.

NATIONALISM AND IDEOLOGY

Each of these senses of nationalism — self-determination, nation-building, national preference — is compatible with the mainstream ideologies we have discussed. One could be a conservative nationalist, or a liberal nationalist, or a conservative internationalist, or a socialist who is nationalist on economic issues, and internationalist on foreign policy, etc. At the same time, there are certain affinities or tendencies for specific ideologies to be nationalist or internationalist. Liberalism, because it celebrates the individual and not the group, very often favours internationalism and is suspicious of nationalism (which it rightly associates with conservatism). Communism or radical socialism is also internationalist, since it ultimately promotes solidarity with humanity as a whole or at least among the working classes worldwide. On this basis one might regard socialism and social democracy as more susceptible to nationalism than is communism. On the other hand, communist regimes have often been totalitarian authoritarian states, highly motivated to tap into nationalism whenever it has suited their purposes. All ideologies have demonstrated an ability to accommodate nationalism, depending on the circumstances and the context.

Among all the numerous varieties of nationalism, it may be useful to distinguish between those which are exclusive and those which are inclusive. Exclusive nationalism stresses membership in a group which is by some definition "closed," such as membership in a racial group, a linguistic or religious community, or an ethnic group. These are "exclusive" because membership in the nation is denied to those not belonging to (or willing to convert to) the requisite community, or not possessing the ascribed characteristic. Some such categories — like race — may permanently exclude those who are not born into them. These are also exclusive because they wish to preserve the integrity of the nation from others "foreign" in nature, others regarded as enemies to be kept away, if not eliminated. Inclusive nationalisms, by contrast, will stress loyalty to beliefs or institutions which are associated with the state and to the state itself. They are inclusive because they are open to any and all who are willing to subscribe to such beliefs, regardless of their race, their creed, or their language. Inclusive nationalisms are easily adopted or chosen; exclusive nationalisms are much less a matter of discretion. Inclusive nationalism is more likely to be found in plural societies and in liberal democracies; exclusive nationalisms are the basis for many authoritarian regimes, and often rest on a high degree of social homogeneity. An interesting example of difference here is citizenship in Germany as opposed to the United States and Canada. Germany has a largely "racial" understanding of citizenship. Anyone of German descent, no matter how long their family has been away from Germany, can become a citizen with relative ease, while foreigners who have been living in Germany for many years have great difficulty in being naturalized. In new nations like the United States and Canada, citizenship is readily conferred on those who are willing to swear their allegiance to the state and demonstrate some rudimentary knowledge about their new nation. German citizenship is (largely) exclusive to ethnic Germans. Citizenship in Canada or the United States is inclusive of (almost) anyone.

Finally, we may note that nationalism can be defensive or aggressive. In the former case, it seeks to preserve the nation from challenge, whether external or internal, and its mobilization of the public is largely to provide an answer to perceived threats. In the latter case, nationalism is not simply an identity, but an identity of superiority, which is proven in contest with, or conquest of, others.

This, too, is a feature we are more likely to associate with authoritarian rather than with liberal–democratic states. It is also, perhaps, the biggest reason why those in liberal–democratic regimes worry about authoritarian regimes. Often, authoritarian regimes are simply concerned with maintaining a structure of power in place; however oppressive or repressive this may be for those who live in such a system, it does not directly affect others outside the authoritarian regime. In the last three sections of this chapter, though, we will discuss three strains of authoritarianism which are, or are perceived to be, a threat to other systems, including liberal democracy. They pose a threat to the degree that they would extend their power beyond the state, would refashion the world in their image.

C: MARXISM-LENINISM / STALINISM

In the discussion of socialism in Chapter Three, we noted that Lenin took and transformed the Marxian notion of a dictatorship of the proletariat, refining and developing the role to be played by the vanguard of professional revolutionaries (the Communist Party) in the aftermath of the revolution. In the Soviet Union after the Bolshevik Revolution of 1917 and the ensuing civil war, the Communist Party under Lenin eventually took control of the state and did not relinquish control again until 1990 when Mikhail Gorbachev secured an amendment to the Soviet constitution removing Article 6, which had preserved the monopoly of the Communist Party. The state which existed in the Soviet Union in this period, and in those countries which fell under the Soviet sphere of influence after the Second World War, was an authoritarian one and a totalitarian one also. It is fair to note that originally, under Lenin and his immediate successors, the Soviet state was neither as harsh or as closed as it would become under Stalin. Lenin, at least, had reasons grounded in theory, however objectionable, for his brand of "democratic centralism." Stalin's rule became increasingly difficult to distinguish from any other personal dictatorship, except perhaps for its own unique moments of cruelty and barbarism. Even though Stalin died in 1953, his successors from Khrushchev to Gorbachev inherited the state apparatus and structure of power that Stalin had erected, including a powerful military complex, dreaded secret police, and an extensive Party apparatus. Today, the only Stalinist regimes remaining are Cuba and North Korea and, if we use Stalinism broadly to indicate Communist Party dictatorship, China.

D: FASCISM

Another ideology that has become largely marginal, but was once of tremendous significance in this century, is fascism. The first fascism was developed and articulated by Benito Mussolini, who founded his movement in 1919 (the word fascism comes from the Latin *fasces*, describing a symbol of authority taken from ancient Rome). If the communism of Lenin was a left-wing elitism, fascism is a right-wing elitism that combines extreme nationalism, statism, corporatism, anti-communism, and belief in a strong leader. The most striking case of fascism, of course, was the National Socialist (Nazi) regime in Germany under Hitler from 1933 to 1945, but other examples of fascism were Spain under Franco (1939-75) and Argentina under Peron (1946-55).

The nationalism that fascism draws upon is extreme and exclusive in the sense indicated above. In some cases, as in its Nazi incarnation, nationalism becomes racialism; the nation is identified with "a race" (which, like the Nazi notion of an Aryan master race, may be completely mythical). Those who are foreign are not only excluded from membership but, as threats to the "purity" of the nation, are to be eliminated or exterminated. Hence Nazi Germany carried out the Holocaust in which six million Jews were exterminated along with hundreds of thousands of Gypsies, Slavs, Poles, and other minorities deemed a threat to the Aryan race.

In fascism the people are also directed to the state which is conceived as the beginning and end of the nation. Fascism opposes the liberal notion of autonomous individuals and any institutions associated with it, including democracy (many fascist rulers used democracy to win power and then discarded it). Conversely, fascism opposes the class–based politics of socialism, seeking instead to secure the loyalty of all classes to the state. Similarly, the internationalist or cosmopolitan character of liberalism and socialism is rejected as weakness and as subversive to the character of the nation. Fascism is not only exclusive but aggressively so, seeking to prove the superiority and strength of the nation through military victories or conquest. The fascist state not only reflects an extreme nationalism, but constitutes an extreme authoritarianism and, in most cases, a totalitarianism.

Correspondingly, all associations and organizations in society are linked to the state and are allowed to exist or function only as arms of the state. This is known as state corporatism – to distinguish it from the benign societal corporatism that exists in many European societies – or sometimes corporativism. Fascism does not seek to replace the private property capitalist economy, but merely to control it, particularly to direct its production to the ends of the state (e.g. the production of military hardware). Corporativism is a means of linking the state with all sectors of civil society. In some senses fascism combines the organic, collective character of feudalism with the apparatus and control of the modern authoritarian state. This, as much as anything, is what makes it a "right-wing" elitism, or totalitarianism.

Finally, every fascist state has revolved around a leader who is not simply a dictator (an individual holding absolute, unaccountable power) but in addition is held to be the embodiment of the nation, the personal representative of "the race," the most superior example of the superior people which constitute this nation. Of course, no-one matches up to this in reality but fascist states, like all totalitarian and most authoritarian regimes, recognize the value of propaganda. The state uses its control over public communication to spread its misinformation and doctrines and uses secret police and informers to root out private dissent and subversion.

It is debatable whether or not any of today's regimes deserve the name fascist. Certainly few display the total range of characteristics that were embodied by Mussolini's or Hitler's regimes. Commonly, opponents of authoritarian states will decry them as "fascist," and the word is particularly common in denouncing police states. More certain is the incompatibility of fascism with the values of the liberal-democratic consensus we have discussed above. On that basis, so long as and wherever that consensus holds, a future for fascism fortunately seems unlikely.

E: RELIGIOUS FUNDAMENTALISM

One last variety of authoritarianism merits a brief discussion, namely those states where the separation of church and state, or of religion and politics, has no validity. In such regimes, the content of the law which is articulated and enforced by the institutions of the state is dictated by religious commandments or laws. In the most extreme examples, the government is in practice headed by the chief religious representative — whether bishop, ayatollah, rabbi, prophet, etc. — who is regarded as the personal representative of the deity worshipped by adherents of that religion. Such a state constitutes a *theocracy*. Alternatively, the head of state or head of government may in practice remain subordinate to the authority of the chief religious official. What matters is that what the state does conforms first and foremost to the religious code, as interpreted by the authoritative religious figures. Moreover, the state enforces the purely religious law, imposing sanctions on those who "sin" or "give offense" on religious grounds. The state also functions to ensure orthodoxy and conformity to the established religion, not being tolerant of scepticism, unorthodox interpretations, or rival creeds. This is an institutionalisation of fundamentalism, fundamentalism being the strict adherence to the letter of religious law as understood by the paramount religious authorities. Obviously, such an institutionalized fundamentalism is contrary to the liberal democratic consensus. Lest such fundamentalism seem so strange, we could point out that in medieval Europe the relation between church and state was often so close as to satisfy the description made in the last paragraph. One interesting feature of such fundamentalist regimes is that they are often crusading regimes — it is not enough to secure the faith or practice conforming to the faith within the realm, there is a duty to spread "kingdom of God" (whichever God it is) to other apostate (unbelieving) peoples. We should remember that the verb "crusading" directs us back to the Christian crusades to rescue the Holy Land from unbelieving "infidels."

Perhaps mindful of their own distant crusading past, citizens in the once-Christian West now look to Islamic nations, and speculate about the apparent rising tide of Islamic fundamentalism and what it means both inside and outside the borders of Islam. The concerns of the West are captured in the following quote from Max Skidmore:

"Essentially, Islam teaches brotherhood. Its spirit, like that of early Christianity, is internationalist, with a stress on the kinship of all true believers. In the hands of fundamentalists, these beliefs can be interpreted to require war against nonbelievers and to require the establishment of Muslim regimes wherever nation-states exist, which joins with Arab nationalism to add to the hostility against Israel". (1989: 253)

On the other hand, we should make the following observations. Fundamentalist regimes are in a minority within the Islamic world. Where they are in place, they are often embroiled in civil war. In many Islamic states, fundamentalist movements are directed largely against corrupt authoritarian regimes or outmoded personal dynasties (e.g. Saudi Arabia). Even within Islamic regimes there is considerable controversy and struggle about what an Islamic state means, requires, allows, or how it is constituted. As the youngest of the world's great religions, Islam may possess a crusading force and a vitality that often astonishes citizens of the West. Nonetheless, there is in this author's view, no reason, as yet, to view Islamic fundamentalism as a threat to the West or its interests, nor is it clear that Islam is not wrestling with many of the same issues that Christianity confronted at the end of the feudal period. Certainly, the term "Islamic fundamentalism" is too often used to cover a myriad of different beliefs, political systems, and developments that have as much in conflict as in common.

CONCLUSION

This chapter has been concerned with the ideologies or perhaps "isms" which fall outside the consensus fashioned in Western liberal-democracies over the past three centuries or so. We have used the umbrella term authoritarian to describe the regimes associated with these various ideas and beliefs. Conversely, it is often clear that the authoritarian state is not so much a product of ideas and beliefs as that these ideas and beliefs are used to justify or rationalize an authoritarian regime. It is striking, though, that many of the features of these regimes bear more than a passing resemblance to the feudal society against which liberalism reacted, a reaction also at the basis of socialism and liberal-conservatism. Is it an arrogance of the West to believe that authoritarianism will eventually evolve into liberal modernity or post-modernity? Is it an insight of the authoritarian non-West that in a planet increasingly burdened with population and constrained in its options of how to feed, clothe, and shelter this population, more control and discipline is necessary than liberal-democracies can provide?

SUGGESTED READING:

[Publishing information is not provided for texts in political thought which are either out of print or widely available in contemporary editions.]

Brezinskik, Zbigniew. (1990). *The Grand Failure: The Birth and Death of Communism in the Twentieth Century*. New York: Collier Books.

De Felice, Renzo. (1977). *Interpretations of Fascism*. Cambridge, Mass.: Harvard University Press.

Deutsch, Karl W. (1966). *Nationalism and Social Communication*. 2nd edition. Cambridge, Mass.: Harvard University Press.

Gellner, Ernest. (1983). *Nations and Nationalism*. Oxford: Basil Blackwell.

Gwertzman, Bernard, and Michael Kaurman, eds. (1991). *The Collapse of Communism*. New York: Random House.

Hitler, Adolf. (1925). *Mein Kampf*.

Minogue, Kenneth. (1967). *Nationalism*. New York: Basic Books.

O'Sullivan, Noel. (1983). *Fascism*. London: J.M. Dent.

Ward, Barbara. (1966). *Nationalism and Ideology*. New York: W.W. Norton.

Chapter Eight
The Prospects of Ideology

THE DISCUSSION IN THIS BOOK has focused on the broad context of Western industrial societies, with occasional reference, for the benefit of our readers, to the specific manifestations of ideology in the United States and Canada. We need to note here the complex play of broad influences which transcend particular cultures and the presence of particular factors which shape the form ideologies take (as well as which ideologies flourish) in any given nation.

A: IDEOLOGY IN THE NATIONAL CONTEXT

We began by situating ideology within the broader heading of political culture. Let me suggest, for the sake of argument, that each nation has a political culture, even though in some nations it may be more appropriate to speak of political cultures. A political culture shapes the boundaries of the politically possible by transmitting and promoting certain political ideas and, equally important, by suppressing or denouncing others. Within the circle of possibilities articulated by a political culture, public policies are enacted and public institutions created, reformed, or preserved. In return (as we saw most clearly in Chapters Four and Five), once established, institutions constrain and sustain a political culture.

On this basis we can perhaps understand easily how some features of ideology are not unique to any nation, but are found in several. Students of comparative politics talk about "advanced industrial societies," indicating certain levels of economic, political and social development which are common to these countries, and which are reflected in the principal political, and economic institutions. These are also the societies in which the ideologies that we discussed in the first six chapters have flourished. In the institutional setting, in the common historical experiences and currents influencing these societies, and in the similar problems and social structures of these societies, there is a basis for a relatively similar ideological experience. Liberalism, conservative liberalism, and socialism in Canada and the United States are much like liberalism, conservative liberalism, and socialism in Britain, Australia, Germany, or Denmark. It has also become increasingly the case in the modern world that developments in one nation are easily and quickly exported to other countries that have similar problems, a similar culture, or a similar social structure. Mrs. Thatcher's conservative (conservative liberal) revolution in Britain influenced conservatives throughout the Western world, just as the successes and failures of the Green party in Germany have been instructive for environmentalist politics elsewhere. In an age of globalization and electronic mass communication, there are few secrets.

Nonetheless, each country remains to some degree unique. Each has its own history and out of that history, a culture, and within that culture, a more specifically political culture. It is for this reason that socialism in Canada is not exactly the same as socialism in Greece or socialism in the United States. It is for this reason that in some countries certain ideologies do well and others fail to become established. Ideas do not spring up in a vacuum; they are generated in response to problems and situations. Similarly, ideas will only take hold when the conditions are right for them and, having become a part of a country's political culture, ideas may well be changed and shaped by the particular character of that country's experience. There are, then, often quite striking differences between the way ideology is expressed in one country and the way it develops in another. There are also striking cases where an ideology fails to do well in one setting but flourishes in another country that doesn't seem all that different from the first. A prime example of this has been the very different political cultures that have existed in two countries which otherwise have a great deal in common, the United States and Canada. Several different explanations of this difference have been put forward, each of which likely contains part of the truth. Although these explanations have been offered to makes sense of the differences between Canada and the United States, the ideas behind them could easily be applied to account for other national differences.

One explanation (see Lipset, 1965) focuses on the different circumstances surrounding the creation of these nation-states. The United States was forged in a revolutionary beginning, out of the experience of government by an unaccountable monarchy, a beginning paid for in the blood of war. This origin had significant and positive effects for nation-building, for fashioning a common American identity, complete with a history, legends, and myths, and formed the foundation for an homogenizing culture that celebrates individuals, but not necessarily difference. Some of the more political consequences of the American revolutionary origins were an abiding suspicion of government and a concern with concentrations of public power.

Canada, by contrast, had no single formative event like the American Revolution. The Canadian state emerged, as it were, through a gradual process of the transfer of sovereignty from Britain. If anything, the desire for Canadian self-government was stronger in Britain than Canada. Interestingly, the Canadian Fathers of Confederation wished to preserve Canada as *British* North America, in explicit contrast to the republic to the south. American democracy and egalitarianism were particularly suspect for the tories, liberal conservatives, and conservative liberals who made up the Fathers of Confederation. They saw the establishment of the Dominion of Canada as much as a reorganization of the British North American colonies as the creation of a new country. Along with this "gentle" beginning, then, went a considerable deference to authority and a lack of challenge to the often elitist assumptions imbedded in the Westminster model of responsible government. Equally important, there was no strong Canadian national identity created. Indeed, one persistent challenge for (English-speaking) Canadians since Confederation has been to define themselves in some way other than by reference to the ways in which they are not American.

A second way to explain persistent differences in the two political cultures, and hence with the mix of ideologies that each contains, has pointed to the differences in institutions in each country. The United States has had a constitutional Bill of Rights since 1789, providing an institutional basis for limiting state intrusion into certain spheres of individual liberty. Canada had no such constitutional code until 1982 and then acquired one much less categorical and much more subject to qualification than the American example. The United States employs a separation of powers and a corresponding set of checks and balances which ensure a relatively weak national state, reflecting the fear of concentrated power of the constitutional framers. Canada has a parliamentary fusion of powers, with a corresponding dominance of the legislature by the executive and strong (i.e. disciplined) political parties. Through much of their history, the United States presented political culture in some ways more openly democratic than Canada's (although not for Americans of colour or of leftist political persuasion), and there is a vibrant tradition of direct democracy (at least at the local and state levels) that has yet to take hold in Canada.

Finally, one of the most intriguing explanations for the political cultures of these two nations has drawn upon the "cultural fragment" theory of Louis Hartz, which proposes that the political cultures of new nations (such as Canada, the United States, Australia, South Africa, etc.), can be explained as partial or incomplete embodiments of an ideological whole represented by the European culture created by the liberal revolution: "all of them are fragments of the larger whole of Europe struck off in the course of the revolution which brought the West into the modern world" (1964:3). The United States, in Hartz's argument, was a liberal fragment settled in the main by refugees from the organic absolutism of late medieval Europe. Toryism had no place in the New World, which lacked the aristocratic tradition and corresponding institutions of organic hierarchy. Colonial victory in the War of Independence meant that any tory loyalists to the British Crown were soon gone — back to Britain, or to Britain's remaining North American colonies — thus cleansing the American liberal fragment which flourished in the absence of opposition. In Hartz's thesis, the absence of toryism in the United States accounts for the lack of (and hostility to) socialist ideas in this political culture, because both toryism and socialism are collectivist by contrast with liberalism's individualism. In a uniformly individualist political culture, there was no basis on which socialism might build.

As far as Canada is concerned, the seminal article applying Hartz's fragment theory has been Gad Horowitz's "Conservatism, Liberalism and Socialism in Canada" (1966). The fundamental thrust of Horowitz's article is to explain (contrary to the application of Hartz to Canada made previously by Kenneth McRae) the viability of socialism in Canada, especially given its marginality in the United States. While conceding that Canada is a predominantly liberal nation, Horowitz points out that it is not monolithically liberal like the United States, making the case for the presence of a "tory touch" in Canada. This tory presence was rooted in the organic, feudal character of the French colony in Quebec prior to 1759 and the migration of United Empire Loyalists from the new American nation following the War of Independence. This tory presence meant that collectivist ideas were acceptable in Canada (while ceasing to be so in the United States). Horowitz argues that the survival of toryism in Canada was crucial in allowing socialism to be regarded as a legitimate option within the Canadian ideological landscape, a reception which socialism could not find in the United States. Horowitz also outlines in considerable detail how American liberalism, conservatism, and socialism differ from Canadian liberalism, conservatism and socialism, in some measure, but not exclusively, because of the "tory touch" in Canada.

Horowitz's article was based on the historical experience of Canadian ideology and, while some have challenged his reading of that history, an altogether different question is whether or not that history needs updating. In the original article, Horowitz presents a Canadian ideological landscape very different from that of the United States It is sometimes difficult to see that the difference is so pronounced today, especially as Canadian conservatism seems increasingly beholden to American conservatism for platforms and rhetoric, and as Canadian socialism — like socialism in many places — shifts towards the centre. An interesting concept in the Hartz-Horowitz treatment of ideology is the notion of "congealment": that is, when a political culture becomes "fixed" and thus impervious to outside influences. The United States is seen to have "congealed" soon after the War of Independence. Canada, on the other hand, appears never to have "congealed" and it may well be that over the long haul, the national differences in ideology between these neighbouring political cultures will be more in name than in substance. Ideological convergence is not a surprising development given the ever-closer political, economic, and cultural ties between these two countries.

B: IDEOLOGY AND PARTY

A more problematic relationship than the one between ideology and political culture is that between ideologies and political parties. It is very tempting to identify parties and ideologies, particularly when political parties often have ideological names like Liberal, Conservative, or Socialist. The confusion is less likely in the United States, where for most of the post-war period one has expected to find conservatives and liberals in both parties. In the last fifteen to twenty years in American politics there has been more of a polarization and more of a correlation between ideology and party. While not all conservatives are Republicans, it is increasingly unlikely that a Republican will *not* be a conservative, just as it is increasingly unlikely that a liberal will *not* be a Democrat. Nonetheless, in the United States, as elsewhere, there is no certain link between ideology and party. For example, one could easily be misled in Canada by equating support for the NDP in Canada with the presence of socialism. Many supporters of this party are reform liberals, or western populists, or even disenchanted conservatives. On the other hand, since socialists are unlikely to vote for any party but the NDP, declining support for the NDP may indicate a waning of socialism. Similarly, electoral support for the Conservative party in Canada says little or nothing about the strength of toryism and is only partially indicative of the strength of Canadian conservatism. In Europe, surviving Communist parties in countries like Italy have renamed themselves and embraced platforms that are socialist or even social democrat, having moved considerably from the Leninist model of a vanguard party. By contrast, Communists in formerly communist countries have not only renamed their parties Socialist or Social Democratic to escape the notoriety of their past, but have made strong commitments to democracy and to the capitalist market economy. Most socialist parties in the west have moved to social democracy or even reform liberalism; in some cases (e.g. New Zealand), parties once socialist have adopted policies of economic management normally identified with liberal conservatives such as Margaret Thatcher or Ronald Reagan.

As noted, the temptation to identify parties and ideologies is certainly understandable. We expect ideological beliefs to inform political actions like joining, working for, or supporting a political party, and in the absence of surveys, we rely on public activity like voting for evidence of ideological dispositions. As we have noted though, modern parties are rarely ideologically pure. Indeed, they are often not driven by ideological concerns at all and may be regarded better as associations of activists and supporters drawn from various locations in the ideological landscape. Individuals with identical ideology may support different parties, while individuals with divergent ideologies can unite behind a candidate, platform, or leader. Finally, we may recall the earlier breakdown of ideology into a perspective, a program, and a destination. In the practical world it is the programs we encounter and, commonly, policies in the program of one ideology can be found in the program of another ideology, albeit for different purposes or justifications. Red tories and socialists alike may support policies of the welfare state against liberal conservatives who wish to dismantle it. Reform liberals, social democrats, feminists, and progressive red tories may all support policies that conservative traditionalists oppose. For all of these reasons, we can only speak generally or tentatively about the current ideological landscape of Canada, the United States, or any other nation.

One final set of observations will confirm this last point. Just as parties are rarely ideologically "pure," so too individuals (generally) are rarely exemplars of just one ideology. Many people have a full range of ideological beliefs drawn from across the ideological spectrum or from at least a couple of different locales in the ideological landscape. Our discussion has indicated that the ideological universe has expanded and become more complicated as modern society has become more complex, and as the role of the state has steadily grown. So too the ideological belief systems of individuals can be expected to have become more complex and comprehensive. It is also the case that, for many, beliefs about the political world are not explicitly formulated or conceived in ideological terms; ideology is for them at most implicit. Few people then may be accurately characterized as ideologues. This term "idealogue" can be used simply to signify one who adheres consistently and completely to a specific ideology, and there is no reason that one cannot do so rationally and critically. Often though, ideologue is used pejoratively to indicate someone who relies upon an ideology to determine their stance on issues. Why this is problematic leads us to discuss the larger question of the role ideology can or should play in our political world.

C: BEYOND IDEOLOGY?

As indicated above, ideology is often viewed unfavourably; to be called an *ideologue* is rarely a compliment. The supposedly negative features are that ideology is simplistic and one-sided, dogmatic, biased, and emotional. There is enough truth to each of these claims to merit a closer examination. We have noted that ideology is simpler than philosophy, and this is something that makes it accessible to the public. It is not far from simpler to simplistic, to the claim that the world is more complex than the picture ideology typically presents, a picture which for that reason is inadequate. This view of ideology as one-sided is related to the particular perspective that is often unique to an ideology. The example drawn earlier concerning Marxism and class on the one hand, versus feminism and patriarchy, suggests that there may often be validity to the characterization of ideology as one-sided. *Both* class and patriarchy may be features of contemporary social relations, but to take either by itself as the whole or dominant truth *is* one-sided. It may be then that part of the price ideology pays to be popular or accessible is to remain one-sided or at times simplistic. Is this too large a price to pay?

To call ideology dogmatic is to say that its adherents insist on the truth of their belief system come what may and will admit no exceptions, accept no challenges, or rethink no principles. This is of course an observation that speaks more about those who believe in an ideology and about the way they believe, than about ideology itself. To adhere uncritically to an ideology may not be uncommon, but neither is it something necessarily entailed by ideology. To identify ideologies as biased is significant only if there is by comparison some "unbiased" way of thinking that is somehow more "objective" than ideology. With the demise of the myth of "value-free" enquiry years ago, it is not clear what that more objective way might be. Ideologies are no more or less biased than philosophies, theories, or any other systematic bodies of beliefs or ways of thinking. Ideologies *are* partial in the sense we identified above given that they entail a specific way of seeing, but that is as much their strength as their weakness. Finally, the claim that ideologies are emotional is like the claim they are dogmatic; it is a claim about those who hold an ideology and about how it excites them. Ideologies often make emotional appeals on the strength of the symbols and slogans they employ, and one of the strengths of ideology may well be that as a simplified system it is capable of appealing to affect rather than intellect. Nevertheless, there is no reason to assert that this is the only appeal of ideology, or even necessarily its strongest appeal.

Criticisms of ideology come down to one point which is well taken; ideology can become a substitute for independent thinking, for analysis, and for

reflection. The individual attaches herself to a belief system and thereafter allows her judgement to be determined more or less automatically by the prescriptions of the ideology. Like all uncritical forms of thought, ideology employed in such a manner is deserving of disdain. However, there is nothing in
the nature of ideology that requires it to be employed uncritically or dogmati-
cally. At stake here may well be the manner by which we come to have an ideology; do we adopt it ready-made and complete as others have fashioned it, or
do we construct for ourselves an ideology out of the numerous options available? Is our ideology a passive product of our socialization, a byproduct of our
experience, or the active result of questioning, debating, and subjecting our
own answers to challenge? Do these distinctions matter at all, or is it just a question of whether we think with our ideology, or let our ideology think for us?

Again, it is possible to distinguish between the aspects of ideology identified
above. The greatest danger of an uncritical use of ideology attends its perspective, the particular way of seeing the world unique to an ideology; if we let an
ideology become a substitute for thinking hard about the world, then the very
partial character of the ideology, its tendency to be one-sided, becomes our
prison, albeit one of our own making. There is an argument to be made that
most successful ideologies survive because there is an element of truth in the
partial picture of the world which they present. The danger of ideology is to
present this important partial truth as the whole truth, thereby keeping other
truths from our attention and our concern. It may well be that class as Marx and
his followers described it is a problematic term, but that does not mean that
there are not social relations to which "class" better draws our attention than
other terms. To deny that the fundamental structure of social relations is patriarchy does not eliminate the possibility that a great many social relations have
had and continue to have a patriarchal character. There may never have been a
state of nature such as the liberal philosophers Hobbes and Locke presented,
but an atomistic individualism certainly speaks to some dimensions of our experience in modern societies. The challenge is to make one's way critically
among these ideological visions, perspectives, and programs, to arrive through
discourse and enquiry at some conclusions about their relative merits and
weaknesses. If we do not have ideology, then what? Moving in the direction of
a *more* systematic, consistent, multi-perspectived way of thinking about politics
brings us to political philosophy (although as noted, where the line is crossed
from ideology to philosophy, or vice-versa, is not clear). In some utopias, perhaps all citizens can be philosophers, but this is simply not a possibility in the
society in which we now live, whatever might be the merits of such a state of
affairs. In the opposite direction we move towards what might at its best be
called an expedient approach to politics and what is at worst a wholly unprinci-

pled, often inconsistent thinking about politics. Expedience can well avoid some of the pitfalls we have identified as possible companions of ideology, but it can also mean losing two of the central virtues of ideology. First, ideology is principled; fundamental propositions about what is right or wrong in the social and political realm run through an ideology and structure it. This means that its adherents are also guided by such propositions, and the consequence of this is that their political judgements and activity are not simply the product of the most narrowly defined or circumstantially constrained calculations of self-interest. In this way political judgements gain some measure of objectivity, and in this way they become subjects for public debate, challenge, and re-thinking. These latter activities, of course, are at the heart of any meaningful democracy. Secondly, and not wholly unconnected with the last, ideology is goal-directed, animated by a vision of what is the best world, the best of all possible worlds, or the best we can make of this world. Political judgments informed by ideology then, are oriented towards making the world in some way a better place (or preserving it from forces that would make it worse). Here too, then, politics becomes more than simply reacting to circumstances or accepting the world as it is and surviving in it; instead of being the passive product of social and technological forces, ideology expresses our desire to shape our world, to engage in the kind of purposive action that is essentially human.

In our view then, ideology has an important role to play in the real world of political citizenship, ideology that is employed and acquired critically, in a manner that remains open to debate and challenge. The catch, and there always is a catch, is to appropriate the good points about ideology – its systematic, principled, goal-directed approach to politics – while avoiding its pitfalls: its one-sidedness, and the temptation it can bring with it to cease thinking for oneself.

In 1960, the American political scientist Daniel Bell proclaimed "the end of ideology" in a book of the same title, and the notion that ideology was dead or dying in the West caused considerable debate in the 1960s. It seems obvious now, thirty-five years later, that the pronouncement of the death of ideology was premature; certainly the resurgence of conservatism *and* the depth of the bitterness that seems to mark exchanges between contemporary liberals and conservatives confirm that ideological difference is alive and well. It is also clearer today that the 1950s in America (the period about which Bell was writing) represented a time of convergence, when the two dominant American ideologies – reform liberalism and liberal conservatism – moved towards each other, reflecting a general peacetime consensus about means and ends. During the 1960s and 1970s, a variety of events – the Vietnam War, the OPEC oil crisis and its economic aftermath, Watergate, Roe vs. Wade – provided the issues on which the mainstream ideologies would again diverge; in the meantime, some of the new ideologies that we discussed above, such as feminism and environmentalism, began to find a voice. These specific events in the United States serve to illustrate a more general proposition that has guided the approach to ideology in this book: namely, that ideologies develop in reaction to changing contexts. Under certain conditions, the ideologies in a political culture may well converge upon a consensus, such that real differences are submerged or obscured. To expect, though, that this will remain true, to believe that ideology is dead, is like believing that nothing new will happen tomorrow, that history has come to a close. For many years, we have written of fascism as an historically important, but essentially finished ideology. The rise of neo-Nazi groups and the electoral success of the extreme right in Europe suggests that we may have been too hasty in signing the death certificate of fascism. It is certainly fashionable today to proclaim the death of Marxism, if not of democratic socialism, as a vital movement offering an alternative to liberal capitalism. Whether or not we will look back differently in twenty years will depend less on what Karl Marx said and more on what the modern disciples of Adam Smith and Milton Friedman do. Without offering either prediction or prophecy, we can suggest that political contexts will shift and develop, and that as they do, the appeal of some ideas will be enhanced, the record of others will be tarnished. Such will be the basis of the ideological currents of tomorrow, just as it has been throughout our experience

SUGGESTED READING:

Hartz, Louis. (1962). *The Liberal Tradition in America*. New York: Harcourt Brace and World.
Christian, W., and C. Campbell. (1990). *Political Parties and Ideologies in Canada*. 3rd edition. Toronto: McGraw-Hill Ryerson.

Bibliography

[Publishing information is not provided for texts in political thought which are either out of print, or widely available in contemporary editions.]

Andrew, Edward. (1988). *Shylock's Rights*. Toronto: University of Toronto Press.

Avineri, Shlomo. (1968). *The Social and Political Thought of Karl Marx*. Cambridge: Cambridge University Press.

Bakunin, Mikhail. (1873). *Statehood and Anarchy*.

Barber, Benjamin R. (1984). *Strong Democracy: Participatory Politics for a New Age*. Berkeley: University of California Press.

Bell, Daniel. (1962). *The End of Ideology*. 2nd edition, New York: Collier Books.

Benn, S.I. and R.S. Peters. (1959). *Social Principles and the Democratic State*. London: Unwin.

Berlin, Isaiah. (1969). *Four Essays on Liberty*. Oxford: Oxford University Press.

Bookchin, Murray. (1980). *Toward an Ecological Society*. Montreal: Black Rose Books.

Brezinski, Zbigniew. (1990). *The Grand Failure: The Birth and Death of Communism in the Twentieth Century*. New York: Collier Books.

Buckley, William F., ed. (1970). *Did You Ever See A Dream Walking? American Conservative Thought in the Twentieth Century*. Indianapolis: Bobbs-Merrill.

Burke, Edmund. (1790). *Reflections on the Revolution in France*.

———. (1791). *An Appeal from the New to the Old Whigs*.

Carson, Rachel. (1965). *Silent Spring*. London: Hamish Hamilton.

Christian, W. and C. Campbell. (1990). *Political Parties and Ideologies in Canada*. 3rd edition, Toronto: McGraw-Hill Ryerson.

Cunningham, Frank. (1987). *Democratic Theory and Socialism*. Cambridge: Cambridge University Press.

Dahl, Robert. (1956). *A Preface to Democratic Theory*. Chicago: University of Chicago Press.

De Felice, Renzo. (1977). *Interpretations of Fascism*. Cambridge, Mass.: Harvard University Press.

Deutsch, Karl W. (1966). *Nationalism and Social Communication*. 2nd edition. Cambridge, Mass.: Harvard University Press.

Dewey, John. *Liberalism and Social Action*. New York: G. B. Putnam's Sons, 1935.

Dobson, Andrew, ed. (1991). *The Green Reader*. London: Andre Deutsch.

Dworkin, Andrea. (1976). *Our Blood: Prophecies and Discourses on Sexual Politics*. New York: Harper & Row.

Dworkin, Ronald. (1977). *Taking Rights Seriously*. London: Duckworth.

Eccleshall, Robert, and Vincent Geoghegan, Richard Jay and Rick Wilford. (1984). *Political Ideologies: an Introduction*. London: Hutchinson.

Eisenstein, Zillah. (1981). *The Radical Future of Liberal Feminism*. New York: Longman.

Esberey, Joy, and Larry Johnston. (1994). *Democracy and the State*. Peterborough, Ontario: Broadview Press.

Fried, Albert, and Ronald Sanders, eds. (1964). *Socialist Thought: A Documentary History*. Garden City, N.Y.: Anchor Books.

Friedan, Betty. (1963). *The Feminine Mystique*. New York: W.W. Norton.

Friedman, Milton. (1963). *Capitalism and Freedom*. Chicago: University of Chicago Press.

Funderburk, Charles, and Robert G. Thobaben. (1989). *Political Ideologies: Left, Center, Right*. New York: Harper & Row.

Galbraith, John Kenneth. (1973). *Economics and the Public Purpose*. Boston: Houghton Mifflin.

Gellner, Ernest. (1983). *Nations and Nationalism*. Oxford: Basil Blackwell.

Gould, James A., and Willis H. Truitt. (1973). *Political Ideologies*. New York: Macmillan.

Green, Phillip. (1981). *The Pursuit of Inequality*. New York: Pantheon.

Greene, Ian. (1989). *The Charter of Rights*. Toronto: James Lorimer.

Groth, Alexander J. (1971). *Major Ideologies: An Interpretative Survey of Democracy, Socialism, and Nationalism*. New York: John Wiley.

Gutman, Amy. (1980). *Liberal Equality*. Cambridge: Cambridge University Press.

Gwertzman, Bernard, and Michael Kaurman, eds. (1991). *The Collapse of Communism*. New York: Random House.

Harrington, Michael. (1989). *Socialism: Past and Future*. New York: Plume.

Hartsock, Nancy C.M. (1983). *Money, Sex, and Power: Toward a Feminist Historical Materialism*. New York: Longman.

Hitler, Adolf. (1925). *Mein Kampf*.

Jagger, Alison M. (1983). *Feminist Politics and Human Nature*. Totawa, N.J.: Rowman & Allanheld.

Hartz, Louis. (1964). *The Founding of New Societies*. New York: Harcourt, Brace & World.

Hayek, Friedrich A. (1957). *The Road to Serfdom*. Chicago: University of Chicago Press.

Hearnshaw, F.J.C. (1933). *Conservatism in England*. London and Basingstoke: Macmillan.

Hegel, G.W.F. (1820). *Reason in History*.

Heilbroner, Robert L. (1970). *Between Capitalism and Socialism*. New York: Random House.

Held, David. (1987). *Models of Democracy*. Cambridge: Polity Press.

Hobbes, Thomas. (1651). *Leviathan*.

Horowitz, Gad. (1966). "Conservatism, Liberalism, and Socialism in Canada: An Interpretation," *Canadian Journal of Economics and Political Science* 32, no. 2.

Howe, Irving, ed. (1982). *Beyond the Welfare State*. New York: Schocken Books.

Huntington, Samuel P. (1957, June). "Conservatism as an Ideology," *APSR* 51, 454-73.

Jefferson, Thomas. Selections in Merrill D. Peterson, ed. (1975). *The Portable Thomas Jefferson*. New York: Viking Press.

Jones, A.H.M.. (1986). *Athenian Democracy*. Baltimore: Johns Hopkins University Press.

Kolakowski, Leszek. (1978). *Main Currents of Marxism: The Founders*. Oxford: Oxford University Press.

Kristol, Irving. (1983). *Reflections of a Neoconservative*. New York: Basic Books.

Kropotkin, Peter. (1886). *Law and Authority*.

Lenin, V. I. (1902). *What Is To Be Done?*

Lindblom, Charles. (1979). *Politics and Markets*. New York: Basic Books.

Lipset, S.M. (1965). "Revolution and Counterrevolution: Canada and the United States," in Thomas Fond, ed. *The Revolutionary Theme in Contemporary America*. Lexington: University of Kentucky Press.

List, Friedrich. (1837). *The National System of Political Economy*.

Locke, John. (1685). *Second Treatise on Government*.

——. (1666). *A Letter Concerning Toleration*.

MacIntyre, Alasdair. (1978). *Against The Self-Images of the Age*. Notre Dame, Indiana: University of Notre Dame Press.

——. (1984). *After Virtue*. 2nd edition, Notre Dame, Indiana: University of Notre Dame Press.

Macpherson, C.B. (1977). *The Life and Times of Liberal Democracy*. New York: Oxford University Press.

Mannheim, Karl. (1936). *Ideology and Utopia: An Introduction to the Sociology of Knowledge*. London: Routledge & Kegan Paul.

Mansfield, Jane. (1980). *Beyond Adversarial Democracy*. New York: Basic Books.

Marx, Karl, and Friedrich Engels. (1976). *Collected Works*. New York: International Publishers.

Mayer, J.P. (1961). *Political Thought in France: from the Revolution to the Fifth Republic*. London: Routledge & Kegan Paul.

McLellan, David. (1983). *Marxism after Marx*. London, Macmillan.

Mill, James. (1820). *On Government*.

Mill, John Stuart. (1859). *On Liberty*.

——. (1869). *The Subjection of Women*.

——. (1861). *Utilitarianism*.

——. (1861). *Considerations on Representative Government*.

Millet, Kate. (1970). *Sexual Politics*. Garden City, N.Y.: Doubleday.

Minogue, Kenneth. (1963). *The Liberal Mind*. New York: Vintage Books.

——. (1967). *Nationalism*. New York: Basic Books.

Mishra, Ramesh. (1990). *The Welfare State in Capitalist Society*. Toronto: University of Toronto Press.

Mulhall, Stephen and Adam Swift. (1992). *Liberals and Communitarians*. Oxford: Blackwell.

Nisbet, Robert. (1986). *Conservatism: Dream and Reality*. Minneapolis: University of Minnesota Press.

Novack, Michael. (1982). *The Spirit of Democratic Capitalism*. New York: Simon & Shuster.

Nozick, Robert. (1974). *Anarchy, State, and Utopia*. New York: Basic Books.

Oakeshott, Michael. (1962). *Rationalism in Politics*. London, Methuen.

O'Sullivan, Noel. (1983). *Fascism*. London: J.M. Dent.

Parenti, Michael. (1978). *Power and the Powerless*. New York: St. Martin's Press.

Pateman, Carole. (1970). *Participation and Democratic Theory*. Cambridge: Cambridge University Press.

——. (1978). *The Relevance of Liberalism*. Boulder, Colo.: Westview Press.

Phillips, Anne. (1991). *Engendering Democracy*. Oxford: Polity Press.

Plamenatz, John. (1970). *Ideology*. London: Macmillan.

——. (1963). *Man and Society*. London: Longmans.

Raphael, D. D. (1975). *Problems of Political Philosophy*. Rev. ed. London: Macmillan.

Rawls, John. (1971). *A Theory of Justice*. Cambridge, Mass.: Harvard University Press.

Ringen, Stein. (1987). *The Possibility of Politics*. Oxford: Clarendon Press.

Rousseau, Jean-Jacques. (1753). *Discourse on Inequality*.

——. (1762). *The Social Contract*.

Sandel, Michael J., ed. (1984). *Liberalism and its Critics*. New York: New York University Press.

Sargent, Lyman Tower. (1987). *Contemporary Political Ideologies*. 7th edition. Chicago: Dorsey Press.

Schumacher, E.F. (1974). *Small is Beautiful*. London: Random Century.

Schumpeter, Joseph A. (1962). *Capitalism, Socialism, and Democracy*. New York: Harper & Row.

Shaw, George Bernard, ed. (1958). *The Fabian Essays in Socialism*. London: Allen & Unwin.

Smith, Adam. (1776). *The Wealth of Nations*.

Soltau, Roger Henry. (1959). *French Political Thought in the 19th Century*. New York: Russell and Russell.

Stirner, Max. (1845). *The Ego and His Own*.

Stockman, David A. (1987). *The Triumph of Politics: The Inside Story of the Reagan Revolution*. New York: Avon Books.

Sunstein, Cass, ed. (1990). *Feminism and Political Theory*. Chicago: University of Chicago Press.

Taylor, Charles. (1991). *The Malaise of Modernity*. Concord, Ontario: House of Anansi.

Walzer, Michael. (1983). *Spheres of Justice: A Defense of Pluralism and Equality*. New York: Basic Books.

Ward, Barbara. (1966). *Nationalism and Ideology*. New York: W.W. Norton.

Watkins, Frederick. (1957). *The Political Tradition of the West*. Cambridge, Mass.: Harvard University Press.

Wolff, Robert Paul. (1970). *In Defense of Anarchism*. New York: Harper Torchbooks.

Woodcock, George, ed. (1977). *The Anarchist Reader*. London: Fontana.

Index

Marx, Karl 17, 18, 28, 63, 65, 67, 70, 71, 72, 79, 104-7, 155, 156-9, 162, 173, 177, 221, 223

Marxism 15-6, 63, 73, 113, 185-6, 220, 223

Marxist-Leninism 158-9, 202, **209**

McRae, Kenneth 26

Meny, Yves 99

Mill, James 40-1, 46, 47, 77, 83

Mill, John Stuart 43, 45, 77, 85, 87, 91, 138, 155, 185

Millet, Kate 182

Mishra, Ramesh 164, 167

Mitchell, Juliet 182

mixed government 41

monarchy 22, 23

monetarism 168-71

Montesquieu, Charles 43, 46, 76

Moral Majority 101

morality 43, 45, 59-61, 71, 121

Mussolini, Benito 210

nationalism 22, 45, 62, 83, 173, 184, 205-9

nation-building 206-7, 215

New Deal, the 26

Oakshott, Michael 51, 60, 94, 95

obligation - see legitimacy

Okin, Susan Moller 181

Owen, Robert 63, 69, 78-9

Paine, Thomas 128-9

patriarchy 16, 182, 185, 220

Perot, Ross 181

Plato 120, 143

political culture 11-3, 214-5

Pope Leo XIII 99

popular sovereignty 37-8, 139, 198

populism 22, **179-81,** 184

prescription 54

proletariat 16, 109, 155-9

property 40, 86-7, 111-3, 133, 150-1, 164, 210

Proudhon, Pierre 63, 68, 78-9

public ownership 70, 111-3, 158

rationalism 45

Rawls, John 83, 88

Reagan, Ronald 170, 219

redistribution 70, 113, 164

Reformation, the 31-2, 34-5, 197, 203

religious right, the 101-3

representative government 41, 45, 94, 139, 144-5

republicanism 22, 23

responsible government 22, 39-41

revolution 105-8, 109-10, 127, 155, 158-9, 183

Ricardo, David 155

rights 22, 37, 67, 89, 91-2, 122, **123-34,** 136, 201

Roberts, J.M. 24

Roosevelt, Franklin Delano 90

Rousseau, Jean-Jacques 134, 139, 141, 142-3, 175

rule of law, the 22, 50, 87, 122, **123-7,** 132, 136, 146, 201

Saint-Simon, Claude Henri 63, 73, 78-9

Schumacher, Fritz 192-3, 195

Second International 107

self-determination 206

separation of powers 41, 46

sexism 182

Skidmore, Max 212

Smith, Adam 76-7, 83, 93, 152-3, 159, 161, 223

social contract 39

social democracy 113-6, 167, 170, 208

social science 82

socialism 19, 22, **63-73,** 74-5, 91, **104-16,** 118-9, 127, 132-4, 154, 158, 168, 208, 210, 213, 215, 218

democratic 71, 107, 109-13, 133, 136, 145

evolutionary 107-8

utopian 63, 65, 69-70

sociology of knowledge, the 16

Stalin, Josef 209

state of nature, the 35-7, 175

Stirner, Max 178

sustainable development1 91

Suzuki, David 191

Taylor, Harriet 185

Thatcher, Margaret 170, 183, 215, 219

theocracy 211

Third International 108

PRINTED IN CANADA